WHEELS AND PADDLES IN THE SUDAN
(1923 – 1946)

The Author
C. R. WILLIAMS, C.B.E

C. R. Williams, C.B.E.

WHEELS AND PADDLES IN THE SUDAN (1923 – 1946)

The Pentland Press
Edinburgh

© C. R. Williams 1986

First published in 1986 by
The Pentland Press
Kippielaw, By Haddington,
East Lothian, Scotland

All rights reserved. Unauthorised
duplication contravenes
existing laws.

Typeset by Scottish Studios & Engravers Ltd. Glasgow
Printed and bound by M. & A. Thomson Litho Ltd.
Cover design: Ann Ross Paterson

ISBN 0 946270 24 4

This book is dedicated to the Sudanese people in whose country I spent my working life and to my wife and family who have encouraged me in the writing of this account.

I also wish to express my gratitude to my Grandson, Guy Carswell, for his help with the illustrations, and to my Son-in-law, David Carswell, for his help with the production of the maps.

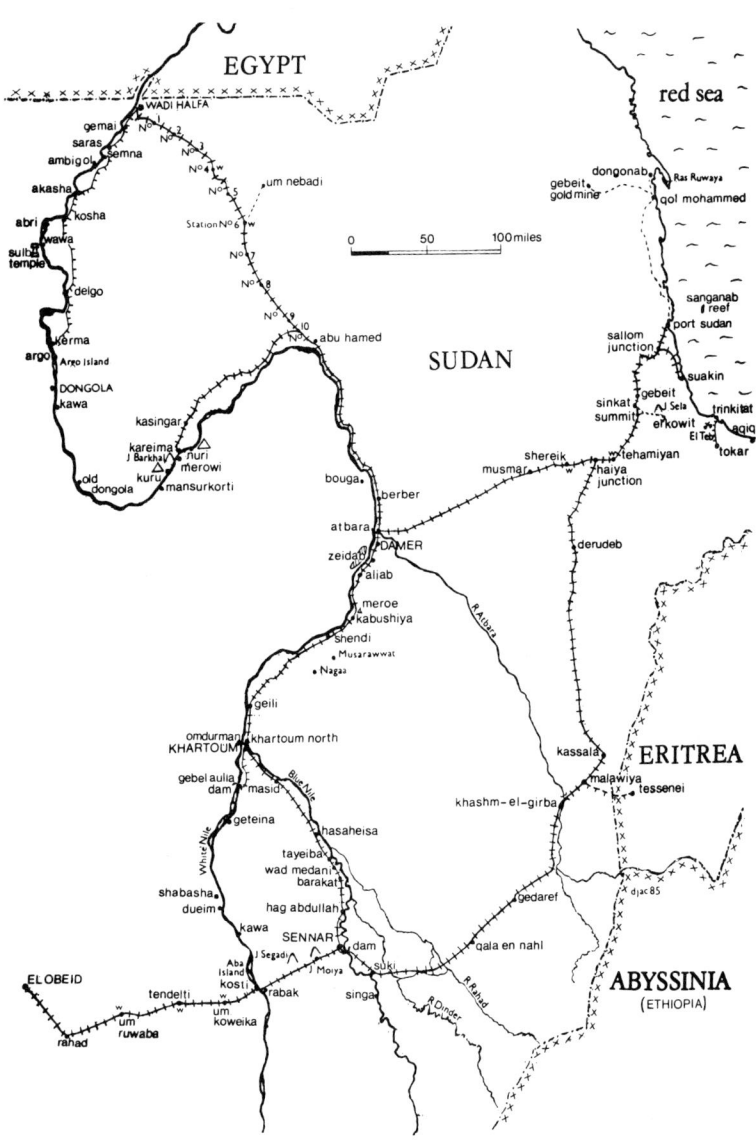

Contents

Chapter		Page
1	Early Experiences in the Middle East	1
2	In Khartoum	15
3	Move to Atbara	31
4	Moving Around	56
5	Port Sudan and the Coast	77
6	Dongola and the 'Batn-el-Hajar'	87
7	The War Years 1939–45	95
8	Khartoum to Juba — August 1945	121
9	Down south	151
10	Up the Bahr-el-Ghazal	168
11	Into the Jur	183
12	From Meshra-el-Req to Juba	203
13	Into the Sobat	219
14	Up the Pibor	237
15	A Journey up the Blue Nile	242
16	Sennar to Malakal by Road	249
17	Through the Nuba Mountains	287
18	Farewell	301
	Appendix — Jongelei	306
	Glossary	312

Preface

When laid up sick recently, I was given *A Pattern of Islands*, by Arthur Grimble, to read. My evident pleasure prompted a suggestion that I should write about my own experiences in the Sudan. I hesitated as 38 years have passed since my departure, diaries and notes are scarce, and memory is not what it was. However, the matter was not allowed to drop and I have been persuaded to try.

My particular area was transportation. I served 23 years in Sudan Railways, from 1923 to 1946; 16 years in the Mechanical Department and 7 in Headquarters. Thus my recollections fall into two parts. For the first period, for which I rely mainly on memory, I was largely concerned in the running, and later the repair, of locomotives and rolling stock. For the last 7 years I added two new dimensions. First of these was the waterways of the Southern Sudan. I was greatly interested in this subject, and in Headquarters detailed knowledge was required, but I had had no previous experience since the Steamers Section was handled by 'The Admiral' at Khartoum North, who was directly responsible to the Chief Mechanical Engineer. The second new dimension was membership of the Governor General's Council for the last 5 years. This involved me in schemes outside transportation, for example the Zande Development Scheme, requiring visits to the south for which I have copious notes. I ask that the compartmentation (what a word!) may be accepted; it is the way it happened.

Chapter One

EARLY EXPERIENCES IN THE MIDDLE EAST

My first taste of this part of the world came in 1918 when, after initial training at Oxford and Uxbridge as a Flight Cadet, I was posted to Egypt for flying training. On arrival in Egypt I was sent to Aboukir, 12 miles east of Alexandria. Flying training was slow in starting and it ceased in 1919 before I had graduated. However, I liked Egypt so I became Clerk in charge of Demobilisation. When the two squadrons at Aboukir had been dealt with, I was posted to Heliopolis to continue demobilisation work at Wing Headquarters.

Only three Flight Cadets remained: one whose parents lived in Cairo, one interesting chap named Roy Langford, who had been a mercenary in South America and had a bullet lodged in his liver, and myself.

Life at Heliopolis was pleasant, and the work was interesting. I shared quarters with an American Rhodes Scholar, who had represented his state at tennis, and we had a regular four on three days a week. I had a horse to ride and two monkeys as pets. I also discovered a curious financial phenomenon! One of my duties was to preside at the paying-out of the unit. I sat with a sergeant on either side of me, and piles of Egyptian £E1 notes and great bags of silver coin in front of me. Entries in army pay books were made in sterling but payment was in local currency. The exchange rate was £E1=£1 0s 6½d sterling, and we were supposed to convert each £E5 on the basis of three at £1 0s 7d and two at £1 0s 6d.

The silver bags were weighed and not counted and contained a mixture of sterling 1 and 2 shilling pieces and Egyptian 5 and 10 piastres. Sterling coin and Egyptian piastres were equally valid but were noticeably different in size and weight. The unexplained phenomenon was that I always had money in hand at the end of the day. When I took over the job there was in the office safe a bag containing £E35. To this I added the profits from pay days, and

1

WHEELS AND PADDLES IN THE SUDAN

from it I provided money for all sorts of minor squadron social occasions. When I handed over it contained £E81.

In September 1919 I was sent on a job to north Syria, with time allowed en route for sight-seeing in Jerusalem, Damascus and Baalbek. The line from Kantara on the Suez Canal to Haifa was laid during World War I to standard gauge (4 feet 8½ inches) and it intersected at Ludd, the 105-centimetre gauge line laid by the Turks from Tel-Aviv–Jaffa to Jerusalem. I arrived at Ludd at 08.00 hours. The locomotive that would pull me up to Jerusalem was in the livery of Sudan Government Railways but I paid little attention to this at the time. Jerusalem was quiet and a Thomas Cook chief guide made sight-seeing easy. The Grand Senussi, Sidi Idris, was on pilgrimage, staying at my hotel, and I received a command to visit this man of considerable personality.

Another interesting experience occurred as I was being shown round the Church of the Holy Sepulchre. We were in the Greek Orthodox Chapel at the commencement of the Festival of the Holy Cross. A dignitary asked my guide if he could borrow me and I was hustled off to join a gathering procession of clerics and given a 2½-foot long candle and a posy of flowers. In the procession I was advised to copy my neighbour, a venerable old priest who made signs that he would see me through. We started a long, slow perambulation of the building with much singing and frequent stops. My self-consciousness gradually wore off. The ceremony lasted 1½ hours after which I received the Archimandrite's thanks for my participation.

After four days in Jerusalem I continued northward. From Haifa the line ran up the Yarmuk Valley to Deraa on the plateau, where it joined the Damascus to Ma'an Pilgrim Line. It was of Turkish origin and 105-centimetre gauge. It had suffered heavily during the war and all its bridges over deep ravines were wooden trestles constructed by the Australians. We reached Deraa at about 16.00 hours and after tea set off for Damascus. It was a lovely evening and I sat on the last flat wagon of the train, with my legs dangling over the end. We were travelling slowly up an incline, when a shadowy form appeared and heaved a small sack on to the truck. He called for assistance to climb up and joined me on the tail-board. He offered me quinces from his sack, but these are most unpalatable when raw, so I surreptitiously ditched many of mine, partially eaten, over the side into the increasing gloom!

WHEELS AND PADDLES IN THE SUDAN

This part of the world is full of interesting characters. One of my contacts in the hotel at Damascus was the Khedive's trainer, who was completing the purchase of Arab horses for the Khedive's racing stable. The transaction took place at the mansion of Hassan Ibisch Pasha, a famous big-game hunter, and I was shown his extensive collection of trophies, many from the Sudan. At the stables I saw the seven beautiful animals involved in the transaction and £8,200 were counted out in sovereigns for them. One was a mare in foal, and I was told that the seller would be on hand when the foal was born, to claim possession.

My luck continued when in the hotel I met an expert on Persian rugs. He took me to the Great Mosque to see nearly an acre of them. Through the ages important people have come to pray and left a rug behind them. My guide named the variety of each rug, and told me where and by whom it was woven, as evidenced by the details of design or shade of wool. It was a wonderful introduction to a subject of which I had very little knowledge.

We also visited the Bazaars and 'The Street called Straight'. The Hamidje Bazaar was open to the sky as the Germans had stripped off the roof covering. I purchased quite cheaply a Hittite cylinder seal then set out to explore. I arrived in a handsome Jewish quarter, where on all sides I was invited to 'visit'. I eventually came to rest in a large courtyard with a fountain and a lofty sitting-out terrace with a large *sala* (sitting-room) behind, and some beautiful, fair daughters, which is unusual in Jewesses.

I was in Damascus on 1 October, the first anniversary of its recapture. By kind invitation of the Emir I was present on the saluting base for the Ceremonial Parade. On the way there I passed two jovial policemen, swinging between them a man's dirty *galabiya* (robe). They invited me to inspect the contents. It was the gory head of a man and with pride they announced: 'Him, very bad man'. For me the highlight of the Parade was the ride-past of two companies of Arab Horse, one on greys and the other on pale chestnuts, with several foals at foot.

The Railway Transport Officers were assiduous in involving one in escort duty; no female was allowed to travel alone on the Damas–Hama–Homs Prolongement, as the railway was called. That fact involved me in several interesting encounters. My first was with an elderly lady missionary who had spent half her life helping the Armenians in their various bouts of trouble. Another interesting

WHEELS AND PADDLES IN THE SUDAN

moment occurred at the point where the railway line traverses the Pass of Abilene on the way to Rayak. Someone of influence was travelling on the train so at this spot the train was stopped to allow inspection of an inscription cut in the rock recording the camping of a legion, I think Decima Victrix, Lysanias being Tetrach (see Luke 3:1).

Baalbek, in due course, was a great thrill. I was the only visitor and the Curator gave me his undivided attention. The Kaiser Wilhelm had, after his visit, caused some important holding repairs to be carried out, and placed a large tablet to record his action in the Temple of Diana. The Australians had effectually dealt with it and it lay on the ground in pieces. In the area where the Crusaders had tethered their horses, I saw carved on a step a 'nine men Morris court' and, incidentally, I also noticed one carved on the floor of Pontius Pilate's Palace in Jerusalem, which might have been in use at the time of our Lord's trial.

I spent the night in the mess of a Pathan Regiment. After dinner we attended a performance of 'Hamlet' in Urdu, and I shall never forget Hamlet's rig, which was slashed wine-coloured breeches and hose, a French cavalry breast-plate, a Sam Browne belt and an Admiral's cocked hat. Altogether an amazing show!

On the return trip a Railway Transport Officer loaded me with two dames from Occupied Enemy Territory Administration. These ladies were skilled in securing for themselves the best that was available. We were approaching Rayak Junction where the line to Beirut takes off, and I had been instructed to take them to a rest camp presided over by a Colonel of the Indian Army Medical Service. I introduced them, and they took over! In five minutes the whole establishment revolved round them, and they extracted from the Colonel an invitation to miss the connection to Damascus, and 'rest awhile'. The Colonel extended the invitation to me but I declined, hoping to lose the ladies, as I had jobs to do in Damascus and limited time. However, three days later, as I was boarding the train for Haifa, the Railway Transport Officer detailed me for escort, and it was these same two ladies!

At Haifa we changed trains. I put my haversack on a bunk to reserve it and bade the ladies farewell, saying that I hoped to be asleep when they detrained at Ludd. However, my haversack was stolen, and so I had to report the loss at Ludd, and put up with mild badinage from the ladies!

WHEELS AND PADDLES IN THE SUDAN

It was now mid-October 1919 and our Service time was running out. The Flight Cadet from Cairo was demobbed, Roy was ill in hospital and I was job-hunting. Efforts to join the Egyptian Irrigation Department failed for lack of an engineering qualification. I liked the work of the Frontier Districts Administration with their Hausa policemen and camels, but there was no vacancy and keen competition anyway. I declined two very attractive non-government offers.

Before leaving Cairo I visited Roy Langford in hospital. He was in bad shape from that bullet in his liver, and I had little hope of ever seeing him again. However, nine years later he bobbed up again at a Lyons Corner House and I learned that he was then manager of the Criterion Theatre.

A number of visits to Shepheards Hotel had impressed on me the motto of that establishment. Loosely translated from the Latin, it reads, 'Whoever drinks from the water of the Nile, will return to drink again'. It was in this mood that I left Cairo and started for England. I arrived in London the day before Armistice Sunday

I returned to Oxford and, by switching from History to Engineering Science, blazed a trail for New College. In my third year a college noticeboard called for applications for the Sudan Political Service, so I applied. I was one of 62 applicants from Oxford and Cambridge for eight vacancies. The Sudan Service was probably unique in that entry was by selection. A Board of four Governors of Provinces or Deputy Governors considered the applicants, and chose likely individuals. The 62 candidates were reduced to 32 by consideration of their records presented by college tutors on behalf of their candidates. Surviving that round, I appeared before two members of the Board and reached the last 16. Final selection was in London before the full Board where it was revealed that my age of 27 was higher than desirable. The Chairman told me, however, that one person from Oxford and one from Cambridge were required for consideration by the General Manager of Sudan Railways for a vacancy in his department. The war had obscured normal promotion prospects and so they preferred to give a newly joined official a 'life of opportunity to prove suitability for promotion'. I accepted the Oxford nomination and I was interviewed by the Assistant General Manager. The vacancy, however, went to the Cambridge nominee because my three years of works experience implied too much bias towards things mechanical.

WHEELS AND PADDLES IN THE SUDAN

The door to the Sudan seemed closed. However, three weeks later, the Sudan Railways offered me a similar job in the Mechanical Department, with promotion prospects unclear, on condition that I became a pupil for nine months of the Chief Mechanical Engineer of the London, Brighton & South Coast Railway at Brighton. I agreed and was given what must have been the most intensive course ever provided. In May 1923, I left for the Sudan as a District Locomotive Superintendent.

I have been asked many times why anyone should want to go to the Sudan. I can only answer for myself; I found the idea attractive! It was a large country, over one million square miles. Its personnel were selected. There were three months annual leave, and early retirement at 50 on half-pay. The pay, £E480 per year, was not high although my father, a retired parson, commented that he had never been paid so much for a year's work!

During the voyage to Port Said I sat at table next to a Major Golding who, as a young man, had served in Malta as a warrant officer attached to the Royal Malta Artillery for educational purposes. He invited me to go ashore with him at Malta to visit his old haunts of 25 years ago. We visited the big forts of Saint Angelo and Saint Elmo. His former pupils, now mainly high ranking warrant and non-commissioned officers, showed immense pleasure at seeing him again after all these years. The news that 'The Little Monkey' (for that was his Maltese nickname) had returned spread like wild fire, and the sergeant's mess at Saint Angelo was soon crowded with his ex-pupils. Brandy and coffee flowed with the telling of many anecdotes. We made a triumphal crossing of the harbour to Saint Elmo where it happened all over again and we had difficulty in breaking away for a lunch appointment.

After lunch we visited the hostelry which had been his favourite haunt, 'Le Coq d'Or' in Sliema. It was siesta time and very quiet. The Major asked a bar attendant whether Madame X, who had presided in his time, was still in command. She was, but she was a very old lady and she was resting. Did the Major wish her to be disturbed? He asked her to tell Madame that 'The Little Monkey', using the Maltese words, would, if she could manage it, like to see her. The message was taken up to her and a reply came back that she would be down in ten minutes. We waited and a sweet old lady came into the bar and threw her arms round the Major's neck. Her pleasure at seeing him again was immense. Refreshment followed,

WHEELS AND PADDLES IN THE SUDAN

spiced with anecdote, and I realised that some friendships can survive very long periods of absence.

I enjoyed the journey to Port Said, and also the quaint characters who seem to surface when one travels aboard ship. Disembarking at Port Said I was soon in the train for Cairo. I arrived in the afternoon and presented myself at the Sudan Agency the following morning. Surprisingly I had three days to wait in Cairo before going southwards. Although there was a nightly train to Aswan, the Sudan Government steamer, which provided the next link, only gave a twice weekly service, for the mails. However, I found plenty to do, visiting a tailor I knew from my sojourn at Heliopolis. His shop was in a fine old *khan* or Caravanserai and we drank Caravan tea. He made me a 'palm beach suit'. I also went to see my Armenian clerk from demobilisation days, who had kept one of my two pet monkeys.

The three days passed quickly, and a night's journey then took me to Aswan. The steamer 'Lotus' was a pleasant introduction to the Sudan; its dazzling white paint, cleanliness and efficient staff impressed me. Passengers were few — half a dozen tourists, a Deputy Governor from the south, and a commercial traveller.

We arrived at Abu Simbel at daybreak. The temples gleamed magnificently in the sun. Guides showed us round, but the tourists knew one piece of information not found in the guide books. Between the two temples was a long slope of golden sand. Suitable approach to the *suffragis* (waiters) on the steamer produced a large plated tea-tray which made a splendid toboggan before the sand became red-hot. After half an hour's sport the revellers rejoined 'Lotus' for the short lap to Wadi Halfa.

I was met there by the Dockyard Manager. In these days Sudan Government Railways and Steamers, to give its full title, operated a dockyard to maintain a fleet of four large and five small steamers. I was shown round the dockyard, and then boarded the train, which was white and very clean, with white-clad attendants. We started across the desert, which is so featureless and unpopulated that the stations were numbered 1 to 10 instead of being named. At No. 4 was a well of very brackish water used only in dire emergencies. No. 5 was at the highest point, and at No. 6 was a locomotive shed, a slightly better well, a spare engine, a Decauville track to the north east and a British couple, whose significance I did not appreciate at the time. No. 10 was a junction with a line extending to the west

WHEELS AND PADDLES IN THE SUDAN

towards Dongola. I was to learn later the story of the Desert Line.

We reached Abu Hamed and the Nile after dark, and Atbara, the Headquarters of the Railway, at about 07.00 hours. I was taken to the Headquarters of the Mechanical Department. The Heads of Department, and most Assistant Heads, had been with the Railway from the earliest days and had a kind of aura. They were to be approached with deference. First, I had audience with the Assistant Chief Mechanical Engineer, Mason, who was to be my host for the day. These were still the days of donkey transport, with only one car in private use. This was a 9 hp Bianchi, belonging to Midwinter Pasha, the General Manager, and in later years I became the owner of this car. For this first morning, however, I had to hurry on foot to keep up with the fine white donkeys.

After breakfast I met my 'Chief', Rupert Fawkes, from whom I was to learn my job. He had a striking face and a twinkle in the eye. We got on well together. He was a fine engineer who taught me a lot.

Later in the morning came audience with the Great Man, Midwinter Pasha, with his considerable reputation. As a young Sapper he had laid the line across the desert with his own hands, burning them badly in the process. It had been a standing contest between him and the Saidi labourers to see who could hold on to the rails the longer and they had loved their mad *Englezi* officer. Progress was up to three miles per day, a very high figure for manual methods. It was a dash to get a supply line from Wadi Halfa across the desert to Abu Hamed on the Nile by the time Kitchener had fought his way around the great Dongola Bend. From Abu Hamed, Midwinter carried on the line to Atbara, and eventually, after the Battle of Omdurman, to Khartoum North. About 1904 Midwinter became General Manager, succeeding Macauley Bey who left to take over the Egyptian State Railways. On the outbreak of World War I Kitchener was recalled from Egypt, and Wingate, the Governor General of the Sudan, had to go to Cairo, and so Midwinter became, quite literally, the Government. In addition to his Railway responsibilities he became a veritable Pooh-Bah, with all sorts of new problems, such as rationing and closing down the Gezira Cotton Project and the building of the Makwar Dam. He was said to work 20 hours a day for years on end. I found him still a man of vigour, and it was another two years before he retired.

In the afternoon Mason took me out in his launch, and later I went to the Club. I was soon quizzed as to whether I had met the 'Barmaid at No. 6'! I then realised the significance of the couple I had seen at No. 6 station. They were the manager of the Um Nebadi gold mine and his wife. The mine, possibly dating back to the time of King Solomon, was situated 50 miles north-east of No. 6, and reached by the Decauville track. Life there was very boring and, for relaxation they would meet the mail train at No. 6, and offer a warm beer to anyone off the train who would talk to them on the veranda of their little 'office'. Old hands who knew the set-up would call them over for a cold beer in the restaurant car. The mine closed down in the late 1920s, mainly because no-one would tolerate the living conditions.

The following morning I was put on the train to Khartoum. The line passes through the middle of the Meroe, Kabushiya pyramids and temples, where active excavation was in progress. In later years my wife and I spent many a day scratching about there. I was met at Khartoum by J. H. Dunbar, from whom I was to take over at Kosti, the ultimate District of the system. He was a man of few words but not difficult to get on with. The next day was spent buying household equipment and trekking kit. In the evening we hitched our service car to a train and set off for Kosti.

There followed a busy week of getting down to the nitty-gritty of running a stud of elderly engines, and sampling the reactions of a Sudanese staff to a new arrival. I was escorted over my 300-mile section, and warned as to its difficulties. These included the cleaning-out and repair of a deep well bore at Tendelti. I paid a duty call, on 'Sarah' Craig, the Governor of Darfur Province, at El Obeid, before whom I had appeared at the Selection Board the previous year. He was surprised and pleased to see me — enough to come and stay with me in Khartoum the following year. The week passed quickly, and Dunbar then left for Atbara, to take over as Carriage and Wagon Works Manager.

I settled down to survey my first Command. My stud of 16 engines intrigued me. There were 11 Baldwins, bought 'off the shelf' in 1898 from the USA as the only 3 foot 6 inch gauge engines available at the time. They were very like the Cannonball Expresses of later TV fame; wonderful little work-horses, or should I say ponies? They survived rough treatment; the bar-frames instead of the more usual plate frames meant that any collision damage could be remedied with heat and a hammer. They only lacked headlight

WHEELS AND PADDLES IN THE SUDAN

and bell, being fitted with an effective cow-catcher. The other five engines were Kitsons. They seemed vaguely familiar; four years previously I had seen them working on the Ludd–Jerusalem line. That line was 105 centimetres — slightly less than our 3 feet 6 inches — causing heavy tyre wear. As they were at the time the only engines easily available they were requisitioned and, on completion of their war service, duly returned to the Sudan, and so I met them again in Kosti.

An early problem was a crop of 'preventable' failures of locomotives en route. With Locomotive Running Officials, failures were very unpopular, and preventable failures were anathema. Statistics were circulated monthly, and a low figure was much to be desired. My drivers decided to put me to the test, and quickly gave me three preventable failures in five days. I wrote a scorching criticism of each driver involved! I instructed my Sudanese clerk to translate faithfully my sentiments into Arabic. He was shocked — Mr Dunbar would never have done such a thing — so I next enlisted the help of a Syrian Traffic Inspector. Stress between the Traffic and Mechanical Departments of a railway is common, and Baramki Eff, the Traffic Inspector, revelled in this opportunity to revile some Mechanical Department staff. I posted the result on the shed noticeboard. The staff read of their offences in subdued silence. Over the next few days three supplicants begged me to fine them any amount I cared, provided that the notices were taken down. I had got under their skin; the notices remained up for a fortnight, and I had no more trouble.

Life at Kosti was simple. The Departmental representatives were in general interested in the very good duck shooting available. When I was there duck were 'out of season', but it would not have meant much to me anyway. There was no electric light or pressure paraffin lamps, only candle *shamadans*. One problem was a full-grown ostrich that roamed at large! The radius of action of its neck was 7 feet and nothing inside that distance was safe. It was a protected species by law and had survived being tied to the railway lines several times.

Water supply was less of a problem. There were deep bores at two stations, two locomotive sheds were on the Nile and a third close to a small lake, so a 4,500-gallon tank behind the engine met all requirements.

A feature of Kosti was the *radeef*, a sort of Chelsea Pensioners for the Sudan Defence Force. These old nuggets paraded for an annual review before the Governor General. It was the Day of the Year for Kosti. Their uniform was tattered but their skin glowed and their medals shone. Sudan Political Officials indulged in verse at any opportunity, and a former District Commissioner at Kosti, 'Gladys' Bond, who was then Governor of Dongola Province, had composed an ode. I was given a copy. It remains an interesting example of authority girding at itself:

THE GOVERNOR GENERAL'S LAUNCH APPROACHES

Inspector Log
Stand still, Bolis for God's sake people cheer
And say you're pleased — that's why I brought you here.
Form up in line, and let your clean Damur
Attest the zeal of Hadret el Mamur.

Are all the Omdahs Robes of Honour clean?
And have they practised saying Mabsouteen?
See that a lot of people stand about
To hide the places where the flags give out.

Where is the Sub-Mamur, and has he sent
All with long sentence of imprisonment
Well out of reach? Remember any left
Are called Mohd. Achmed — ten days theft.

Is everyone with any just complaint
Out of the way, and under safe restraint?
Where is the claimant as to whom I say
I settled in his favour yesterday?

Do all old soldiers clearly understand
That they are part of that immortal Band
That ended the Khalifa's bloody reign?
The greatest battle of the whole campaign.

See there are lots of little whores to squeal,
See they are nicely oiled from head to heel —
Our credit hangs on how they beat their drums,
Protrude their breasts and wag their little bums.

WHEELS AND PADDLES IN THE SUDAN

GOVERNOR GENERAL REACHES LANDING STAGE

Inspector Log
General salute, now all that man can do
Is done— and luck alone can pull us through —
Surely the labours of the last few days
Will gain the Merkaz credit, win us praise.

Governor General Log
Sheiks, Omdahs, Notables, Officials both
Civil and Military, I am nothing loth
To say that I am very pleased to see
Such flags, such joy, such signs of loyalty,
Such vast increasing of the public wealth —
Chiefly I'm mabsut giddan with myself.

All British officials were on parade to mark the importance of the Governor General's visit. It commenced at 9.30 hours, and I was warned that we should be lucky to be dismissed by noon. The Governor General had served in the Sudan Defence Force in the early days. All Sudanese carried tribal markings on their cheeks, which revealed a lot to the initiated, of which the Governor General was certainly one. He delighted the majority on parade with several minutes of individual history. It was a very moving ceremony.

The District Commissioner was most helpful to me. Whilst Political Officers spend a year, after selection, at Oxford or Cambridge studying classical Arabic, this was not required of Technical Officers, such as I was. We had to acquire a knowledge of colloquial Arabic, and undergo a verbal examination after one year in the country. The District Commissioner suggested that I sit in his office and listen to him dealing with cases. He maintained a most helpful running commentary at the same time. I remember one case, concerning the ownership of water melons planted on a sand bank. It all hinged on whether the land in question was or was not *fazda* (a recurrent sand bank). 'A' who had planted the seed would only surrender his right to the fruit if 'B' and his witnesses would swear on the Koran that the land really was *fazda*. 'B' and his two witnesses gladly agreed to do so, using the Office Koran. 'A' however, required them to use Fiki Ahmed's Koran. This distressed 'B', who took at least one minute to make up his mind to perjure himself. His witnesses, however, would not commit perjury on the Koran of Fiki

WHEELS AND PADDLES IN THE SUDAN

Ahmed; it was only acceptable using the Office Koran. The case was dismissed. It taught me a useful lesson.

Every day, at 11.00 hours, a telegram of news appeared on my office table. It was four or five pages, headed AUN. My clerk knew that these letters stood for 'Army up Nile' but its source required further search. The telegram was Reuters' news for the day. It was circulated free to all stations without a local newspaper as part of a bargain struck by Lord Kitchener with Reuters. In return for this service being provided in perpetuity he allowed Reuters correspondents to accompany the expedition. Thus it was that 25 years later a copy of AUN still appeared daily on my desk in Kosti.

A visit to El Obeid was always interesting. I parked my service car at the far end of the station area and from my end window the sand and gravel stretched for miles towards French Equatorial Africa. Something not infrequently appeared from that direction. For instance, all the pilgrims from west and central Africa converged on El Obeid on foot, and many cattle moved over the same route. One afternoon, from my desk by the window, I saw a herd of cattle being driven in. They became quite assertive after a drink. The drill was to get them into pens alongside the loading ramp and thence up a crush into open cattle trucks. The most awkward time was when the first were in the truck with room to move about, and the 5-foot sides were a challenge that could be satisfactorily negotiated. Several managed it. One great beast refused to enter the crush. Audax, the British vet supervising the entrainment, was summoned. He wound up the animal's tail whilst two men caught hold of the tips of its horns, and the twisting had it in the truck in no time. The rest followed with little trouble, the message understood!

Another interesting memory was of the old man in rags who staggered towards my service car with a 4-foot square of four sticks suspended from his shoulders by two ropes, he was walking in the centre of this. On the sticks were perched 22 red-tailed grey parrots. I was invited to buy two parrots. Why two? Because the old chap was determined to avoid having the most scruffy ones left on his hands as his stock decreased. One had to take a good one and a less desirable one. I declined, but it was not to be the end of my contact with those parrots. Later I became involved with no less than four of them!

In early summer unexpected patches of colour may be met with

13

in the Sudan. I was taking an engine out on trial when I noticed a half-acre patch of vivid red and yellow colour fairly close to the track. I was thrilled to find it was a non-climbing type of a lily, *Gloriosa abyssinica*. Next day we filled a Tate Sugar packing case with the tubers and I sent them to a nursery which specialised in hot-house plants. They were delighted, especially at finding an albino variety amongst them.

Sooner or later in the East, Middle or Far, one becomes aware of the 'grape-vine'. In my case it was sooner! After five weeks at Kosti, my boy told me that we would be moving to Khartoum on the Saturday of the following week. It was a precise date. I took little notice of the remark, but on the following Thursday received instructions to hand over Kosti District on the Saturday and take the night train to Khartoum. My boy was overjoyed. I was left wondering just what was the source of such news? The best suggestion I could come up with was a combination of overheard conversation and the very extended nature of the Sudanese family. All servants were loosely connected, and greatly interested in each other's movements. I encountered this kind of happening several times in my service.

I duly handed over to Jones, my Locomotive Inspector, and on Saturday evening set off for Khartoum.

Chapter Two

IN KHARTOUM

I arrived on Sunday morning. Stenning, my predecessor, greeted me. We spent most of the next week together. There was quite a bit for me to pick up as the Khartoum post was in theory a divisional one, to which the Kosti District was rather loosely attached.

An early job was to meet the folk at Khartoum North Dockyard, who were of the Mechanical Department but directly responsible to the Chief Mechanical Engineer. The Railways ran a steamer link between Khartoum and Rejaf, situated 1,000 miles away on the southern border, and a dockyard at Khartoum North for their maintenance. In command was the 'Admiral', Commander Yates, a taciturn individual. His No. 1 was Bob Gordon who became a life-long friend. Stenning arranged for us to dine at the Sudan Club, combining his farewell and my introduction. After dinner we played bridge. The Admiral maintained a running commentary and Stenning complained that if he behaved like that in the Cavendish Club he would be chucked out. The Admiral's reply was typical; 'The Cavendish Club! (loud snort) — I founded it!'

The railway station at Khartoum Central was situated on the outskirts. The town was laid out like a Union Jack, with two main streets intersecting at right angles. The whole area was divided into rectangular blocks with two diagonal avenues. The station was at the south end of the shorter main street with the Governor General's Palace, on the river bank, at the north end. At the intersection of the main streets stood the Gordon Memorial Statue. It was about half a mile from the statue to the station. The five Railway Officials lived there in departmental houses, a little community within the community, all save myself with at least 15 years of service and well known to each other. They were kind to me, the new arrival. The senior, and our 'frontman', was 'Buggins' Bayley, the Divisional Traffic Chief, with his charming wife Norah. His District Officer was 'Squiffy' Scaife, who had a distinguished war record and was a keen philatelist. We were friends for many years. The Engineering Department had 'Pinkeye' alias Pinckney, for Divisional Officer, who was a bachelor, with only two more years to serve, and was contemplating matrimony. 'Rabbie' Moore was his No. 1. 'Pinkeye' went on leave in July, and it fell to me to look after Polly, one of those parrots that I had seen at El Obeid. Polly had a real ability to talk and continually declaimed a telephone conversation routine. One evening a friend suggested that we should train him to salute 'Pinkeye's bride when she arrived in three month's time. The parrot quickly became word-perfect, repeating, 'Hullo! Hullo! I am Polly Pinckney. Who are you? Are you Mrs Pinckney? Have you your marriage lines?' When the Pinckneys arrived, I put Polly on their veranda and went to the station to meet them. When they got back to the bungalow Polly was in good voice. The bride took it very well — and I was much relieved!

In Khartoum I soon learned that life was more than a '9-to-5' job with time-off which was divorced from the job. We were, after all, in the Sudan for a limited period to achieve a definite purpose, which was to bring the Sudanese from primitive conditions to self-government.

It seemed to me that these ideals were a little higher than in many places and that support in their pursuit was a common experience. The presence of the British in the Sudan was the result of the tragic end of General Gordon's life of service. In the late 19th century 'service' still had an accepted value and the basic purpose of our presence after Omdurman required that ingredient.

I felt that this sprang from four sources. These were the memory of General Gordon and of Lord Kitchener, the cathedral and its Bishop and the palace with the Governor General. As mentioned already, the Gordon Statue stood at the main crossroads of the city. Behind it was the palace built on the site of his murder with the cathedral built in his memory some 200 yards away. On the river front was the Kitchener Statue to the memory of the man who made the purpose of our presence possible, bringing freedom to the Sudan, instituting Government, giving high priority to the rebuilding of the palace and founding the Gordon Memorial College in front of which his statue stood. The cathedral, with its Gordon Memorial Chapel paid tribute to General Gordon, as did the fine example of 'service' shown by Bishop Gwynne, who was the senior British resident. The presence of the palace, and the Governor

WHEELS AND PADDLES IN THE SUDAN

Governor General's Palace from garden.

Khartoum Cathedral.

WHEELS AND PADDLES IN THE SUDAN

General, was felt by every member of the 'family' for it was, in my view, a very paternalistic government.

The government considered the other person's point of view in making the 'day-off' in the week the Muslim Friday rather than the Christian Sunday, though 'time-off' to attend Christian Service on Sundays was allowed. Consumption of alcohol before sunset was not common and at noon on Friday was almost invariably confined to 'a beer'. Being 'happily married' was also the usual state. In a job which kept me fully occupied the atmosphere was helpful.

One of my earliest memories of Khartoum was a farewell dinner party at the Sappers' Mess for a District Commissioner from the south who was the author of that charming book 'Engato the Lion Cub'. A few months before, in the far south-east corner of the Sudan, he had come across two parties of natives, each 1,000 strong. Tribe 'A' came from over the Kenya border. Tribe 'B' lived on the Sudan side. 'A' had raided 'B' and carried off women, children and cattle. 'B' had just caught up with them, and were about to engage. The District Commissioner had a sergeant and five policemen with him. He thought that 'A' would win, and declared that the matter should be decided by single combat. 'A' would choose their champion, and he would represent 'B'. Fortunately he was victorious, and 'A' honoured the agreement and handed over the booty. The District Commissioner made laconic mention of the episode in his monthly report to his Governor, who added a brief comment that the outcome was fortunate. The Civil Secretary, on hearing of the episode, was greatly worried. An international incident had been narrowly avoided. Had the District Commissioner lost, a military column, at least, would have been required. Such a man was too great a responsibility and must go. It seemed to me that the Political Service was losing a shining light!

I soon made some acceptable teak furniture for my extensive bungalow sited between the residences of 'Pinkeye' and 'Buggins'. This equipment lived with me throughout my service. My early start was fortunate as at Christmas 'Sarah' Craig, the Governor at El Obeid, wrote asking me to put him up during his coming visit to Khartoum. I was thrilled that a high-ranking Political should choose to stay with a newly joined Technical. I was not yet fully aware of the great gulf which many in the Political Service, and even more their wives, felt existed between themselves and the lesser mortals in the Technical Services. That authority on the Middle East, C. S.

Jarvis, noted it in his book 'The Back-Garden of Allah' where he remarked that the Political Service was composed of 'Cock-Angels — nidification value low!' The Governor's visit went off very well.

In December Felix Pole, General Manager of the Great Western Railway, conducted an in-depth examination of Sudan Railways. In Khartoum he visited the Traffic and Engineering Departments and then, the Mechanical Department after which I ferried him the two miles to the Mogren Quay in an elderly and temperamental motor trolley. Mogren was the terminal for the Steamer Services on the southern reach to Rejaf. It had some simple equipment, just two cranes and two grain-cleaning plants. Felix Pole was well satisfied. He asked my Chief whether my title of District Locomotive Superintendent ought to be Divisional Locomotive Superintendent. The Chief grinned: 'Yes — but don't tell him!' It was the beginning of a long friendship with Felix Pole. The Railway derived much satisfaction from his eventual report. Suggestions for improvements were indicated but generally our General Manager, Midwinter Pasha, was relieved, and I too was happy. Felix wrote telling me to look him up when I arrived on leave.

In February a fire occurred in the Sudan Plantation Company's cotton ginning factory at Wad Medani. I received a wire from Headquarters Atbara reading 'Attach service car to 16.00 hours train. Proceed to Wad Medani. Report to Poyntz-Wright, Manager SPS. Advise on preparation insurance claim. CME concurs' signed 'Midwinter'. It was unusual to receive an order direct from the General Manager so I wondered what lay ahead. I had never been inside a ginning factory before. Its purpose is simply to convert the cotton as picked into lint and seed. The fire had destroyed all the heavy conveyor belts that disposed of the seed. The roof and framework lost the festoons of lint in one flash. The box of the great press was reduced to cinders, and the gins had lost their rollers and suffered cracked frames.

The place was greatly under-insured. I calculated the cost of replacement, and the possibility of repair to machinery. After three days I decided to go to Atbara for estimates on local costs of material, and to ascertain availability of specialist facilities such as welding. The General Manager took great interest and wrote a note: 'Mr Williams will expect a fee for his services, and has my permission to accept it. He should not negotiate the claim.' The sting lay in the tail. Poyntz-Wright was disappointed and begged me to go as far as possible with the negotiation. On Saturday morning the insurance people arrived from Cairo. They were young Topliss of Topliss and Harding, and an assessor named Delaney, who took one look at the havoc and said 'You are in trouble.' And so I was.

I had estimated the cost of repair at £8,000, and salvage value not less than £16,000. It seemed to me that against a strict assessor we might get £2,500, but no more. This depressed Poyntz-Wright who said that any figure above that would give him joy, and so I knew what I had to do.

Delaney said that they did not want to be hard on the Sudan Plantations Syndicate; with four new ginning factories under construction at Hassa Heissa, they wanted the insurance business. He asked me what figure would satisfy the Syndicate. I said £4,500, to which he replied 'No difficulty about that!' We worked on adjusting the figures that morning, and Delaney called it the most honest claim that he had dealt with in 25 years in the Middle East. That made me wonder what insurance life in Cairo, Alexandria and Beirut, which were his main theatres, was really like.

I had lunch with a much mollified Poyntz-Wright, who asked me about my fee. I hesitated between £5 and £10 then murmured that I had my pay and travelling allowance, and after all it had been a pleasant experience. The next day a cheque for £50 arrived with a grateful letter. The question of my negotiating the claim fortunately never surfaced!

I was soon to learn the truth of the Arabic saying that 'To lie is the salt of a man; the shame is to him who believes'. My senior locomotive driver Mahmoud Zaki, on a goods train for Khartoum, stopped at Turabi, the station next to Wad Medani, to drop off a wagon. He retired for coffee with the Station Master leaving the fireman to do the shunt. Although against the rules this should have presented little difficulty. However, lacking the Station Master's supervision, the pointsman made a mess of the switch, and the fireman ran the engine through the points and bent the switch rail. Zaki thought that by carefully driving the engine to and fro he could iron out the damage. He was only partially successful so he told the Station Master to send a message, with his compliments, to the blacksmith at Turabi Pumping Station, asking him to come at daybreak with a sledge-hammer and complete the cure in time for the up passenger train due at 09.10 hours. Neither Zaki nor the Station Master were aware of any down train due during the night

WHEELS AND PADDLES IN THE SUDAN

— and it was a down train that would be in any danger. At daybreak the blacksmith arrived, but decided a large forge fire was needed. So, it was agreed that the *Osta*, the chargeman of the Permanent Way gang, just had time to dash the ten miles to Wad Medani, pick up a new switch rail from Stores, return and fit it. However, luck was out! The run to Wad Medani was so fast that the pump trolley derailed on entering the station, scattering the crew, and the *Osta* broke his leg. No-one else knew which switch rail out of a number of variants was required, and so the Permanent Way Inspector was called in to restore the track. He made his report and the Mechanical Department was blamed. I held a 'Court of Enquiry', which revealed that on the night in question two down trains had passed through Turabi. A Guardian Angel must have been on the alert as neither had split the facing points and been derailed. The Enquiry took two and a half days. Zaki refused to admit any fault and denied my reconstruction of events. A heavy fine was imposed.

The story had a sequel. Several years later I was travelling this section during the 'Rains' with Zaki on the engine. It was nearly dark and there had been some rain. Under the regulations we could not proceed until the section ahead had been patrolled in daylight. So, we had to spend the night. I told my boy to put out two chairs and prepare coffee. Drinking coffee we chatted about this and that and I asked Zaki if my reconstruction of the Turabi events had been correct. Zaki admitted yes so I asked why he had wasted two and a half days of my time. He replied: 'I was unlucky on that occasion; another time I might be believed.' Then the matter was dropped.

About May time I received orders to prepare an armoured train, against a possible emergency. I was not to employ any Sudanese or Egyptian staff on the work, so I had only the help of two British and one Maltese foremen, a Greek fitter and a Greek electrical apprentice. It was very hot, and I had jaundice. Basically we had to protect two flat 30-foot trucks with a fence of old rails about 5 feet high, build a platform for a three-pounder gun at one end, and a second storey 'lookout' at the other, and fix as much armour plate as practicable on a shunting engine, paying special attention to its water tanks. It took us about a fortnight of hard slog. The armour plate came from one of General Gordon's gun-boats still lying at Khartoum North, and cutting it was very tedious. On completion the Kaid and his Aide-de-camp came for a trial run, and firing practice was safely carried out. I then went to hospital about my

WHEELS AND PADDLES IN THE SUDAN

jaundice and the Senior Physician welcomed me thus: 'Come here, I can see your spleen standing out!' I was put on Calamine for a long spell.

The building of the Makwar Dam on the Blue Nile caused the Mechanical Department the most worry on my patch. The dam was to provide irrigation water for the cotton crop on the Gezira Scheme. Alexandrini and Perry had started work about 1912 on a cost-plus basis, and spent heavily on the easier parts of the contract, which were the main canal and the foundations for the first half of the dam. With the outbreak of war, work stopped and after the war restarted under a new contractor with Gibson as Engineer-in-charge. Work was in full swing when I became involved. Stone was quarried at Jebel Segadi, a lump of red granite 25 miles away. Six 600-ton train loads of stone had to be moved every day, with terrific wear and tear. The Saidi and Sudanese labourers treated the trucks harshly, knocking the pins and cotters out of the doors with sledge hammers. Even with care the job involved risk; as carried out the risks were colossal, as doors bursting open en route produced derailments, and affected the tight work schedule. Gibson was an absolute tyrant on the job, apparently unwilling to co-operate over the matter of door cotters and pins. I was hard put to it with a daily consumption of over 100 such items. I was having them made in all sorts of places, but had difficulty in fitting them, as the wagons were seldom still. One morning, at the approach to the dam, with a labourer to carry them, I picked up 32 cotters in some 200 yards of track. I walked on to the gantry to see one of my trucks hanging at an angle, half over the end of the gantry. I sat down with my baskets of salvaged cotters, to watch events. Shortly Gibson arrived, and ordered me to remove 'that bloody truck', so that he could get on with the job. I pointed out that in theory I was trespassing on his gantry, and said that as soon as he had restored the truck to the track, I would have it pulled away — but if, as seemed likely, he dropped it into the drink, he would be minus one truck and I would see that it was not replaced! In the event he did get it back!

The closing of the Sudd a month later was a touch and go affair. Two 30-ton trucks, full of stone and encased in wire-rope nets, went in first, followed by four train loads of stone and over two million sandbags. The Sudd held, and a tiresome unpredictable rise of the river passed.

Makwar was the first dam I ever saw under construction. I

thought the work left a lot to be desired, but later learnt that the design had taken this possibility into account. The face of the openings and sluiceways was of nicely tooled ashlar, but the rest of the face was in random stone, and the filling was by skips of stone and cement mortar, shot into the hole, with very little bedding on mortar. It was, however, laced with drainage channels to deal with leakage through the face. A considerable number of jets spurted from the downstream face, when the difference in head was only about 4 feet. The Resident Engineer once asked me what I thought of the design. Stupidly, thinking of these shortcomings, I replied: 'A brute force design,' and he replied: 'I'm sorry that's how you feel. I was largely responsible for it.' I felt very small and contrite. However, more about the dam in due course!

My boss, the Chief Mechanical Engineer, seemed to delight in non-routine jobs. One day a wire came: 'Arrange to dismantle and send to Atbara all machinery and plant from Gordon Memorial College workshop. Don't drop the tank.' I went off to reconnoitre. The machine tools, shafting and so on were easy enough. The tank, however, measuring $30 \times 5 \times 3$ feet, was perched on a 20-foot high brick wall, and contained about 1 foot of Nile mud. It presented some problems as it was wanted for further use.

I set some men on to cleaning out the mud, and went off in search of tackle. I found a 33-foot baulk of timber, a heavy hand winch, some suitable blocks and tackle, and plenty of rope for guys. Transporting all this to site occupied the second day. The centre of the tank, at the point of hoisting, had to be strengthened to prevent crippling by means of struts and it was not easy to get the baulk vertical, but we managed it, and were ready to start the big job on the next day. It was tricky getting the tank down between an inclined post and the wall on which it had been sitting. The site would not allow of it being lowered on the side away from the post. However, we managed it, and the rest of the job provided no problems.

One day I found an old Indian sitting on the veranda with a pile of carpets beside him. My boy said that after lunch the old man wished to display them. Apparently he came to Khartoum each summer offering his rugs to a list of clients in strict order. After lunch the very nice Turkoman rugs were displayed. I would have liked any one of them, but the pecking order was firmly fixed, and I had no chance. Perhaps another year I might be lucky.

WHEELS AND PADDLES IN THE SUDAN

One curious duty of the District Locomotive Superintendent at Khartoum was that, if possible, he should be present when the north-bound mail train departed at 08.00 hours on two mornings in the week. This sometimes proved amusing. One morning, a small elephant, about 4 feet high, arrived on foot, to be entrained in an empty open cattle truck, waiting at a cattle loading ramp. He walked into it, looked at a bucket of water there, and turned his head in my direction. I am sure that I saw a wink in his eye before he took a run at that bucket, which he almost kicked right out of the truck, deluging a number of onlookers. I hope he wasn't too thirsty on the first leg of his journey!

Next Bairam holiday my boss thought I ought to know something about boat-building. With the skilled help of Hassan Yacoub, a nephew of the Khalifa, he was building a double skin, double diagonal planking design in teak. Hassan Yacoub had discovered a simple, satisfactory method for generating the curved lines of a boat, which our Drawing Office adopted for the future. It was a privilege to work with such a fine craftsman.

One day, I received a cryptic telegram from the Station Master at a station with a pump. It said: that the pumpman was just sitting down. He seemed to be very sad, and there was no water. Could we please help'. I set off with a spare pumpman by the next train, and found a sad state of affairs. The pumpman's wife was very ill, he had leprosy, and they had a little boy aged three. I had never seen leprosy before, but from what I saw, I had no difficulty in accepting that he was a leper. Fortunately there was an empty truck at the station, so I brought them back to Khartoum and got the woman into hospital. The father and son needed more time to sort out, and so I had the wagon put at my end of the station where I could keep an eye on them. In the early 1920s medical science was doing little for lepers, and I discovered that all known sufferers in Khartoum and Omdurman were consigned to a cattle *hosh* (a sort of courtyard), on the outskirts of Omdurman, and depended on food supplied by Bishop Gwynne and his friends. It seemed the boy would have to go with his father and therefore contract leprosy too. I felt that something had to be done and found some American missionaries running a girls' school in Khartoum North. I went to see them, and they took the boy in whilst his father went off to become No. 10 in the *hosh*. That was my first contact with leprosy and it made me a keen supporter of work for lepers all my life.

WHEELS AND PADDLES IN THE SUDAN

The most far-reaching decision in the development of the Sudan had been that to grow cotton. It was approached with humility via a series of pilot schemes. The first was at Zeidab, 25 miles south of Atbara on the west bank of the Nile. In its final form it consisted of an area 25 miles long and 3 miles wide. It used American short staple cotton, and pump irrigation. Results had been encouraging. The alluvial mud, south of Khartoum, was considered suitable for the second pilot scheme, using steam-driven pumps at Turabi, and the plans for the dam at Makwar, that I have already mentioned, and an extensive irrigation canal system, were put in hand. The Turabi scheme was quickly followed by a third effort at Wad el Nau, with diesel-driven pumps and sowing of long staple cotton. Work on the dam had started in 1912.

The cotton scheme was designed as a co-operative venture with three participants. These were the tenant farmers, the Sudan Plantations Syndicate and the Government. Basically, the Government had to build the dam and main canal. The Syndicate was responsible for the smaller canals, ploughing and seed, transport, supervision of crop, ginning and marketing. The tenants had to plant, water, tend and pick the crop and then clean out the dead plants. The proceeds were split as follows: Government 25 percent, Syndicate 35 percent, and tenants 40 percent. This was modified slightly over the years as circumstances changed. If cotton fetched 9 pence per pound, the scheme satisfied all parties. The tenants had 10-acre plots, of which one-third was in cotton, one-third in *dura* (millet) and one-third fallow. The *dura* crop belonged wholly to the tenants, and the plot was generally worked by the whole family. Participation was very popular and inspection was done scrupulously. It became an altogether thriving scheme and a main source of revenue for the railways.

A Ruston Bucyrus excavator used on the main canal was the largest of its kind at the time. It had a 5-cubic-yard bucket and an 80-foot boom. I became very interested in this machine and its three-member crew. I was allowed to drive it with a driver alongside giving copious advice. I needed it, since with five levers, three pedals and a lever-operated throttle, driving was a highly co-ordinated process as both hands and both feet were in action all the time. My efforts left much to be desired. These men, Irishmen as usual, were artists at their job and typical of the professional backbone of the contracting industry.

WHEELS AND PADDLES IN THE SUDAN

Stone for the Makwar Dam came from Jebel Segadi, which I visited regularly to keep an eye on working conditions for my wagons. Blasting the granite was spectacular, with several thousand tons of rock falling at one blast. One day after watching this I decided to climb the back of the jebel. My path wound round a large boulder projecting from the cliff, in which there was a cave. In its mouth, in the sunshine, with one leg cocked over its shoulder, performing its toilet, was a fine leopard. It gave me a malevolent look, but was unable to spring instantly. I was — and did — and covered 40 yards very speedily. I made my way to the top and after enjoying the view returned to my service car for a well-earned breakfast.

The cement needed for the dam was sufficient to warrant creation of a cement factory close to the dam site. It worked for seven months in the year, and then closed down. The machinery was driven by two fine Corlis drop-valve steam engines, fed by wood-fired Babcock and Wilcox boilers. The limestone was reduced to powder, mixed with local red sand and pressed into briquettes which were fired in vertical furnaces, yielding the clinker, which was then crushed, and reduced to powder in a horizontal ball mill. Probably the hardest work in the process was to clean up the cement dust at the end of the seven-month run. It covered everything, and if not thoroughly removed, the plant would never have started up again. When the dam was finished, the factory closed down for good, as the total demand for cement did not warrant its continuance. Later I had to prepare a report on this factory.

The third raw material for the dam was the sand. It came from a source nearby, and was red in colour. When mixed with cement, the resulting mortar was referred to as 'Roman' cement.

About July 1924 I was called into Atbara, and informed confidentially that I would be moved there in October. That evening I attended a quite remarkable dinner party, with the General Manager at the head of the table, and Bishop Gwynne at the foot. At the four corners were the Heads of Department; 'Buzz-Buzz' Newcombe, Traffic Manager, Peter Lord, Chief Engineer, Rupert Fawkes, Chief Mechanical Engineer, and Harry Hawkins, Controller of Stores. John Hunter, a prominent Traffic official, sat on one side, and I sat on the other. The conversation of these old-timers was superb. The Bishop in particular had a marvellous repertoire of anecdotes, known to them all, but they

WHEELS AND PADDLES IN THE SUDAN

wanted to hear the stories again. A lot of the stories were about 'Drago', Colonel Drage, who had been Kitchener's Quartermaster and was a typical example of the breed. It was an unique experience, and a great pleasure.

The late leave period in July saw 'Polly' (Pinckney's parrot) entrusted to my care again, and also his wife's pair of bull terriers and a sealyham. I soon sought out the Chief Vet who took over the bull terriers! Sally, the sealyham, was less of a problem and accompanied me to the office. Daily de-ticking was needed but I handed her back in quite good condition. I was not so fortunate with Polly. Montague, Pinckney's District Engineer at Wad Medani, was staying with me, and he also had a parrot, in fact the second one that Pinckney had bought from the pedlar. Montague proposed that we should let the two birds enjoy a get-together on the veranda rail. Polly, sadly pecked at the climbing Antignon plant that adorned the veranda and during the evening he died. The vet confirmed that Antignon was poisonous to animals. And so Polly was decently buried. My boy and the gardener sewed him up in a basket and dug a hole alongside an evergreen hedge. A little while later, arguing, the two exhumed the basket saying that whilst they had been careful to orient the grave towards Mecca, they were not sure about the corpse being pointed feet-first. The parrot, they said, was special because he could talk, and therefore must be buried feet-first and pointing to Mecca like a true Muslim!

In August came the 'Rains'. They were very regular — 8 August, plus or minus three days, generally covered their onset. They could be very heavy, and a wash-out report telegram could run to four pages. It consisted of a series of three groups of figures, followed by aaa. Thus 162 7 3 aaa signified a wash-out at kilometre 162, extending over seven rail lengths on a 3-foot high bank. Generally two wash-out trains would be standing ready at each Engineering District Headquarters, complete with dry rations, thousands of baskets, plenty of shovels and *fasses* (hoes), and a water tank. At daybreak, with a pump trolley in front, they would set off with a horde of labourers, and work for days on end, if necessary, until the line was restored. During this time ordinary rail services were at a standstill. It was our practice to fit culverts or a bridge at 50 percent of the wash-outs every year, and so progressively reduce the vulnerability of the line. If the abutments of a bridge were damaged, a temporary diversion was needed, involving some days work, to allow time for rebuilding.

With the rains the cotton soil of the section Khartoum — Wad Medani could become treacherous and engine derailments were likely. I had one serious mishap during my spell at Khartoum. When I reported it to my Chief his laconic reply enjoined me to be quick about getting the engine back into service. Our breakdown procedure was basic; we only had a 25-ton breakdown crane which

Derailment in rains.

was not much use in dealing with an engine lying on its side though it could help with coaches and trucks. We would shunt a breakdown van with quantities of jacks and packing on to the line close to the front end of the engine and isolate it there whilst the Engineering Department would lay a diversion round the mishap. Then followed several days, perhaps even a week, of very heavy toil, jack and pack, amid prayer for fair weather. When we had restored the engine to an upright position the Engineering Department would lay temporary track under it to enable us to tow it out on to the main line and get it away amid deep sighs of relief.

Khartoum Central Station was protected by a 2-foot high *bund* (earth bank). The ground sloped gently towards the station and the *bund* diverted the water safely away towards the Blue Nile. We had a terrific downpour one evening, the *bund* broke, and the station area was flooded to a depth of 18 inches. I was worried because the main fuses were only about 2 feet above ground level. I set off for the workshops in the midst of the deluge and when crossing the shallow drains, up to my thighs in water, lightning struck the big 50,000 gallon cast-iron water tank, and ran along the water surface like a giant snap-dragon. I could feel my back hair stand on end. When I got across, it must have been about the peak of the flood, and I found the water only 4 inches below the circuit breakers, but not rising. I was greatly relieved and after a while floundered back to my bungalow, and a bath.

In July the *Kaid* went on leave; there was a parade of army cadets for inspection at the station, the band played, and the *kaid* departed. The army cadets did not return quickly to Barracks. They demonstrated, and generally upset the apple-cart, before returning to Barracks and challenging the world at large. News of the awkward position was telegraphed to the *Kaid* at Atbara, where he arrived at 15.00 hours. His engine was refuelled and by 16.00 hours he was on his way back to Khartoum. Such was the capability of the Atlantic class engine that, with this light load, they were back in Khartoum by 20.30 hours. The *Kaid* quickly dealt with the 'insurrection', and the driver asked to be allowed to work the 22.00 hours train to Atbara, and so enjoy his normal rest at home there.

Shortly after this there was trouble at Atbara. The Egyptian Railway Battalion mutinied. From the earliest days, the Railway had enjoyed, and relied upon, the support of the men of this Battalion, who supplied many of the Station Masters, and Permanent Way staff, as well as many Locomtive drivers and skilled artisans in the Works. In general they were better equipped for skilled work than the Sudanese whose emergence had been more recent, and who had shorter contact with these technical matters. Egyptian army pay was low, and the men employed by the Railway received up to 4 piastres a day 'technical pay' which kept them happy. The mutiny was shortlived, but it was decided to send the Battalion back to Egypt immediately, and the loss to the Railway was considerable. Promotion of all suitable Sudanese was immediate, but gaps, particularly in the Mechanical Department, remained. To fill these an order was sent to Thomas Cook in Cairo, to find and trade-test 40 assorted artisans. They arrived in Atbara just shortly after I did, and they were a motley bunch, but included some interesting characters (of whom more anon).

In October 1924 the message came summoning me to Atbara to exchange jobs with Cartmell, the Assistant Mechanical Engineer, Outdoor, who would take over my job in Khartoum.

Chapter Three

MOVE TO ATBARA

The job at Atbara involved responsibility for the locomotives based there. Atbara was geographically the heart of the whole system. Engines from this shed worked northward to Wadi Halfa and Kareima, eastward to Gebeit and southward to Khartoum. The rails were 50 pounds per yard except for the Atbara–Port Sudan section which was 75 pounds per yard, and over this section we were able to use engines with a heavier axle load. Water supply and its quality was one of my main problems.

The original classes of locomotives had been in service for about twenty years and were now used on the extensions of the system, being replaced by more powerful classes at Atbara, to meet the increasing loads. The 4-6-2 'Pacifics' still gave good service northwards over the very trying conditions of the Halfa Desert, and functioned almost entirely on Nile water, only in emergency taking on the saline supply of No. 6, the Locomotive Depot in the middle of the desert. With Nile water, boilers steamed well and were easy to maintain.

On the eastward run, we still used a few of the early 'Port' class, which dated back to their assembly at Suakin in 1904, but the main load fell on the 'Heavy Mikados' — 2-8-2 — which were their replacement, and powerful enough to climb the 'bank' without an extra 'banking' engine. Water, however, was a problem on this run. For the first half, to Musmar, the locomotive had to haul an extra 4,500 gallon tank of Nile water, and for the second half obtain its supply from four pumping stations equipped with water softeners. This was the section with the 1 percent gradient, and maintaining a full head of steam with these water conditions required skill.

Southward to Khartoum we still used some 'Khor' class locomotives. These were the lighter edition of the early 'Ports'. The heavier 75 pounds rail was soon installed and then the main burden fell upon their excellent replacements, the 'Prairies' 2-6-2. For the mail

WHEELS AND PADDLES IN THE SUDAN

trains, I still had four 'Atlantics' which were my joy. They were beautiful locomotives, capable of high performance with a light load in an emergency. They bore massive brass nameplates: 'Sirdar', 'Lewa', 'Pasha' and 'Ferik'. I fought long and hard for their retention in service. They were eventually scrapped in a period of austerity, but I salvaged a nameplate to remind me of their excellence. Water supply on this section was no problem as Nile water was available throughout.

    I soon found that I had inherited some locomotives that could hardly move themselves and could not pull a train as their boilers were full of scale. My suggestion to remove it by electric current was vetoed by our Electrical Engineer. I therefore got permission to try a method described in a handbook written by the Chief Mechanical Engineer of the Federated Malay States Railways for his locomotive staff. It went something like this: 'Obtain a quantity of eucalyptus leaves, macerate them well, place in a large container and boil slowly for not less than four hours. Strain off liquid and add one and a half pints to the boiler water of an engine. Keep the dome cover off. Light up and maintain fire for 24 hours. Cool off and wash out thoroughly. Repeat if necessary.' I had once noticed two fine eucalyptus trees in the Governor's garden at Wadi Halfa so I wrote off and obtained two sacks of leaves. A dictionary informed me that 'macerate' meant 'to soften and separate the parts of a substance by steeping it in a fluid'. I decided to bruise the leaves well before soaking them in water. I found two 8-inch cog wheels with a 4-inch face which I mounted in a frame in mesh, put a handle on it and a hopper above it and set a man to work to bruise, very thoroughly, one sack of leaves. We soon had the concoction cooking in a large copper pot capable of holding a whole sheep. A deep brown liquid was the result. The next day we administered the prescribed dose to the ailing patient, lit up the boiler, kept the fire going for 24 hours, and then let it cool off. We then washed out huge quantities of scale, enough to fill two barrows. We complied with the prescription to 'repeat if necessary' and this time collected nearly a full barrow of scale and could see a lot of the copper of the fire-box sheeting on inspection. The locomotive performed well on shunting duty and the following day it hauled a goods train to Khartoum. We therefore prescribed half a pint of the brew with each filling of the boiler and soon noticed considerable improvement in coal consumption figures. The limiting factor was the supply of eucalyptus leaves so I

WHEELS AND PADDLES IN THE SUDAN

150 Class Engine (Heavy Mikado).

110 Class Engine (Atlantic).

WHEELS AND PADDLES IN THE SUDAN

wrote to the Botanical Gardens at Giza near Cairo for a supply of young trees. We quickly established these in a little plantation alongside an irrigation pump. They grew rapidly and we were cropping them carefully after one year. There was no more excuse for dirty boilers!

Soon my Chief sent me to Port Sudan to meet 'The Count', the old peppery Divisional Locomotive Superintendent there, who was nearing retirement and had fallen out with my predecessor. I was warned to tread lightly and to take with me a newly joined District Locomotive Superintendent, Yorke, who would shortly be posted to Gebeit, which came under Port Sudan. 'The Count' met us, all smiles, and the visit started well. We met the Governor and his staff, and then the Port Manager and all the railway staff. We spent the next day discussing the details of the job, and on the last day of our visit 'The Count' graciously offered us the use of his pony and trap, a very smart equipage of which he was justly proud, for a drive around. With hesitation we accepted, and returned safely, despite the fact that I had never driven a pony and trap before. Memory of 'The Count' lived on after his retirement, as he brought from Mauritius four sprouting coconuts to the Sudan. One, in my garden at Atbara certainly bore fruit.

Shortly after I arrived in Atbara the Egyptian Army battalions in Khartoum mutinied. All males were armed for defence of the Palace and the 'armoured train' took up position outside the barracks which were close to the railway line. Most of the Egyptians were fortunately contained inside their barracks and surrendered. Egypt was requested to withdraw the battalions.

The 40 assorted artisans soon arrived and most came to the Mechanical Department. Some very useful individuals were still serving when I retired twenty years later. I remember one (who was with us for a year and a half), a fine, practical engineer from Budapest. I found him very useful as I had to set up a number of pumping stations on an extension to the line and I gave him the drawings, list of materials required and a service car to live in and told him to draw his material from store, pick up a gang of men and go and do the job. In, perhaps, a fortnight's time a message would come reading 'Water supply installed am returning Atbara next train'. It was too good to last. With Bela Kun's exit my engineer hurried home. Another outstanding craftsman was an Austrian-Czech, Josef Lukavsky. He had what I would think was the unique distinction of having fought on four sides in the 1914–18 war, with an aptitude for being taken prisoner and escaping. He had particular skill with wood-working machinery and was soon put in charge of the sawmill and was a key man in all coach-building work. He was still holding the post when I retired. Another interesting character was Oshood, a Turk, who was a wonderful locksmith. A fourth generation cracksman, his skill had earned him a lowly position on General Harrington's staff where, when required, he used to abstract papers from VIP's briefcases. When the British left Constantinople the army took him, for his own safety, to Egypt. One day ten years later, a file arrived on my desk containing a letter from the British Ambassador in Constantinople to the Foreign Office. The Ambassador stated that he had that day interviewed the Turk's widowed mother who complained of the treatment of her son by the British Army which he had faithfully served. She stated that he had been removed from her circle and she was entirely deprived of his support and that she had not seen him for ten years. Would His Excellency do something about it! I sent for the Turk and explained the letter to him. He said it was true; he would like to visit Constantinople but would be killed on sight and he told me the whole story. I was rather fond of the little man; his ability to open any of our safes in under two minutes was one of the showpieces of a tour of the works for VIPs. His answer to my offer of help, however, was a sad but definite 'no'. We had then to compose a suitably phrased reply. He never went home.

One could talk about many of them. Henry Courdji, for example, responsible for turning the white stock out in apple-pie order. He never sat down to breakfast without first spreading a white tablecloth and setting the table. Pavlos was in charge of the Carriage and Wagon Machine Shop and his Armenian wife was renowned for her crystallised fruit. Poblonski, our 'Tame Bolshevik', also deserves mention. He was a Pole on whom we always kept an eye but we never found anything amiss. One morning when going round the coach shop I found him flashing £E300 in notes. I told him to put the money away and asked what was its purpose. He said he was going on leave later in the day. I wondered from whence the money came so I rang up the District Commissioner and asked if he knew anything about Poblonski. He asked for time and later, somewhat agitated, said that Poblonski was on the proscribed list of persons denied entry to the Sudan! When I pointed out that two years previously he had passed through frontier-control at Wadi Halfa in both directions there was consternation. He went on leave that same afternoon with a large and unexplained amount of money and did not return.

Just before Christmas the Governor from Damer came visiting. On the return journey his steamer *Louise* ran onto a sharp rock and sank. Small steamers always had a barge lashed alongside for safety, so no-one got wet. The next morning the Chief Mechanical Engineer told me to salvage *Louise*. I got the required gear together, took one of the '40 assorted artisans' and a squad of labourers and set off. The site of the wreck was about seven miles south of Atbara but everything had to be ferried across the River Atbara which lay between. There was a strong rumour that a 'sahhar' had recently appeared. A 'sahhar' is a man who can, at will, turn himself into a crocodile. When a 'sahhar' was said to be about no native would swim in the river, and I felt that much swimming would be necessary.

The cotton folk at Zeidab lent me their steam tug and a barge. The wreck was half submerged by the stern with the bows cocked up on a sharp rock which had penetrated the bows about 15 inches. I had no experience of ship salvage!

Louise was about 70 feet long, say 4 feet draft and a stern-wheeler with boiler forward. It had about 1 foot 6 inches free board, and an open lower deck with scarcely any gunwales. As she lay, the stern half and the engine room were submerged to a varying degree. I felt that my best chance was to de-water the engine room and reduce the possibility of in-flow at the point of penetration. I retired to Atbara to have some wooden shutters, about 8 feet by 6 feet made and ballasted with fire bars to make them ride vertically in the water. The Works were very co-operative and made them in about 4 hours. We hung these shutters from the upper deck and they overhung the lower deck to which they were wired. I had brought with me two 4-inch Pulsometer Pumps and hose so we quickly connected them to the tug's boiler.

The stern end was dealt with and flotation improved but the problem of the rock penetrating the bow remained. *Louise* was facing upstream and I felt that it needed to be securely anchored. A very convenient palm tree was available. In theory I knew that a 'cement box' must be made but experiment had to show the way of making it. The hole was about 3 feet from the stem and the plates were very curved in that area. I could see that the edges of the box had got to conform as accurately as possible to the contours of the ship and that it would need to be at least 6-inches deeper than the height of the rock penetrating the ship. To the bottom edges of the box hessian would be loosely attached which, with the box in position, would be sufficient to cover the rock. When completed the box would have to be shored-up from any available ship members. This done we would pour in a generous amount of concrete which, hopefully, would be retained in the box by the hessian and fill up any gaps between the box and the sides of the ship. I expected considerable difficulty in shaping the edges of the box to conform with the contour of the ship but my carpenters quickly managed a very creditable production. After it was in position the pumps worked well, the cement box held, and the anchoring was sufficient to hold her over the rock while she rose in the water and eventually floated clear. We towed her back to Atbara and beached her on a flat, sandy shore. The Chief Mechanical Engineer came to have a look and was satisfied and then informed 'The Admiral' of the events of sinking and salvage. I have little doubt that the news had travelled to Khartoum North rather more quickly by grape-vine. Anyhow, 'The Admiral' said he would come and inspect. He did and he was most gracious. His only complaint was that we had beached *Louise* on a falling river and he would not be able to collect for repair at Khartoum North until June or July.

I had inherited a nice riverside bungalow on arrival in Atbara — but the Electrical Engineer soon pinched it for his bride to come to. I doubled up with Dunbar (from whom I had inherited Kosti District) as there were not enough houses to go round. The cantonment was planned with the original houses along the riverbank with a small *midan*, or open space, behind and then rows of bungalows facing north with roads between them running east and west. The Headquarters and the Works lay a further half a mile inland.

Port Sudan came into existence after it was realised that the historic port of Suakin, 20 miles to the south, could not be developed with deep-water quays and was in fact slowly closing up with a growth of the coral. An alternative port had to be found and a creek at Sheikh Barghout seemed a possibility. The spot took its name from the small 'guba' or tomb at the creek entrance in which Sheikh Barghout was buried. He had died of thirst at sea — and, in my time, no fisherman sailing out of harbour would think of passing the tomb without pouring out a small libation of fresh water.

Work started around 1905 on a quay of five deep-water berths on the north side of the entrance. Warehouses were built, and four coal transporters and four 5-ton cranes installed with a power station to run them, two tugs and a small dockyard to maintain them, and a port was in being in a small way. A difficulty was fresh water. There was a narrow coastal plain, two to four miles wide, and only a few feet above sea level, with no visible water. In the Red Sea Hills behind Port Sudan, which rise to 4,000 feet, there was a small surface stream, Khor Mog, which disappeared into the ground when reaching the plain. A well was sunk at this point from which a supply was taken, but was insufficient for expanding occupation and three large sea-water condensers were installed. These gave me trouble because of very heavy corrosion. The cargo handling was by Yemeni contract labour under the supply and control of one Sheikh Ali Yahyia, who grew to great wealth from the contract which he held until the late 1920s.

Movement in the Sudan for first, second and third class passengers was attuned to the mails which arrived twice each week. There was a third service in the week for fourth class passengers, and over some routes for third class as well. Visitors sometimes arrived in the country without being aware of this. An American once arrived at Port Sudan shortly after the mail train left and, on learning that he had to wait three days until the next one, exclaimed: 'Say! In this country you don't need a timetable. What you want is a calendar!' That irksome three-day stopover was eased by our providing him with a glass-bottomed boat to view the great beauty of the Red Sea and at 20 piastres for a half-hour trip along the reef it was good value. He could also fish — we hired out the gear — and the sport was excellent.

The way inland to Atbara and the Nile was up a rocky valley where, after much survey, a route was found which did not exceed a 1 percent gradient. It was about 60 miles to Summit, at about 3,300 feet, divided into nine sections. Each section was equipped with a sand-trap outside the upper end of the station to deal with any breakaway. It was laid with 75 pounds per yard flat-bottomed rail. Two engines were required to work a 600-ton train up the 'bank' to Summit. The wells on this stretch of line yielded very hard water which caused a lot of frothing and boiler trouble; later this

WHEELS AND PADDLES IN THE SUDAN

was eased by installing water softeners. Occasionally an ibex could be spotted but there was not a lot of animal life to be seen from the line and vegetation was sparse.

From Summit the line descended, at the same gradient, for three sections, to a sandy-gravel plateau which fell gently to the Nile at Atbara, 220 miles from Summit. There was no cultivation other than an occasional small patch in a *khor*-bed after the rains. A few palms dotted the *khors* on the hills but otherwise there were just a few bushes. Occasional ostrich and gazelle would be seen and occasionally a small herd of camels owned by the Hadendoa, the 'Fuzzy Wuzzy' who inhabited the hills. Their wealth lay in their camels which they exported on foot to Egypt for the meat market. The Hadendoa were proud and handsome, with hair in solid ringlets. They were frequently seen in characteristic pose, gazing into the distance with one foot on the ground and leaning on a stick. I always felt that, rather like a Spanish gendarme in his triangular hat, they gave warning that they were not to be taken lightly.

After four sections from Summit there was a junction at Haiya from which a line ran south to Kassala and then west to Sennar to afford an alternative route from Kosti and El Obeid to Port Sudan without competing with the cotton traffic of Wad Medani via Khartoum and Atbara. When I came into Atbara the line was under construction from the Haiya end. The idea was to reach the site for the Butana Bridge over the River Atbara and allow construction of the bridge to go forward while the Makwar Dam was being built, as when completed the dam would carry the railway across the Blue Nile. On our return journey I had a look at the first section, to Derudeb, where a locomotive depot was to be established. This line would carry the rain-grown cotton crop to be grown in the Gash Delta near Kassala, as soon as transport became available.

By my time nearly all the British and European locomotive drivers had disappeared. I just missed the celebrated Billy Bottles, a hard drinker, whose water bottle when on duty was always duly fortified. One moonlit night, when midway between Atbara and Khartoum, looking westward over the Nile, he saw a long silver cigar-shaped object in the sky. It was a great shock to him and he reported it in Khartoum. The reply from Atbara was 'tell him to take more water with it'. The criticism was undeserved as he had sighted the Zeppelin endeavouring to carry much-needed supplies to the forces in German East Africa. I only recall having two British and one Greek drivers. Of the British, Lampard became a Locomotive Inspector and Clarke, who had been a crane-driver at Gibraltar, in due course retired. The best of the British drivers had become Locomotive Inspectors and were responsible for training the Sudanese. They did a fine job. Their Chief, Jones, was an ex-Great Western Railway man from Didcot. He was an indefatigable worker, generally rising at 03.00 hours. He smoked a 50-size tin of cigarettes before breakfast and had a habit of appearing in my office to make a striking statement. One day he exclaimed: 'Sir! I have had a £5 per month rise.' I said that I did not recall signing the authority for it. 'No Sir', he said, 'I have given up smoking!'

A scheme I had started at Khartoum was soon implemented in Atbara. This was a 'most efficient engine' competition on a monthly basis. The reward was a 9-inch brass engraved plate mounted on the smoke-box door, carried by the winner for one month. Competition was keen on account of the publicity. Points were awarded under headings such as Punctuality, Coal Consumption, and Cleanliness with a deduction for preventable failures. It was implemented in all districts.

We had our lighter moments in Atbara. There was the annual Fancy-Dress Dance at the Sports Club. I remember my first one; I was sharing a house with Dunbar and we decided to go as 'Hall's Distemper', with plank, buckets and white coats. At Christmas there was the Chief Mechanical Engineer's Children's Party. My boss involved us in its production. The resources of the Mechanical Department were widely called upon in preparing sets and the garden with its several large trees on the Nile bank was ideal. We also had the Annual Race Meeting. One year I spotted in Stores Yard the pensioned-off Port Sudan Hotel bus. It offered possibilities. Its loan was easy to arrange but its movement presented more difficulty. I settled for four sanitary cart mules, with their drivers acting as walking grooms to assist in maintaining direction. We kept our intentions in the dark and 'Venture's' progress down the course on the day caused surprise.

For a while I ran the 'Players' and also acted as Stage Manager, probably because it was thought I could arrange technical assistance when necessary. We had two productions each year and one year we attempted a 'Co-optimist' type show. Just 30 hours before the first performance the juvenile lead went down with appendicitis. There was no understudy but 'the show must go on'. It was decided that as compiler and prompter the Stage Manager must step in. I cannot sing a note, but I talked my way through my numbers. The audience was charitable and the production was not curtailed.

The Chief Mechanical Engineer was a fine craftsman and could handle a file with the best. He could not abide slovenly work nor allow the mishandling of tools to pass unchecked. Once, when passing through the Fitting Shop at Khartoum North Dockyard, he spotted a fitter letting up the big-end bearing of the connecting rod of a stern-wheeler. The fitter, who was well paid and experienced, was doing a poor job and not even holding his file correctly. Rupert, the Chief Mechanical Engineer, seized the file and showed the man just how it should be done. Having finished the first half of the bearing he told the fitter to start on the second half. Thoroughly shocked, he started carefully. Rupert watched him till satisfied then left. The fitter at the next vice said quietly to the transgressor: 'You are a fool! Why did you not continue to do it wrong? He would then have done the other part for you'. However, I would not like to suggest that the taking of such a liberty was a frequent occurrence as, in general, the staff held him in high regard. When, some years later he took his final leave of the Atbara Works staff, they presented him with a life-size portrait bust, carved by a Coach Shop carpenter. It was a wonderfully good likeness, complete to his handkerchief in his breast pocket. No sittings had been given and it was entirely the result of acute observation. I think the boss was both touched and surprised.

Coming back from my first leave, I took over the monthly magazine, *The Atbarabian*, which contained about 30 roneoed foolscap sheets. Production entailed a lot of work as the editor had to produce 20 to 25 pages himself. We had at this stage a circulation of 250 copies per month. When I took over I thought it was for four issues but the responsibility remained with me for one and a half years. Then I too succumbed and, with no-one else wanting the job, I closed it down. Each of my helpers received a nice silver memento and the inscription on our silver tea service bears record to its source.

I spent my first Bairam holiday with an old friend, John Humphrys, District Commissioner, Shendi, whom I had known at Oxford, visiting the temples at Musawwarat-es-Sufra and Nagaa. We set off at dawn in a T Ford box-car with one policeman to help push and a lot of spare tyres as we expected much trouble from thorns. Musawwarat lies about 25 miles south of Shendi at the foot of a chain of hills. Its full name is 'Musawwarat-es-Sufra' with 'Sufra' meaning a coffee tray. It aptly describes the position of the ruins in a flat golden expanse of sand one and a half miles across, almost encircled by two 'breakwaters' of low hills with an opening of 250 yards. The buildings of red sandstone are extensive and date from about AD250. Their exact purpose is uncertain but they have many interesting features. For instance, the rise from one level to another in the buildings is by inclined plane rather than by steps. We made fair progress, only changing one tube, to arrive for breakfast.

After looking round for two hours we set off for Nagaa which lay due south, over the range of hills. We tried a direct route but could not descend on the far side and had to return to find a way round the end of the ridge. Much shovel work was needed at Khor crossings and numerous tyre changes.

We arrived at Nagaa with its four small temples about 16.00 hours. There was great activity at a deep well with herds waiting their turn. Natives haul up the water in goat skins, whilst larger

Hadendoa with their camels.

containers, made of cattle skins, are hauled up by a donkey being driven away from the well-mouth; meanwhile the herds stand by, waiting to be watered in turn. We left at dusk along a track to Wad Ben Naga Station, and thence alongside the railway line northward to Shendi. At 21.00 hours we met a police party on camels setting out in search. It had been a hard but interesting day, if rather expensive in tyres and tubes!

One day the Chief said: 'I've a holiday job for you, go down to Port Sudan and take over the new Pacifics. Just watch out that they do not get knocked about during unloading.' The locomotives were a repeat order of an existing class so the main interest was that they had been shipped fully erected; up till now all locomotives had arrived in parts and packing cases, requiring transport to Atbara for assembly. After World War I a Swede, Christen Smith, built a fleet of ten ships, whose names all began with Bel, designed for bulk carrying and equipped with very fine lifting gear with a capacity of 100 tons. When freight like locomotives and rolling stock was not available they could be used for grain in bulk. I hooked my service car on to a train and got down to Port Sudan in readiness. The 'Bel----' arrived at about 14.00 hours, tied up and immediately began assembly of lifting gear. The tenders were loaded on the bows and the locomotives amid-ships on deck. I was surprised at their well-cared for condition, without salt spray or rust. By 16.00 hours they had the lifting gear rigged and made a start by lifting off two tenders. Port Sudan is humid, as well as hot, and the 16-stone Chief Officer seemed to be finding things difficult. After two lifts they called a halt till next morning.

We gathered on the quay at 06.00 hours. The skipper was in command of operations. The Chief Officer was suffering from heat-stroke. To handle unloading seven officers were required and with the Chief Officer *hors-de-combat* the Skipper had to lend a hand. The gear consisted of a very strong boom from which the beam was suspended and a powerful winch, all designed to handle a load of 100 tons. The accurate control and positioning of the beam was obtained by four winches placed at the four corners of the mid-ships section with tackle running from a strong post at each corner to the ends of the lifting beam. The load was slung under the beam. We had provided a 15-ton block of concrete which was slung out on a boom from the side of the ship away from the quay to act as a counterpoise. An officer standing on the quay side using a 9 inch × 2 inch plank as a lever and the edge of the quay as the fulcrum was able to make an accurate final positioning of the engine over the quay rails. An officer in charge on the quay gave the orders.

Getting out the first engine was a ticklish job as they were closely packed, but it was inched out without damage as the five winches completely controlled all movement. When clear, the engine was

Unloading locos at Port Sudan 'easing out'.

turned through 90 degrees by hand and lowered until it was about 1 inch above the quay rails. The officer with the plank lever then tilted the ship quite easily to allow lowering the engine accurately on to the rails. The engine was then unslung from the beam. The whole procedure took 45 minutes; one of the two tenders previously unloaded was brought up and attached and then the complete locomotive was towed away. The second engine was handled in the same way. Then they turned their attention to the eight tenders still on the bows and unloaded them so as to be ready for the remaining engines. By dusk they had unloaded both eight tenders and another five engines. It was a very good day's work.

Unloading locos at Port Sudan 'setting down'.

They started at dawn on the third day and by 10.00 hours the job was completed. The Chief Officer reappeared and the whole job had gone very well; it had taken about 17 hours. The only damage was to one corner of a cab roof and that had happened during the voyage. I could find no shortages and everything had been cleaned up thoroughly. Before they sailed the Skipper invited me on board to see the rest of the cargo. It consisted of locomotives and rolling stock for several Indian railways.

WHEELS AND PADDLES IN THE SUDAN

The only problem now was to transport them to Atbara without incurring any hot-box trouble. The locomotives had not been run in and the Sudan earth-ballasted track and sandy atmosphere cause hot-box problems at any time. However, we paid a lot of attention to axle-box packing and lubrication before setting off. I sent a rake of five locomotives off with a Locomotive Inspector in charge, whilst I followed with the second rake of five locomotives. We took it gently and got to Atbara, 525 kilometres away, without incident. We had paid £500 per locomotive for freight and had saved the cost of packing cases, a quite considerable item, and we were spared the work of assembly of the parts at Atbara after transport from Port Sudan. We decided that in future, whenever possible, our locomotives would come out from England fully erected.

The main purpose of our railway was to haul freight but the passenger side had its own importance, in the form of two or three trains in each direction weekly. They may have been few in number, but they certainly looked good, with their ivory-white paintwork, and they were maintained to a very high standard of cleanliness. When I was at Khartoum, I frequently would walk through the stock before it left the Stock Shed for the station. I remember discussing the subject of cleanliness with a Sudanese notable in my later years, and he said: 'You British pay a lot of attention to cleanliness, and I know that when you go, and we take over, it won't be the same, but it will be good enough for us.'

The original coaching stock was, in the main, built in England, of teak inside and out, on a pitch-pine frame — and they lasted very well. Immediately after World War I a number of all-steel vehicles, with a minimum of upper internal woodwork, were tried for third and fourth class. They certainly helped in providing improved cleanliness. I only remember one big fire on a train, involving four coaches, on the Kosti District. Among the casualties was one all-steel coach. It was a write-off, except for the bogies, as it broke its back under the heat of the fire. The underframes of the other three survived to carry new bodies, and gave quite a fillip to local production, with my boss getting very interested in the matter. Two of his main points for reconstruction were strength in the framework to combat impact, and smoothness of the finish to minimise dust nuisance.

Quality of timber used was vital in fabricating a good design and we went to great trouble to obtain good timber. It was still the days

WHEELS AND PADDLES IN THE SUDAN

110 Class on train.

200 Class on train.

when reliable suppliers could obtain material to a high specification, and continue to supply it. The pitch-pine for the sole-bars and main pillars came from New Orleans, the former in 32–35 foot lengths, and it was beautiful stuff. The material for the other pillars, struts and roof members was 'No. 2 Clear and better' British Columbia pine from Vancouver. Each was supplied by one of the leading timber merchants in London, and with great mutual satisfaction. Our teak came from Rangoon. Just before World War II supplies of pitch-pine for sole-bars to our specification became so difficult that we made trials with pau from the Andaman Islands, as a possible replacement. In the mid-1920s we were early experimenters with 'Masonite' to provide the smooth external surface to our rolling stock. Over-belief in its strength led to an unfortunate demonstration. His Excellency was visiting Atbara Works, and was shown a coach under construction in the Coach Shop, with a 'Masonite' outer skin. The Foreman, in his enthusiasm to demonstrate the strength of this material, picked up a hammer and dealt it a sharp blow — and the head of the hammer punched out a neat hole in the skin! It was some time before this episode was forgotten.

We came to the conclusion that 'Masonite', while very useful internally, gave a lower factor of safety against impact than tongued and grooved matchboarding, which we retained for the outer skin. The stock was finished in ivory-white, and looked superb. It took many years of close collaboration with our suppliers, Indestructible Paint, now defunct, to obtain these end results, and I remember having their chemist once staying with me in Atbara for a month, to sort out some problems. When a party of officials was returning off leave, a rake of gleaming white-painted stock would be standing on the quay side at Port Sudan to greet them, and to convey them inland. The liner passengers too, many of them Government Officials returning from leave to their posts further East, also had a good view of the stock, and we received many requests for information and painting schedules.

However, in addition to looking good, the coaches had to be resistant to impact. One year, during the rains, a wash-out occurred near Derudeb and several coaches rolled down an embankment during a stormy night. When the rescue party arrived soon after daybreak, they found a third class coach lying on its roof, and most of its occupants asleep. They thought that they had experienced a particularly robust shunt, and had only bruises and a few cuts. The coach was intact and no-one had suffered any serious injuries.

The sleeping cars and first class coaches were very comfortable. These were the days before air-conditioning, although I had a works-made experimental unit in my own service car. It was a drawback that no shower was provided, but perhaps just as well, because the temperature of the water from the roof tank could be dangerous. Freedom from pests was achieved only by regular disinfection. The dining and kitchen cars provided excellent catering, maybe on the plain side, but their breakfast kippers were highly appreciated, and the kitchen cars would stand any detailed inspection. The Sudanese notable quoted earlier was probably right — our standards were high — but we liked it that way.

One day the Bishop came into the Chief's office; he was smiling and we guessed he was in search of something. It soon transpired that what he wanted was a 'Church on Wheels'. What could the Chief do about it? The idea was well received and backing was forthcoming from many quarters; authority was given, the Drawing Office got busy, an underframe was made available and before long we saw it taking shape. It consisted of a little church accommodating a congregation of, say, twenty persons combined with living quarters for a parson.

Clerics were thin on the ground in the Northern Sudan; we had an Archdeacon and one other in Khartoum, a Mission to Seamen parson in Port Sudan and one based on Atbara, who had to travel round the whole of the Northern Sudan ministering to scattered folk rather than congregations. With this mobility he would become much more effective.

The idea of the Mobile Church received support from several of our suppliers. The firm from which we obtained all our train-lighting dynamos and batteries kindly gave us an installation for the vehicle. When the Church Saloon, as it was called, was completed the Bishop performed the Consecration. As he was about to commence the service a *murasla* (messenger) rode up with a telegram addressed to the Bishop from London: it read 'May your light never fail — Stone'.

On looking back I find it is so often little things that come to mind and one sometimes wonders how that comes about. One night during the Rains I was en route for Khartoum when rain was reported ahead of us. We had to stop for the night where we were — at Aliab. It was a beautiful evening and I suggested that the other

The Church Saloon.

passenger on the train join me for a drink and told my boy to set out chairs. My fellow traveller was one Pennington, of the Agricultural Department. He was a great authority on bird lore. We were enjoying the cool when a plover's call could be heard in the distance. Pennington asked me if I knew how the spur-winged plover got his spur. I did not know and he unfolded the tale. Nebi Suliman, King Solomon, summoned all the birds and beasts to a great feast. When all were assembled, the plover's seat was still unoccupied. Nebi Suliman asked if anyone could offer an explanation for his absence. At this point the plover arrived and stood in front of Nebi Suliman, with head bowed down in shame. Nebi Suliman asked why he was late for the party and the plover replied that he had overslept. The sentence was that in future the plover would carry a 'spur' feather on its wing which would effectively prevent it from tucking its head under its wing and enjoying deep slumber — and that is how the plover got its spur!

At the end of my second year I went on leave, and having tea in the dining car, I was joined by a young man. In due course I learned that he had been on an interesting expedition. The Citroen company had offered a desert vehicle to the British army; two young officers had been chosen to accompany a demonstration run and he was one of them. They had driven from Cairo to Qena and then by the old Roman road to Safaga on the Red Sea and then down the coast to Berenice and the Sudan. He had been thrilled by what he had seen on that journey. It was as if time had stood still for nearly 2,000 years. In the marble quarries there were great blocks of stone destined for the Forum, labelled Caesar Nerva Trajan, just waiting for Carter Patterson to pick them up. In the emerald mines at Berenice he had seen two Europeans looking round and he had picked up a piece of emerald matrix which he showed me. They had driven on through Port Sudan to Aqiq and then through the hills to Kassala and on to Khartoum, where he found his recall awaiting him. The vehicle had behaved very well.

Returning from leave, my table companion was a man who had seen a lot of the world. A remittance man in British Columbia in the 1890s, he had been turned out of Dawson City in 1897 and then led the Rush in 1898, remaining in the Klondyke till 1914 when he was evacuated with typhoid. On recovery he joined up, fought on many fronts, finishing up on General Harrington's staff at Constantinople. There he met a Turk who held the concession for the Berenice emerald mines and wanted him to reopen them. My friend agreed to tackle the job after completion of his present task — to establish a potash plant on the Dead Sea. He remarked that he would like to know what was happening at Berenice. I told him what I knew and he said it would make him very keen to get the potash plant off the ground. He asked if I would like to see the *'firman'* (licence) and fetched it from his baggage; it was on parchment, a wonderful example of Turkish calligraphy.

With three days to wait in Cairo I put up at the Continental, which was full of Americans. One, whose table in the dining room was 10 yards away from mine, had a very strident voice. She would sit with her right hand obviously displayed, and her many friends would remark, as they passed, on a ring on her finger. She would answer: 'Mr Blanchard says it is the cutest scarab he has ever seen.' Pieced together, her story was that with a dragoman she had recently visited the interior of Cheops, the Great Pyramid, bumped her head and with his assistance found the (dud) scarab on which Mr Blanchard had pronounced. I never met the lady in person during the three days but I felt I knew quite a bit about her.

In March 1940, just 15 years later, whilst en route for Cairo travelling passenger, I was awakened at 02.30 hours in the middle of the Nubian Desert to be told that a sleeping car had a very hot box. As the only railway official on the train I had to act quickly. The head *farash* told me there were only two spare sleeping compartments on the train and with 11 passengers in that coach, that meant seven problems. The car must be left behind, its occupants given 20 minutes to get packed up, whilst the *farasheen* endeavoured to find some occupants of double compartments willing to admit the dispossessed. With the first six passengers I was lucky, they accepted the position philosophically, but at the seventh I ran into trouble. A night-capped head appeared, and consigned me to a distance. At length I made her see sense and she agreed to get herself in working order. The remaining four passengers were co-operative. As I went back to my compartment to pack up I felt there was something familiar about that voice. On returning to the scene I found that the other passengers had vacated and some progress had been made with No. 7. She started to hand out her bits and pieces, ending with a green parrot in a cage. I told the *farash* of my sleeper to take her to my compartment and, after checking that the move was completed, I told the driver to proceed, whilst I spent the rest of the night in the dining-car. On arrival at Wadi Halfa I handed No. 7 to a Traffic Official to get her and her bird onto the steamer. As we started she gravitated to my table for breakfast and I thought I recognised that voice. At Abu Simbel most people went ashore, but No. 7 remained on deck so I tried to solve the mystery. I asked if this sentence had meant anything to her: 'I bumped my head and then found a scarab at my feet — I took it to Mr Blanchard and he said it was the cutest scarab he had ever seen!' Her eyes sparkled: 'How the hell do you know that?' She said that the Continental was still her base and she was the representative in the Middle East for *Chambers Journal*. In the couple of days we spent on the steamer, I learnt something of the hard life of a representative. I saw her back to the Continental. When I enquired for her at a later date, she and her parrot were away on assignment.

One irksome aspect of my job as Locomotive Running Superintendent was that I had to be easily contacted at any time. This meant having a telephone alongside my bed. One night a second call proved tiresome. A voice from Kassala, a very distant station announced that a man sleeping on the rail, using it as a pillow, had lost his head. I am reported as having said: 'Who the hell would want to run a railway! Thank God he did not derail the train!' The natives, and particularly pilgrims from West Africa, were very prone to walk between the rails as this was more level and free of obstruction than a path alongside the track. They would use one rail as a pillow when they lay down to sleep. I have never been certain just why. Many natives like a hard pillow and carry around with them a little wooden 'horse', rather like a diminutive gymnasium horse, which is essential if an exotic hairstyle is not to be ruined, but this would not apply to a pilgrim with a plain coiffure. I wondered whether the attractions were warmth and being coveniently situated or whether it was to be made aware, by the drumming sound in a rail, of an approaching train.

The Chief Engineer held strong views on the impropriety of walking along the track. If when out on his motor trolley he met anyone so doing, he would invite him to board his trolley. Continuing on his way for about 10 miles, he would point out the folly of the practice and the unforgiving nature of the locomotive. He would then put his passenger down and politely wish him good-day in the hope that 10 miles of additional walk might drive the advice home and that they would never meet again.

Camels were more frequent casualties than humans, for our track was entirely unfenced. All locomotives were fitted with cow-catchers which very often threw the animal, be it cattle or camel, clear. Sometimes they got thrown upwards to get lodged on the buffer beam and against the very warm smokebox. A wounded camel in this position was an unpleasant sight and its removal could be difficult. Collisions with camels were frequently the subject of my night calls. The railways accepted liability for killing camels because the track was unfenced. We paid out £E5 on production of the tail of the dead animal. I used to wonder how many tail-less camels there were roving around but I was told I had a suspicious nature!

Early in 1926 the Makwar Dam was due to be opened. It was to be a great occasion; it marked the completion of a major decision to link the fortunes of a young country to the production of cotton by providing the necessary water. The Dam and the main canal cost more than two years' entire revenue. The High Commissioner of Egypt, Lord Lloyd, was coming to the Sudan to perform the ceremony. From the railway's point of view it was essential that nothing which was our responsibility should go wrong and we spent a lot of time on detailed preparations. Four special trains for VIPs were required, but the greatest attention had to be paid to Lord Lloyd's train. The ceremonies would mainly be conducted at a site immediately below the Dam where the folk from all the special trains were to assemble. Later in the ceremonies Lord Lloyd and a select few had to travel on his train to the centre of the Dam to unveil two plaques. This part of the proceedings posed the greatest problems. The deck of the Dam carried a rail track, a crane track, a roadway and a vast number of winches and bollards required in connection with the sluices; these were situated between the rail track and the roadway. A week before the event I had this special train assembled and, with the driver and locomotive that would pull it on the day, and my Chief Locomotive Inspector, we set out for Makwar. We had to try to find a series of gaps between the winches and other gear which would allow wooden flights of steps to be placed opposite the doors of the coaches of the special. After a lot of movement backwards and forwards a fair working compromise was achieved. The site of each flight of steps was painted on the deck of the Dam and the exact position of a line on the footplate of the locomotive marked on the upstream parapet of the Dam. We had a safety margin of only plus or minus 3 inches. It called for very accurate handling of the locomotive, but we did two test runs making excellent and accurate stops and I felt that we should be OK on the day.

The Day dawned and we all assembled at Makwar. The two leading notables, Sir Sayed Ali Merghani and Sir Sayed Abdel Rahman el Mahdi, were travelling on separate trains. The former notable held officially in slightly higher esteem, was in No. 2, and the latter was in No. 3. The Sayeds, and more particularly their followers jockeyed for position. No. 2 ran into trouble en route; it arrived 30 minutes late and after No. 3 with consequent seating difficulty as poaching had taken place.

All political officials were resplendent in levee dress, but I being on duty in a technical role was excused. I hovered in 'whites' on the fringe. My Chief Locomotive Inspector was on No. 1 train and I awaited his arrival. The Governor of Blue Nile Province was in command. He was a massive figure to whom I owed my job in the Sudan as he had recommended me to the railways. He had been Chairman of the Selection Committee which turned me down for the Political Service. Twenty minutes before No. 1 train was due 'Pitch-fork Arthur', for such was his nickname, stood reviewing his dispositions. He was well known to railway folk for he had served for some years at Damer, the Province Headquarters near Atbara. Satisfied with what he saw he gave one of his characteristic 'humphs' and then it happened — his tight-fitting, white overall trousers split at the rear. We had provided him with a service car which was near at hand but no spare pair of trousers was available and no one of his staff was built on the same generous lines. It was decided that he must be sewn into the rent garment. Fortunately needle and cotton were to hand in the service car and the repair, as far as we know, survived the proceedings and was largely hidden by the tails of his levee coat.

Lord Lloyd arrived on time and the first part of the proceedings passed off according to plan. Lord Lloyd then again boarded his train to proceed to the centre of the Dam for the unveiling ceremony. I was on the footplate on the fireman's side watching for any trouble with the steps, which had to be placed in position as we stopped. My Chief Locomotive Inspector was behind the driver; he got the wind-up about making a dead accurate stop, pushed the driver out of the way, applied the brake himself and overshot the mark by about 4 feet. We were in real trouble. Frantic efforts were made all along the train to fit steps by some means or other and it was quite unsafe to endeavour to set back. We just had to make the best of it and all the trouble taken had been to no avail. Very real inconvenience was caused at a number of points but Lord Lloyd made a fairly dignified descent from his coach and the unveiling ceremony passed off without further incident. That I never received any official complaint was a matter of some wonder and much gratitude!

Chapter Four

MOVING AROUND

And now, a momentary digression from my theme of 'wheels and paddles' while I remember just one or two of my many other Sudanese experiences.

In the early years of the re-occupation several antiquarians worked in the Sudan. Wellcome, for example whose permit to excavate was conveyed in that terse telegram 'Burrow and welcome'. He became interested in the culture which had existed on Jebel Moiya, hills west of Sennar Junction. On a dais 60 feet above the surrounding area, a ring of hills enclosed a site where a civilisation had existed in isolation. He employed 2,000 men here, as a relief measure and had wide archaeological interests in other countries. In Paraguay he met a firing party leading out a prisoner for execution; he offered 5 shillings for his release and acquired one Colonel Uribe who became his assistant in the Sudan.

Wellcome's great achievement at Jebel Moiya was the construction of the 'House of the Rocks', intended to last for ever. About 60 feet square, it was built like the Pyramids, using the roller, the inclined plane and abundant labour, to a height of 40 feet. The courses, 3 feet high, consisted of granite boulders, roughly hewn to shape. Exterior and partition walls and a central pillar were laid at one time. Sand was heaped on it to provide working space and an approach ramp up which the rocks for the next course could be rolled. As each course was laid the procedure was repeated. The roof of 2-foot reinforced concrete was carried on a grillage of 8 by 18 inch steel girders and when set, all sand was removed to expose the resulting structure. A corner of the main part was furnished as a dining-room with fine antique oak furniture, including a magnificent bulbous leg refectory table. In later years I sat at this table inside Sayed Abdel Raliman el Mahdi's Palace on Aba Island but how it got there I don't know! Before withdrawing Wellcome had a plaque fixed to the central pillar — Wellcome Uribe 1911–1938—

WHEELS AND PADDLES IN THE SUDAN

House of the Rocks.

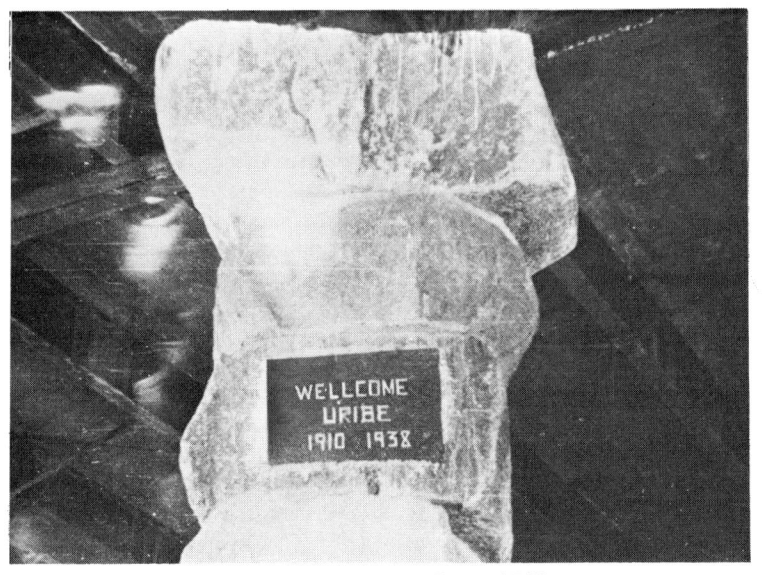

House of the Rocks — Central Pillar

WHEELS AND PADDLES IN THE SUDAN

and left two very fine incinerators. The many years of excavation did not reveal the precise date. On our last visit my wife picked up a scarab which, if genuine, would be a valuable guide. I took it to the Khartoum Museum. They were thrilled; it put the excavations on a time-scale and they gave me another scarab in exchange.

There were interesting antiquities at Kabushia – Meroe, 45 miles south of Atbara. The railway track went right through the middle of them. To the west, between the railway and the Nile, was a considerable town excavated by Professor Garstang immediately before World War I. He spent five years on the site and uncovered a Temple of Amon and the Royal Baths, with curious ornamental seats and much of the gear of a bathing establishment of the second or third century AD. He also excavated the Temple of the Sun, to the east of the railway, dating from the sixth century BC.

The three groups of pyramids, lying to the east of the railway, were excavated by Doctor Reisner immediately after World War I. One group lay close to the town while the other two were some 2½ miles out, on the hills. The pyramids were quite small. They were of a mildly stepped profile and an active person could climb a corner, placing one foot on each side. They were rather steep. The pyramids generally had a small chapel on the east side.

We spent several holidays scratching about here and collected yards of mummy beads of all colours. The finest object we found was a white crystal bumble bee with wings extended, about 1½ inches long. We found a bead factory containing dried clay cylinders of pencil dimensions ready for cutting up, discarded conical ends and lumps of various minerals used to make glazes and colours.

The area around the pyramids was believed to be haunted. My wife heartily endorsed that belief. One day, when riding donkeys to the pyramids from Kabushia station, my wife's donkey bucked violently and threw her. It then set off into the desert braying loudly. The verdict of the donkey boy was that his charge had seen an *afrit*, or devil.

Mentioning Kabushia reminds me of scout camps. I was Commissioner for the Atbara District for many years. We had seven troops in Atbara and several British scouts. At Kabushia was a pleasant site, close to the Nile, and superb for a three to four day camp.

A yearning for past enjoyments was sometimes strong, and I remember one example of this at Gebeit, a small locomotive depot in the Red Sea Hills near the top of the climb up from Port Sudan.

WHEELS AND PADDLES IN THE SUDAN

Vegetables were scarce and the Locomotive Inspector's wife yearned for watercress. She came from the foot of the Chilterns. The hard-water supply needed a water-softener to make it possible for use in locomotives. It was impossible to grow watercress on it. I saw, however, a tank of lovely watercress growing alongside the pump-house and wondered how it had been achieved. A small condenser had been fitted to the exhaust from the pump and it provided sufficient distilled water, slightly warm, to keep a tank three parts filled with gravel well moistened. I was given a fine bunch of watercress to take back to my service car for tea.

In the Sudan it is these small things that one remembers. I have already mentioned that the northern section of the line crossed a featureless desert where the stations were numbered rather than named. No. 6, where there was a small locomotive depot, was presided over by Osman Oshi, a lump of polished ebony with a wonderful smile. Osman decided that the station needed flowers to brighten it up. He had a shallow trench dug, running the whole length of the station between the two lines, ran a lot of water into it and sowed cosmea. They germinated well and he kept them well watered. I passed through en route to Wadi Halfa to judge the Flower Show. They were a wonderful sight, a 300-yard wall of shades of pink and white. I congratulated Osman and said that it was a pity there was not a class in the Wadi Halfa Flower Show for the most colourful garden as he would have been a strong competitor. He asked if I would like some seed. When I returned three days later he handed me a 4-gallon petrol tin full of seed. I told him I did not want to plant up Atbara with cosmea, nice as they looked at No. 6, and handed him a cigarette tin to be filled. I think he was rather disappointed but still smiling.

I think it was at No. 7 that the station staff had a frightening experience. It was about 17.30 hours, the day's work was over and the staff were sitting about, seeking any slight breeze to counter the sodden heat. They were a tiny community. The station building and five *tukls* were made of mud. Miles of flat desert surface extended in all directions with distant hills to the east. The coffee tasted good and as they sat there with their backs to the wall of the station building someone noticed a dark line on the eastern horizon. The line swiftly increased in size and they soon realised it was water. By great good fortune there was a mound 10 feet high close by and just in time — the whole party crowded onto its top. About 2 minutes later the 7-foot wall arrived. The mud buildings collapsed but 3 feet of the mound, which was partly rocky outcrop, remained above water and here the party spent the night. At dawn little of the station remained, just a sea of mud. The wooden table from the station office was recovered in Dongola about 150 miles away.

Our District Commissioner was a countryman; he decided that the *nass* should have an agricultural show. There was an agricultural scheme for small tenant farmers at Bouga, 25 miles north of Atbara, so it was held there. Many traditional skills could not be included but ploughing with oxen attracted keen competition and knowledgeable spectators. The animal classes were hardly up to Bath and West standards but they stimulated the aspirations of the tenants. My wife used to present the prizes.

Royalty travelling by train required special care, not to mention luck, if a hot-box was to be avoided. The Duke and Duchess of York came through in the 1930s and I spent a very worrying time as a heavy sand storm was blowing. My Chief Locomotive Inspector was travelling with them and I had every confidence in his ability but we were relieved when the news came through that their train had arrived on time.

If the Chief Locomotive Inspector was not available I would travel myself. On one such occasion I accompanied the Earl and Countess of Athlone across the desert to Wadi Halfa. I was lucky, we had no trouble and arrived on time. They expressed their appreciation graciously as they left the train. I would not like anyone to think from this that a train journey in the Sudan carried considerable risk of a breakdown! The contrary was the case but luck was always needed with the most important occasions in adverse weather conditions.

Not everyone loved the Sudan Railways. Some persons, in fact, had an almost pathological dislike for us. One of our sternest critics over the years was the Governor of Kassala Province, 'Ras' Bailey. Until the railway reached Kassala in 1924 that Provincial Headquarters maintained an aura of splendid isolation. It was 250 miles to Khartoum and rather more to Port Sudan, which had to be reached by tracks rather than by roads. The fact that it was very close to the Abyssinian border probably accounted for some similarity of outlook to that of the very independent Barons of that country and to the Governor acquiring the pre-nomen of 'Ras'. It was easy to see that the arrival of the railway was not welcome. When the 'slump' came in the 1930s and we were all called upon to state where we saw possibilities of economy, it was current belief in Atbara that the 'Ras' had volunteered to carry out all Sudan Railway functions in Kassala District himself. He required the assistance of a British Locomotive Inspector and a Traffic Inspector, thus allowing two senior British railway personnel, the District Locomotive Superintendent and the District Traffic Manager, to be retrenched (their houses, of course, to be handed over to his staff!). Strangely he made no mention of the District Engineer and his Permanent Way Inspector. Perhaps he was unaware of their existence or, less likely, felt unable to assume their responsibilities. His suggestions were not acted upon.

As a young official I experienced his wrath over a disciplinary court. A young Sudanese clerk in the Traffic Department at Kassala had drawn a cheque that 'bounced'. The Governor wrote to the Civil Secretary demanding the young man's scalp: 'just the sort of thing one expects from a railway's employee!' I sat as President of a Court of Enquiry on the young man. In the Sudan families are very close, and as his brother was getting married he had to assist with the finances. The cost of his share of the entertainment was £E14, so he drew a cheque for that sum and, as his credit balance was only £E11, the cheque was marked 'Refer to Drawer' and it came to the knowledge of the Governor. I investigated and came to the conclusion that the young man was rather the victim of the system. The Government was virtually insisting that young officials like him should be paid by cheque but did nothing to teach the necessity of seeing that the account contained sufficient funds to meet any cheques drawn. Moreover, these young officials were usually a first generation to hold a bank account. They did not have the advantage of a father's stern advice when starting. The finding of the court was a stern reprimand which filtered back to Kassala via the official channels. The 'Ras' exploded and called for disciplinary action on the President of the court for his calculated ineptitude. The General Manager replied to the Civil Secretary. I have in my papers a letter informing me of acceptance by the Civil Secretary of the finding of that Court.

When waiting at Haiya three years later, I saw another service car being attached to the train next to mine and was told it was the Governor of Kassala. A quarter of an hour later the Governor got out of a Province box-car and approached the train. I 'made my number' and asked if he was ready to leave. It was a goods train and therefore its timing was flexible. He saw my wife at the door of our service car and said he would like to make her acquaintance. He was invited to tea and I told a waiting station master to despatch the train. Tea went well and unless I stopped the train it was booked to run through four sections, about 2½ hours, before stopping. After tea the Governor asked my wife if she played 'noughts and crosses' and she brightly replied: 'I'm very fond of it'. Paper and pencils were produced and they settled to earnest conflict. When we arrived at Derudeb I excused myself to see to some Mechanical Department business and the Governor decided to make a move too, asking if I would arrange for a message to be sent to his Headquarters, Kassala, for a car to meet him I said I certainly would and he departed in affable mood and told us never to pass through Kassala without coming to see him. We thought that, perhaps, something had been achieved.

Our service cars in my earlier days had no electric fans and frequently no electric light so the afternoons could be very hot. I remember one day in particular over the Kassala section. It was 16.30 hours, and very hot. We were going to the site of the Butana Bridge over the River Atbara and I suggested that we should travel for the next section on the buffer-beam of the engine. There was an extensive flat space there on which the fireman could stand when shovelling out the ash from the smoke-box. A rug and two cushions allowed one to sit there quite comfortably with feet on the rungs of the cow-catcher. Of course this had to be in daylight and with a wide-awake driver as the results would be serious if one ran into a cow or a camel. With these provisos, however, a ride was very pleasant and a cool change after the furnace-like interior of a service car on a really hot day. No animals showed up and we felt much refreshed by the time we reached the bridge-construction site.

Two years later, a few miles beyond the Butana Bridge, the District Engineer had an awkward experience. He was inspecting the recently constructed line from Gedaref to Kassala on his motor-trolley. He stopped for a picnic lunch under a shady tree 40 yards from the track and his trolley. After his lunch, his trolley boy had disappeared so he settled down to await the boy's return and was, perhaps, even on the point of closing his eyes in the heat when a movement surprised him. It was a lion appearing from behind the motor-trolley which he had used as cover for his stalk. The problem

WHEELS AND PADDLES IN THE SUDAN

was a nice one! Starting from a recumbent position, could a District Engineer, aged about 35 years climb sufficiently high into the boughs of the tree above, in the time that it took an interested lion to cover 40 yards. Also, was the lion of the tree-climbing variety? Fortunately the District Engineer won the race and the lion was not of the tree-climbing variety! When the trolley-boy got back to the trolley there was no District Engineer in sight, just a lion lying down in the shade beneath the tree! It was some seconds before he spotted the District Engineer up aloft waving his arms. The boy had the good sense to sound the klaxon on the trolley as loudly as he could. The lion slunk away allowing a grateful District Engineer to return to earth and continue his journey.

Dawn behind the Kassala Jebels was a wonderful sight, and those jebels were the home of jackals. One could hear them most nights and had to be careful sleeping out in the open. The siding on which our service car stood was about 40 yards from the railway houses and if we were dining on the *mustaba* (veranda) at the front of one of the houses, with our daughter's cot outside under a mosquito net near the service car, we would have an Aladin pressure lamp on either side to illuminate a wide circle. This dissuaded any visit but they would still prowl around, close enough to make one occasionally rise from one's chair.

Gedaref had a long established *merkaz* garden with some fine custard apple trees. These were good-tasting sub-tropical fruit. One morning, before breakfast, we were looking round the garden and I showed pleasure at the sight of these trees so the gardener picked some fruit for me. As we left I wanted to write in my notebook and so handed the custard apples to my wife. She dropped the biggest and it burst open but, never having tasted a custard apple, she was unaware of what she had wasted. Back in our service car, however, the first course at breakfast was custard apple. Very definite approval of the taste of a custard apple and passing the *merkaz* garden happened simultaneously and my wife exclaimed: 'Could you stop the train and let me pick up that custard apple I dropped?' I later planted a tree in our garden; and before long we enjoyed these fruits in Atbara.

Bees are widespread in the Sudan and they sometimes choose unlikely homes, such as in the locomotive shed in Gedaref. In my early days the chargeman, Antonio, one of the '40 assorted artisans', told me that bees had taken over his office and prevented him from getting his books in order for my visit. I inspected the rest of the depot before looking at these temporary residents. The office was a lean-to building adjoining the shed, constructed of corrugated-iron and with a match-board lining. This meant that there was a space of about 4 inches between the inner and outer skins. It was into this space and at 7 feet from the ground that a knot hole provided a front door. Antonio asked my permission to deal with them. I told him that he must not burn them out. He said that he would wait for dusk and then tear off the match-boarding and scoop out the nest. I suggested that it would be painful but he said that taking bees held no terrors for him. He asked for a new *tisht*, a tinned iron pan used for washing clothes, which is about 5 inches deep and 3 feet in diameter, and I gave him money to buy one.

At dusk I anointed myself liberally with citronella oil to repel bees and went to inspect. A big hole had been torn in the match-boarding and great quantities of comb were being scooped out. There were bees buzzing about but the brave warrior and an assistant battled on and soon carried out a very full *tisht*. The comb was standing up nearly a foot in the centre and I wondered if the honey would be contained. They considered that the taking had been worthwhile; they had been stung but not too much. It was quite a while before the bees lost interest in the site though they did not reconstruct on the old site. The honey was excellent.

One day a Financial Secretary arrived in Atbara handicapped by the loss of a denture between Port Sudan and Atbara. It appeared that he had left his sleeping compartment to go to the dining-car for breakfast, leaving his denture in a tooth glass. The sleeping car *farash* (attendant) had tidied up the compartment and thrown the contents of the glass out of the open window! Apparently it was his first contact with a denture and he thought it was rubbish for disposal.

The Financial Secretary at breakfast had soon realised that something was missing and returned to his compartment — but no denture could he find.

The position, however, was not entirely hopeless. The toothless one knew the time he had sat down to breakfast. The train arrived on time. It happened fairly close to Atbara. The window was on the south side of the train and the ground surface was sandy and without vegetation. The General Manager and the Financial Secretary requested the Chief Engineer's help. It only took a few minutes to discover what the approximate position of the train, to 3 kilometres, had been. Messages were quickly sent along the line to arrange for a pump trolley manned by a permanent way gang, to patrol each of the sections in which the denture might be found. Within an hour one of the gangs was back at the station with the missing denture and it was conveyed over the next two sections to Atbara with commendable speed. The safe return to the owner was much appreciated. Such was the versatility of talent on Sudan Railways!

One morning, as I was completing an inspection of Shendi Locomotive Depot, the Syrian chargeman told me that an old man was at the station wanting to show me something interesting. He was a 'seller of charms'. He unslung a leather ditty-bag and pulled out a horned viper — not at all a nice creature! It was the one snake in the Sudan for which I kept a lookout; it had a tiresome habit of winding itself round the base of a latrine bucket with a desire not to be disturbed. Musmar, a locomotive depot between Atbara and Port Sudan, had a bad reputation for this nuisance, and a fatal accident. My first action in such places was always to lift the seat and make sure that I was unaccompanied. The pedlar demonstrated how docile his snake was and invited me to purchase a 1½ inch piece of hardwood twig as a charm against trouble with horned vipers. My chargeman urged me to take one and said he always carried one. I suggested that the poison sacs had been removed from the snake but the pedlar opened wide its mouth to reveal the sacs.

He then produced a charm for scorpions. He drew a 3-foot circle in the sand and shook out from a cigarette tin two fine 4-inch scorpions! The circle effectively contained them. He allowed them to crawl all over him and then returned them to the circle. I was invited to purchase a charm and do likewise. The charm was a small piece of soft 'wood', rather like a dried broad bean stalk. The chargeman obliged but wisely shook off the scorpion just before it took cover in his clothing. I paid 5 piastres for the two charms and still have them. I have never been bitten by horned viper or scorpion, but I do not attribute it to the charms! My wife, however, was bitten by a scorpion; she made the mistake, when in sandals, of putting her foot on a scorpion's head instead of its tail.

Atbara, until about 1930, was short of citrus trees though Lord Kitchener established citrus trees and also mangoes of excellent quality and avocado pears in the palace garden in Khartoum.

A farm north of Atbara, at Darmali, had acquired some of these trees (a rare concession) and had excellent mango trees and two avocado pears. The old General Manager's house also had mangoes and a grapefruit grown at the palace from the original Kitchener trees.

In 1930, however, the Government obtained a large quantity of citrus trees from, or through, Cairo Botanical Gardens at Giza. Any official could have up to five trees at 20 piastres each and there was a big response.

The trees were good value and in three to four years the fruit position had changed. Some lesser help was also given with mangoes. The General Manager's grapefruit tree bore 2,000 fruit, but it required much protection. During the night a donkey would be driven from the *suk* with a couple of panniers on its back and my tree would be lightened by 200 fruit. I built a 10-foot high hexagon wire fence with padlocked door round the tree and greatly reduced the nuisance. Commercial planting of citrus in Dongola also produced some fine fruit.

Personal presents from suppliers, being discouraged, were seldom received in the Sudan. The Chief Mechanical Engineer received a large Stilton cheese which caused some heart-searching. It was decided to keep it, hermetically sealed, for the departmental Christmas party, six weeks away, and it was deposited in the store room of the Chief Mechanical Engineer's house. About a month later, he and his wife, sleeping on their lawn, were awakened at 03.00 hours by an explosion. The store room was covered with a layer of 'goo'. Their boys spent three days scrubbing up, and no-one would have credited the destructive power of a Stilton prior to this offensive demonstration.

Two of those parrots, whose arrival in El Obeid in 1923 I witnessed, came to Atbara; the Chief Mechanical Engineer took a pair and passed one on to the Assistant Chief Engineer. During leave the Chief Mechanical Engineer entrusted his bird to me and as it survived its first sojourn, the same arrangement was made in the following year. Unfortunately one morning we found Polly lying dead, from a clot of blood on the brain. The second one, Congo, lived to a ripe old age, and retired to Somerset with his owner. Living 15 miles away I saw him frequently; he lived on until 1978 so our acquaintance spanned 55 years.

In 'Rabbit Hutch Row' as we called our residences, a plane tree was a prominent feature of the garden and the focus of several 'happenings'. It housed the permanent nest of a *shawk*, a common scavenging hawk which took a dislike to my wife, and used to dive-bomb her. She had to wear her topee at all times and eventually the *shawk* had to be shot.

Another visitor to my garden was a serval. I was sitting there reading by the light of a standard lamp, when he walked into the circle of light and lay down. The serval was about the size of a lightly built Dalmatian, more square in aspect than a cheetah, with a background colour slightly darker than a leopard. He lay about 20 feet from me and was aware of my presence. I refrained from movement but he was quite aware of my presence. After five minutes he retired back into the shadows.

Four nights later the same thing happened. The serval was less at ease and walked about in the pool of light before lying down, listening intently. After five minutes he walked over to the large tree, and, in a flash, had climbed up into its lower branches, which only began some 25 feet from the ground. I never saw him again.

I had no fondness for ostriches and so I was not pleased to return to Atbara after a trek to find that one had been presented to me in my absence. It was about one-third full grown, and already a nuisance if allowed to roam, so I asked the Director of Khartoum Zoo to accept it. The Works prepared a travelling box and we made the journey to Khartoum. The Zoo adjoined the Grand Hotel on the river front, and a fortnight later, after completing some work I had to do, I asked after the health of the ostrich. The Director was apologetic; someone had fed a nasty piece of wood with a needle stuck through the centre, projecting by an inch on either side, to the ostrich, causing a most painful death.

My wife ran the thriving Atbara Sunday School which also interested itself in the orphanage at Abu Rof in Omdurman. Two of its inmates were Peter and a little girl called Melka, who seemed to have a 'romance'. The children were later moved to Salara in the Nuba Mountains and on our visit we discovered that Peter and Melka had married. Sadly, Melka had died giving birth to their first baby.

In about 1935, as an extra job, I was appointed Chairman of a Committee charged to report on the Weights and Measures of the Sudan. Egyptian, Imperial and Metric systems were all in operation in varying degrees. *Suk* purchases would probably be in Egyptian

WHEELS AND PADDLES IN THE SUDAN

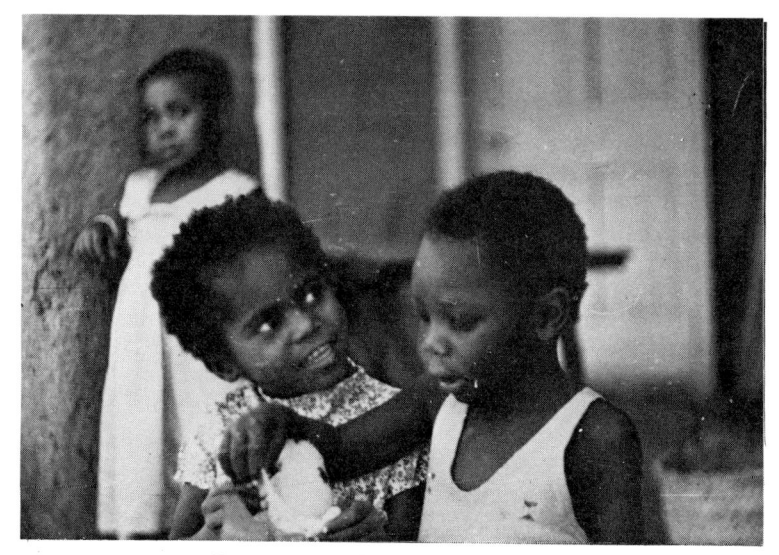

Romance at Abu Rof Orphanage.

rotls, petrol in Imperial gallons and dress fabric in metres. Lord Kitchener, anticipating metric for liquids had ordered two sets of standard measures from 5 litres down to 0.01 litre in copper, together with ten sets of working standards in pewter. However, in many areas Imperial measures continued to hold sway. In submitting our report I received as a memento a set of these working standards which I treasure.

I remember three visitations of locusts during my time in the Sudan. The first time we had warning that hoppers were approaching 70 miles south of Atbara and a large labour force was sent into the desert to dig several miles of trenches, 3 feet deep, in their path; as the trenches filled up, the locusts were destroyed with flame-guns. This invasion was small and adequately dealt with.

Flying locusts were a different story. One day at lunch, about 14.30 hours, it quickly grew dark. The *suffragi* loudly exclaimed *jarradat* (locusts!). The experience was uncanny; a blanket descended and everything green quickly disappeared. Their droppings, as they cleared the trees, could be heard striking the ground. One group of young paw-paw trees about 2½ feet tall and 1½ inch diameter, was devoured to ground level. The *nass* made a

WHEELS AND PADDLES IN THE SUDAN

terrific din to move them on and after about two hours the locusts flew off westward.

The third occasion was while coming up the 'bank' in the afternoon. My service car was next to the locomotive and I was alerted by the fireman to locust trouble ahead. Hoppers were trying to cross the rails over a long distance, which meant 1–2 inches of locusts over each rail. Locomotives had sand boxes to allow sand to be blown under the driving wheels to combat slip, but the quantity of sand carried would be quickly consumed in these circumstances. And quashed locust caused a lot of slip, and on the climb would quickly bring the locomotive to a stop. A spare firing shovel was always carried on a locomotive against accident and, fortunately on this occasion there was a second spare so two of us got to work, the fireman on one side and myself on the other. For the next half hour the toil was backbreaking. There was plenty of gravelly sand alongside the track, though the actual bed was of stone, and one had to sweep the hoppers out of the way, pick up a shovel of sand and endeavour to get as much of it as possible on to the rails under the spinning locomotive wheels, push away hoppers climbing over the rails just ahead, and spread the last of the sand on the rail. Whilst we were thus engaged the driver had to fire as well as drive the locomotive. We had to repeat our cycle as quickly as possible and if we were quick enough the driver was able to keep the train moving at the rate of about 2 miles per hour. The locusts extended for more than 1 kilometre, and the stench of squashed locust was revolting.

Over the years I enjoyed Felix Pole's friendship and always reported to him on leave. On the first time he gave me an all-stations pass for the system, which was a great thrill. In due course he was knighted. This honour was deeply appreciated by Great Western Railway staff, for he was one of them, having started as a clerk in the Traffic Department. His kindness was unbounded; he loved to spring a surprise. On one occasion he asked me when I was returning to Somerton. I replied 'Tomorrow afternoon'. He said, 'Go by the 5.00 p.m. — I'll tell them to stop at Somerton'. It certainly increased my local status immensely.

I think it was in 1930 that Sir Felix Pole paid a short visit to Atbara to see how Sudan Railways had progressed since his inspection seven years earlier. I remember him coming to tea and playing with our youngster.

His first question when you called would be to ask how Sudan Railways was faring, and what could he do to help. One year I mentioned something for which he thought Swindon could supply the answer. 'Can you go the day after tomorrow?' he said, 'I'll see that a foot-plate pass for the 9.00 a.m. is ready for you and a "Castle Class" on the train.' Another year, when I had spent the night at Calcot Place — his home near Reading — it was decided that I should go up to London with him in the morning. When we arrived at Reading station, I endeavoured to break away to get a ticket, but was told to desist and come along with him, and he would see to it. As we neared Paddington a Ticket Inspector appeared, and asked for our tickets. He had failed to recognise his 'boss'! General Managers in England used to hold 'gold passes' for each of the component parts of the railway network. Sir Felix had his passes strung along a gold albert watch chain. He caught hold of his watch, pulled the chain out and swung it through the air towards the astonished Inspector, saying, "Take your pick!" There was a very hasty withdrawal, and the question of my not having a ticket never surfaced.

Another time, after he had left Great Western Railway and become chairman of Associated Electrical Industries (AEI), and I was Works Manager, I told him I could not find a badly needed tool-setter. Quite bluntly he asked why he had not been told of it before. 'What are friends for?' he asked. I was spirited away in the hands of a Director of AEI to Metrovick and given VIP treatment. A visit to Metrovick was always a great experience. Everyone was charming, but faintly amused. They had been instructed to produce a candidate willing to accept what I could offer, and they could not see that happening.

In those days Metrovick must have had one of the most stable workforces in the country. They had a long-service association which you could join on completing 22 years service. I think it had over 1,900 members at the time. The work-shops were most impressive; each bay was large enough to accommodate the *Queen Mary*. I interviewed five possible candidates, but, sadly, none of them was interested in what I could offer.

Towards the end, Sir Felix lost his sight. He had a lovely garden, and knew the position of every tree and shrub, and you would have to act as his eyes. A quarter of a mile away, across a garden and meadow was the Great Western Railway main line. It was fairly general practice for a main-line driver to give a blast on his whistle as he passed Calcot Place, and this remembrance gave Sir Felix much pleasure in his latter years.

The Atbara community took a lot of interest in their gardens. In the late 1920s a Horticultural Society was formed; among its founders were the Horans, Jack and Faith. Jack was its secretary for many years. Their garden, though by no means the largest, was a wealth of colour and interest, as they were keen on introducing new flowers. We were in the habit of gathering plants when on inspection in the south, and giving them to the Horans to see if they could establish them in Atbara. One particular one that we found at the side of the Juba–Nimule road was given the name of *Rodum sidum*. It had a handsome large pink bell-shaped flower and leaves rather like a streptocarpus hybrid, and we both managed to flower them in the following year.

At that time we had the Director of Agriculture and his wife, Doctor and Mrs Tothill, staying with us. Mrs Tothill was a botanist of wide renown and had published a book on the flora of Kenya where they had served before coming to the Sudan. We took her to see the Horan's garden and pausing at these particular flowers she asked their name. I said that the person who was with us when we found them alongside the Juba–Nimule road said they were known locally as *Rodum sidums* Mrs Tothill murmured something about having no recollection of such a name but she would look into the matter. A year passed and the Tothills were again staying with us and we took her to the Horan's garden. The *Rodum sidums* were doing well and again Mrs Tothill paused at them. She gave me a hard look: 'What did you say was the name of those plants?' With a straight face I said *Rodum sidum*. Very acidly she replied: 'I thought so — You might like to know that their proper name is "".' I have forgotten what it was, but she was not amused. I think it was held that I was guilty of 'lese majeste'.

I have very pleasant memories of some of the oldest nuggets who were still in the service. The senior member of staff at Khartoum North Dockyard was First Reis Mohd Abdel Mejid. He had been awarded a big silver watch for particularly meritorious service and it was the custom for every official who met him to enquire what the time was.

Another of the same ilk was First Reis Ali Hassan, the doyen of Kareima Dockyard. His had been a particularly distinguished career. In 1897 he had played a prominent part in working the gunboats up through the Dongola Cataracts and he held a letter of personal commendation from Lord Kitchener for his good work in this connection. You would be asked to tea after which the precious document and a file of bits and pieces would be produced for you to admire.

The third was, I believe, the oldest serving member of the Sudan railways at the time I retired. This was Daoud Hassan, Bandmaster of the Sudan Railways Police Band. His exact age was uncertain but when I retired in 1946 he must have been about 120 years. Like Reis Ali Hassan he came to the notice of Lord Kitchener, who made him bandmaster of a group and in due course presented him with a pair of dark blue mess kit trousers which became his most precious possession and only to be worn on very special occasions.

Without the benefit of Kneller Hall or similar training, he had considerable skill as a bandmaster. He habitually wrote out the band parts for tunes published in the Sunday papers, like 'Round the Marble Arch'. The Police Band had a well established place in the life of the community.

In about 1936, when the Italians were causing trouble in Abyssinia, reinforcements were sent to the Sudan. A second battalion had to come direct from the United Kingdom and, most unusually, a Guard's Battalion — the Coldstream — was chosen. It was not at all a popular decision with the officers.

The battalion came to the Sudan up to strength and we had a company in Atbara. They took part in everything and gave us two shows at the Sports Club; the Guard Mounting Ceremony at St James' Palace and the Ceremony of the Keys. I can still see the figure of the Yeoman Warder, a Guardsman clad in an officer's great coat turned inside out to expose its scarlet lining, proceeding with a lantern and a rolling gait in mimicry of what he must have seen many times in the Tower.

Their interest in the Works was quite surprising. For many weeks, every Thursday morning at 06.30 hours I took a party of 10 round the Works. We ran a Technical School for training young artisans, drawn from all over the country, with the idea of spreading civilisation to untouched areas. Selection was largely by means of intelligence tests — Kim's game, taking down and re-assembling a simple bracket or other similar item where there was only one way to do it correctly, the difference between two drawings of a group of squares differing by the position of one of the squares. I always invited the Guardsmen to test themselves and see how they measured up against lads who had probably never seen a spanner or a drawing before they arrived at the school for a test. The results were not always as one might expect.

One of their biggest contributions to our life was their attendance at our church services. We held our services on the Nile bank in what had been an Army mess in the 1897–98 occupation of Atbara, or Dakhla, as it was then called. The building would have held about 60 people and our average Sunday evening congregation was 15–20 persons. When the Coldstream arrived, however, a squad of 16–20 turned up every Sunday and sat in a solid phalanx around the harmonium. They sang with gusto, and, if the tune played by the organist was not to their liking, they sang another, and left it to the organist to join in. It was my job to take the service on alternate Sundays and I must say I appreciated their support.

About the same time as this a Royal Air Force Squadron was stationed at Damer, eight miles from Atbara, and we saw something of them too. Their Commanding Officer, along with another officer, was taken prisoner by the Turks in 1915 while destroying a telegraph wire. He spent the next three years in detention or prison. His story is told in detail in a book one of the two officers wrote. He bedevilled his captors, alternately feigning madness or mastery of the occult. He caused a lot of trouble to the officers who found themselves in charge of him. He escaped many times and eventually arrived in a psychiatric hospital in Constantinople about five days before the Turks capitulated. He would give us the story of his experiences, as well as entertaining us with a marvellous demonstration of card manipulation and tricks.

About this time, we decided to build an Anglican Church in Atbara. Port Sudan, Wadi Halfa, Wad Medani and El Obeid all had purpose-built or converted churches whilst we had only the old mess. Bishop Gwynne was keen, the Church Missionary Society would make a donation and the Government would help. Several suppliers offered assistance and the Bishop collected money. He also had an architect friend in London who was prepared to produce a plan. It seemed that about half the cost might be covered and so we took the plunge with a lot of local support.

We laid the Foundation Stone, a fine block of granite, suitably inscribed. Beneath it was placed a foundation stone deposit,

Construction of Atbara Church.

consisting of a sealed tin containing a copy of 'The Sudan Herald' featuring the scheme to build the church, the order of service used at the ceremony, a mint set of current coins and a current set of postage stamps. My job was to drive the petrol-electric mobile crane used to lower the foundation stone into position. The ceremony went well, there was plenty of mortar and the Bishop wielded a powerful trowel and mallet. The Coptic and Greek Orthodox priests played their appropriate parts and gave the ceremony an ecumenical flavour.

As an indicator of the funds coming in, I devised a cut-out of a date-palm, 10 foot high with 10 detachable bunches of dates, each marked £100 and 10 rings, marked £10, round the trunk with a movable monkey at the side, and a basket at the base of the palm with the caption 'Please help him to fill the basket.' It was held to be in poor taste and I had to substitute the conventional thermometer.

Building went ahead speedily. The Works produced some beautiful doors using fine local hardwood. Sudan mahogany, though difficult to work, looks magnificent when well finished, and the Forestry Department let us have some lovely timber. Bill Cartmell, Controller of Stores, was interested in church bells and made us a

WHEELS AND PADDLES IN THE SUDAN

carillon with a chime of super-heater flues, which was a great success. Calliangi, our Greek building contractor, gave us white marble steps wherever the level of the floor was changed. Our organist, Bill Cheeseman, completely rebuilt the organ while transferring it from the old to the new church.

Bishop Gwynne performed the Consecration. The church was dedicated to Philip the Deacon, who, in Acts VIII, baptised the Ethiopian eunuch from the court of Candace, who ruled at Meroe, 45 miles south of Atbara. The local connection was felt to be very apposite and it was believed to be the only church so dedicated. We all hoped that the church would serve a community for many years to come. Changing circumstances, however, the withdrawal of the British from the Sudan Railways, as from the rest of Government, in 1956, meant that there then ceased to be a white Anglican congregation in Atbara and there was no longer need for an Anglican church. The church was therefore deconsecrated and turned over to secular use. It was of robust construction so it will be standing long after the decay of all other Sudan Railways buildings in Atbara. It may well pose a bit of an enigma to visitors in centuries to come.

Education is highly valued in the Sudan, and in my time, many youngsters were unable to obtain one of the limited places available. My Chief Sudanese Welfare Officer, Ahmed Hassan Khalifa, was keen on spreading opportunities for the younger people. He was held in high esteem by the railway personnel, and a scheme with his backing was likely to succeed. Primary education started at 6–7 years, and his idea was a sub-grade school for the 4–6 year olds. It had to start with a group of parents requesting a sub-grade school, which they would run themselves via a parents' association. They would find a teacher, to be paid by Sudan Railways. They would find a room in a house, and pay 2 piastres per week for each pupil, which went towards the cost of simple school materials. Welfare funds paid the rent. Power to sack an unsatisfactory teacher lay with the Parents' Association. I made the necessary funds available to Welfare, from 'fines', and we had seven of these schools in Atbara and a number at other railway centres. The standards were most encouraging; we aimed at only teaching the '3 Rs', and many boys profited so well from 2 years of sub-grade education that they went straight into the second year class of Primary Education. It was an interesting example of self-help to achieve results, and even if a boy could not get a Primary School place, he had at least been taught the elements of reading, writing and arithmetic.

Outside of Headquarters we in Sudan Railways knew little about the intricacies of our finances. In the Mechanical Department we regarded Headquarters as 'difficult' during the annual battle over 'Capital and Renewals'. It was not until I moved to Headquarters that I found out that our comparative financial autonomy carried considerable responsibility. The Sudan Government had its financial roots in 'self-help'. I think I am right in saying that its first budget was only about £70,000, mostly from Customs and Excise and the sale of postage stamps. There was no annual subvention from the United Kingdom, and only a small contribution from Egypt, which had reached £E500,000 by my time, and was towards military expenditure in holding the southern frontier of Egypt. The country was run on a shoe-string.

After World War I it was necessary to buy some larger transporters for the docks at Port Sudan, and increase the size of the Sudan Railways Power Station there. It was Sudan Railways itself that had to raise a loan on the Stock Exchange, and be responsible for its servicing and repayment, just as it was for the locomotives and wagons for the Kassala line. By the time I had reached Headquarters the country's budget had risen to £E5 million, and of that I had to provide £E600,000 from the operation of Sudan Railways. Of course I had very little serious competition for freight and passenger traffic, but the cotton crop, my main source of revenue, could be very variable, and a bad year for cotton imposed real difficulties. With loan charges and our contribution to the national budget being the main and inescapable charge, our 'buffer' had to be 'Capital and Renewals'. Adjustment to the salaries and wages bills did not offer much scope for tailoring, but if things got very bad, as they did in the early 1930s, there could be a cut in that area. There was indeed, when we suffered a reduction in pay of between 5 and 10 percent for two years, along with a standstill on Capital and virtually nothing for Renewals. By the time I retired, the budget had grown to more than £E6 million. With all our financial worries in Sudan Railways we managed to remain solvent.

Chapter Five

PORT SUDAN AND THE COAST

Port Sudan was, for most folk, their point of contact with the Red Sea. Whether one went on leave via Port Sudan or via the Nile route was usually dictated by how short one was for time. The Nile route was a 6-day journey to London whilst via Port Sudan took 10 days. The latter route was the more restful and favoured by families. At other times few people visited Port Sudan, unless on business or, like us, they enjoyed the fishing.

The fishing was quite good, with numerous and game fish. I can recall many enjoyable encounters. The Red Sea Hotel maintained a game book, to record notable catches and determine the Champion of the Year. My wife held the lead one year up to 6 hours before the deadline with a magnificent 34-pound bayard but someone in those last few hours landed a shark, and won. Sharks were a handicap to landing any decent-sized fish in the harbour. A shark would go through a hooked fish like a circular saw, leaving only the head on the hook as the last few yards of line were hauled in. We used live sardines for bait, and a Sudanese fisherman in his canoe alongside to catch the sardines and bait the hooks.

One afternoon I had a youngster, aged 10 years doing this job. We had lost three nice fish to a 9-foot shark and he was furious. He tied a 6-inch shark hook to a home-made grass line, baited it with one of the three heads and cast it out to tempt the shark. I was amazed at his spirit. Fortunately the shark, easily twice his size, was not interested.

I kept in my service car my own gear for dealing with such things. It was an 8-inch hook on a length of wire cable, tied to a light rope with an oil-drum buoy; baited, I would tie the rope overnight to an anchor point on shore, and with luck there was work to be done in the morning.

We fished at the harbour entrance using live bait, or took a launch to Sanganeb Light, 4 miles out on the coral reef, trolling a 'dollie'. We would catch enough fish on a trip to Port Sudan to fill the refrigerator on the service car and distribute it widely at Atbara.

An occasional delicacy was the Red Sea prawn. It appeared in the rainy season whenever the *khors* had delivered fresh water into the sea. Within hours the rocks along the shore would have a waving fringe of these 9-inch prawns. With no further rainfall and run-off, they disappeared as rapidly as they came. I always carried a 2-foot shrimping net in the service car when visiting the coast, hoping to coincide with a rainy night, and also to catch sardines for bait.

One holiday we spent days fishing and bathing with the Gordons from Khartoum North at Port Sudan. We parked our service cars at Sheikh Barghout. Bob Gordon and I went over early one morning to the Mission to Seamen's pool, for a bathe, and thence to the quays to see the fishing prospects. It had rained overnight and was a still morning, the water like glass, and the fish flopping in a most inviting manner. I looked down at the water around the rocks and could scarcely believe my eyes. Every rock had its fringe of waving life — the prawns were in! We hurried back for my shrimping net and then waded into the shallow water at the edge of the causeway and simply scooped them off. In half an hour we had filled two 4-gallon petrol tins. Our boys boiled a gallon of them for breakfast and then carried in a large dish piled high with these delicacies, to the surprise of our wives.

Once I was fishing at the harbour mouth, using a grass line with a rock tied to the end of it to anchor the boat. Suddenly I was heading out to sea! I had hooked a fish, which a shark had then swallowed and hooked itself. We set off for Jeddah! The grass line parted and I followed the shark, until mercifully my line broke under the strain.

The Red Sea abounds in the unusual. Such was a remote pearl shell farm run by the Government up the coast. Little was known of it. I acquired some good secondhand wire mesh for making a greenhouse and learned that it came from the closure of Dongonab Pearl Farm. I became interested.

Dongonab was an inhospitable spot, without natural water, situated on the coast, 100 miles north of Port Sudan. It was visited by only one motor car in the 18 years of its existence. The farm was set up in 1905 when there were few resources and many competing demands for almost non-existent funds.

Perhaps the export of pearl shell, which in 1907 was valued at £1,146, raised hope of building up this natural resource. Whatever the reason, Doctor Crossland, and an assistant, and 20 Fuzzy-Wuzzies to do the shore work, started at Dongonab in 1905. Diving was performed by Red Sea Arabs, the traditional pearl fishers.

The pearl oyster had a life cycle of seven years. Only about 1 percent of the eggs survive by making suitable attachments. A first objective was to increase this figure. Baby oysters were tended in nurseries with much protection to three years and then spent the last four years in open water. They were fished by the Arabs, and taken ashore for cleaning by the Fuzzy-Wuzzies. At its height 300 men were employed. Output in 1922 was 225 tons, fetching £68 per ton. Pearls would be found whilst removing the meat; an instant award of up to 10 piastres was sufficient to eliminate retention. Pearls of a good shape and colour from the Red Sea are a rarity. After World War I the price of shell fell, cost of operations rose and the farm closed — and so I acquired my netting.

In this same area was the Gebeit goldmine, the last one in the Sudan after the Um Nebadi mine was closed. It was 50 miles into the Red Sea Hills inland from Dongonab. Its communications with the outside world consisted of an old man who used to ride a camel into Port Sudan once a month carrying the gold output for the previous month. It was reputed to average £3,000. His journey lay through an unsettled area occupied by tough people but the gold only once went adrift, when a crooked Greek bank clerk outwitted the system.

Compared with Suakin, Port Sudan was a modern upstart. Conceived in 1903, as an alternative to spending a considerable sum on improvement to the old port of Suakin, the idea was quickly approved and started in 1905. The Railway reached it in 1906; but the line started from Suakin.

Suakin was an ancient port, it was the port and trading post for African produce. The old part was situated on a circular island, approached by a 2-mile channel through the reef. The newer part of the town with the *suks* and trading activities was on the adjacent mainland, the *gerf*. In 1880 General Gordon was stationed at Suakin and ordered the island to be connected to the mainland by a causeway, with a strong gate at the island end, referred to as Gordon's Gate.

Suakin was the base for two expeditions — for the relief of Gordon, and for the campaign against Osman Digna. As a base it required perimeter walls and detached outlying forts which still

WHEELS AND PADDLES IN THE SUDAN

An outer fort — Suakin.

A house door — Suakin.

Typical Suakin house (Gordon Gate).

exist. The base was constructed on Condenser Island on the northern side of the harbour. The Royal Engineers built quays, and condensers were erected to supplement the water supply, which came from poor-quality wells on the mainland. A stockyard was formed for the materials for the Suakin–Berber railway, and there was much argument about the route and the gauge of track to be employed. Gauge of 18 inch was championed, 3 feet 6 inch decided upon, and standard 4 feet 8½ inch material actually sent, along with 75 navvies, complete with corduroy trousers and bowler hats, to lay the track. Enemy action made it impossible to run a proper survey ahead of the line railhead, and there was great congestion at the harbour, due in part to poor stowage. The climate proved extremely trying. The chosen route led up a *khor*, south of the one finally chosen for the line to Atbara. A section was laid to Handub, and carried forward to Otao, but then the order was given to stop. The navvies inscribed on a rock an advertisement for 'Pears Soap', which was still visible in my time, and then lifted the track, which was reloaded and returned to the United Kingdom.

In 1904 another line was started, this time to Atbara from whence a second party was setting out to meet them.

The two parties met up in 1905, and thus established the railway route from the Nile to the Red Sea. In 1906 the line was laid from Sallom, the second station out from Suakin, to Port Sudan, and the line from Atbara to Port Sudan was complete. This did not cause the immediate demise of Suakin, and it was not until 1922 that the last important office was transferred to Port Sudan. The buildings in Suakin were then neglected, with the Government doing little to preserve them. Public Works Department had an annual provision of £E150, which was of little help, to spend on preservation work. When I knew Suakin most buildings were badly decayed, if not collapsed. The *Muhafaza*, the Governor's residence, which had been Kitchener's Headquarters, was maintained as a Province building. The old National Bank of Egypt building lived on as a Rest House. The *Wakhala* on the *gerf* — a huge caravanserai — was still presentable, as also were a few private residences on the island.

On the north side of the harbour entrance was the Quarantine, which could accommodate up to 600, and was an essential feature in the pilgrim traffic which passed through Suakin to and from Jeddah. It also handled all passport and money affairs. Each pilgrim had to pay £40 in sovereigns to land at Jeddah, and we had to provide the coin. In 1945 the sovereign cost £E4.05, and we also required £E2 from each pilgrim, to be repaid on his return, when he would be in a 'cleaned out' state. Sudan Railways' interest in the Quarantine was the provision of water by condensers, ice for cold storage, and electricity. I was always personally interested in a good supply of ice for our service car. The refrigerating machine was a museum piece; it consisted of two spheres, about 20 inch diameter, mounted at each end of a 3 inch shaft, about 3 feet long, and driven through a central gear wheel. One sphere was half submerged in a bath of brine, and the other in a tank of cooling water, and the shaft rotated. The second sphere contained a compressor, and the other the expansion coils. It was of Swiss manufacture, and had been running for 35 years, requiring very little maintenance.

We spent many a Bairam holiday at Suakin, sometimes bringing 80 boy scouts for a training camp. In return for the camp fire in front of the *wakhala* the locals offered local entertainment.

The fishing at Suakin was excellent. El Fakhi Mohd, our fisherman, knew the haunts of most of the fish and could bring an 8-pound fish from 200 yards to within range of our casts by beating with his hand on the side of his *khouri* (canoe).

A fish that was good to eat was the copper-coloured *safie*, which was particularly adept at seizing bait and dashing back into its lair in the rocks. It normally weighed about 1 pound, but our nannie, Annie Scherkl, caught an unusually large one weighing 2½ pounds.

There was a long thin fish, *terak*, typically 3 feet by 4 inch diameter that was very good eating. They were cut into lengths, popped into the refrigerator and steaks cut off as required.

Best of all was the *bayard*, usually weighing up to 10 pounds, good eating and numerous. They fought well and gave us a lot of sport.

On the south side of the harbour, Graham's Point, near the jetty where our service car was parked, was the depot from which the present railway started. The area was known as 'The Point'. Here all the material was unloaded, and the locomotives and rolling stock assembled. It was my Chief's first job as District Locomotive Superintendent to put the locomotives together. There were many difficulties. The boilers disliked the local water, and frothed inordinately, and the wet steam reduced their hauling capabilities to the extent that climbing the gradient up through the Red Sea Hills needed two locomotives, one hauling and one pushing. However,

Cotton train on Tokar/Trinkitat Light Railway.

they kept going and, in 1905, the railheads met.

Another local feature was the Tokar cotton crop's ginning factory. It was of antiquarian interest, providing the main source of employment in Suakin.

The road from Port Sudan to Suakin was good, but its continuation southwards for the 50 miles to Tokar was not. It ran over the coastal plain, and the last half was through 30 foot high sand dunes, which were difficult to negotiate without local skill, it was always a very difficult ride. I made the journey at least six times, but always with a local driver. Sudan Railways interest lay in running a highly contentious light railway from Tokar to the little port of Trinkitat, carrying the Baraka Delta cotton crop to the coast for transport by our tug and pontoon up to Suakin for ginning. The argument was over whether instead to take it by lorry to Suakin, over the punishing road, with the resulting wear and tear on vehicles. The Province officials wanted the lorries and set the haulage rates to cover the enormous cost of the spares needed. We were against inflicting spares shortages on the country as a whole, and favoured use of the facilities already provided by light railway and sea transport. We generally won the argument.

WHEELS AND PADDLES IN THE SUDAN

The cotton was grown on the Baraka Delta with the winter rain. The seed was issued by the Government. The growing process depended on many variables of rain and flood but usually about 100,000 acres would be flooded and a crop ensured. By the time the cotton was picked, the conditions were awful, with terrific heat and violent sandstorms, and Tokar would become almost deserted.

My first visit to Tokar was late in the season, during a dense sandstorm, when I found the Manager of the Tokar–Trinkitat Light Railway having a novel lunch. His place was laid in the drawer of the dining table. He would open the drawer, take a fork-full of food, and close the drawer again, it was his standard procedure for that time in the season.

The line from Tokar to Trinkitat was 25 miles long, with Decauville track and served by internal combustion engined locomotives. At the beginning of the season, it was quite a job digging out the Tokar end and its workshop from the massive encroachments of sand. Overhauls might be needed if conditions the previous season had interfered with such work, and remedial work might be needed at the other terminal on the jetty. I enjoyed my first trip over that track very much, escaping from a dust-filled atmosphere to another world.

Loading cotton at Trinkitat.

WHEELS AND PADDLES IN THE SUDAN

Midway on the journey, one passed El Teb, the location of one of the battles of the Suakin campaign. It was rather grim, with visible skulls with curly black hair and gleaming teeth. There were also pieces of heavy machinery hauled 40 miles in the 1870s for the construction of a ginning factory at Tokar.

Not far from El Teb, near a well, was a large nursery of fine camels and their young. The *hamla*, the goods-carrying camels of Tokar, had a wide reputation. Before the advent of the Tokar, Trinkitat Light Railway, 1,500 camels were needed to transport the cotton crop to Trinkitat, and the sight of a camel with a huge sack containing 350–400 pounds of seed-cotton tied on both sides of him was one to remember. Most of these camels were owned by three sheiks, who were people of some local consequence. Over the years we came to know one of them, and visited him on his 'country estate' in the foothills.

Trinkitat was approached over a low causeway, leading to the jetty and the two bungalows — one occupied by the manager, and the other a Rest House, known as 'Honey-moon Villa', used by very rare visitors.

At Trinkitat we enjoyed the fine local crabs. There was an old fisherman who produced them until the Italians lured him to Massawa, where, tragically, he fell from the rigging of a ship and was killed. Thus was lost his unique knowledge of the whereabouts and habits of the crabs of Trinkitat, which never again appeared on my menu. At the height of the season, Trinkitat was very busy, with the loading of cotton on to the pontoons to be towed by tugs, and on to *sambuks*, the local sailing craft, for transfer to the Suakin ginning factory.

On one occasion we went on south from Tokar, across the Baraka Delta through the cotton, to Aqiq, 40 miles on. Aqiq was set in a wide bay with a sandy shore. There was a fine Rest House combined with a Police Post which also performed a Customs function. I recollect the remains of Roman water cisterns and a washed-up Italian mine.

We visited Sheikh Shengrai on his 'country estate' up in the foothills. He showed us some of his favourite stock. Our contact continued on after I retired.

On the top of the Red Sea hills, 20 miles south of the railway line, was a little hill resort, Erkowit. Before World War II, it provided a change of air for people who did not go out of the Sudan for their leave. It could accommodate 12–15 persons. The Governor General also had a retreat there. The enterprise was run by our Hotels and Catering Section. We also provided the motor transport link to the railway and so it required inspection from time to time.

Erkowit was situated on a shelf, exposed to the south-east monsoon and enjoyed conditions that were unique. It was well wooded, with rains from December to January, when it was misty, and little *khors* would run, and flowers spring up overnight. It was a wonderful transformation from the usual Northern Sudan scenery. The outstanding landmark was Jebel Sela, the highest visible point in the Hills, and on the lower slopes were the 'Dragon Trees' with their beautiful 2½-foot long bunches of creamy flowers.

With the loss of United Kingdom leave due to the war, Erkowit became more important and accommodation was increased to cope with 50. This involved several visits as we were also mindful of conservation, an interest dear to the heart of the Chief Engineer. The soil on the shelf was of no great depth, and the run-off slope of the shelf was pronounced. It was necessary to prevent the soil disappearing down the hillside. An extensive series of *bunds* and weirs was built to catch the silt, and this worked well. The Chief Engineer built five new accommodation blocks, and a new building to house the dining-room and lounge. He took full advantage of the features of an irregular site, with attractive results.

One year we went to Erkowit on 28 December, taking our oilskins with us. and were virtually the only visitors.

On the edge of the shelf was a spot known as 'Lady Kitty's Leap', from where one could usually see a colony of baboons who resided on a shelf below. We donned our oilskins for a picnic there, but mist obscured any view. Only a few baboons could vaguely be seen and the sound of dripping trees in the mist gave an eerie quality to the experience. It was all so different from normal.

The Governor General once summoned us to a visit at his Erkowit retreat. Life there was more relaxed than at the Palace.

After World War II the main buildings were burned down. Constructed of wood, and with no fire brigade to hand, there was no chance of saving it.

Chapter Six

DONGOLA AND THE 'BATN-EL-HAJAR'

We will first consider how communications in this part of the Sudan developed. Between Wadi Halfa and Abu Hamed were three difficult cataracts, of which the middle one, Semna, was the worst, so that river passage over the whole stretch was impracticable. It was decided that the campaign for re-occupation of the Sudan should follow the river route, and this called for a railway for the first 200 miles.

The railway reached Kerma on 4 May 1897, behind the army which had got to Merawi by September of the previous year. Transport from the railhead had been by boat whilst the railway advanced, and the gunboats were assembled at Kosha, north of Kerma, as soon as the railway reached that point. By these means the Expedition advanced to Merawi, and stayed there until the end of October 1897. However, before the railway had reached Kerma, Lord Kitchener had realised that a direct line from Wadi Halfa to Abu Hamed would save 330 miles, transhipment, and the need for thousands of camels for the section Merawi to Abu Hamed. He decided therefore that a line must be laid as soon as possible. The decision was apparently taken before the railhead reached Kerma, since by that time the first 14 miles of track had been laid from Wadi Halfa. Rail-laying continued through the summer of 1897. Abu Hamed was captured by troops from Merawi on 2 August that year and the railhead reached Abu Hamed on 31 October. Track-laying averaged 1½ miles per day, with a record day of 3 miles laid. These figures are unique in the history of non-mechanical track-laying, and were achieved under terrific problems of heat.

The Sudan Military Railway, as it was then called, was pushed forward to Berber, and then to Atbara, to feed subsequent bases. With the advance south of Abu Hamed based on the direct supply line from Wadi Halfa across the desert, the importance of the rail line from Wadi Halfa to Kerma decreased, and in 1903 the newest

WHEELS AND PADDLES IN THE SUDAN

section Kerma–Kosha was picked up, with the idea of using the rails for the projected Atbara–Suakin line in 1905. In that year a line was laid from No. 10, the first station north of Abu Hamed, to Kareima. It connected with the steamer link from Kareima to Kerma, but there was the gap Kerma–Kosha which subsequently lengthened to Kerma–Wadi Halfa.

Thus, in my day, the circuit would be by train to Kareima, and thence by steamer to Dongola or Kerma according to the time of year and state of the Nile. The last section to Wadi Halfa would be completed by car.

Before we set out let us think for a few minutes about its antiquities. From Dynasties III to VI the Nubians lived well off Nile Valley trade. This changed under Amenemhat I (2,000 BC). The great forts of Semna, the Defufas, and the Circular Grave date from this period. Around 900 BC Southern Libyans settled at Napata and founded the Ethiopian Kingdom. A vigorous race, they conquered Upper Egypt first and then the whole country by 721 BC. For 60 golden years to 661 BC they ruled Egypt, held a prominent position on the world stage and with resources and population probably comparable to that of Israel and Judah — say half a million — waged war with Assyria.

Driven from Egypt the family continued to rule at Napata — hence its monuments — until 300 BC when power shifted to Meroe (Kabushiya). until AD 350.

Napata pyramids.

WHEELS AND PADDLES IN THE SUDAN

Now let us visit Dongola. We branched off the main line at No. 10 Station, and headed for Kareima, where the dockyard which maintained the steamers on the Dongola Reach was situated. Ahead of Kareima, dominating the scene, was Jebel Barkal, the 'Holy Mountain', with Napata at its foot. For six centuries, 900 BC to 300 BC, this was the centre of Ethiopian life. Its temples, partly cut into the mountain have suffered from rockfalls. The two most important are the Temple of Tirhakah and the Temple of Piankhi.

There are five groups of pyramids, three around the Holy Mountain, one downstream at El Kuru and one upstream at Nuri. The former is the older but it was more convenient to visit the latter first. It contained the great Pyramid of Tirhaka. All its pyramids were built of hewn stone throughout, and were not casings filled with rubble. El Kuru, 8 miles downstream on the east bank contained the pyramids of the other four kings of Egypt and the horse graves of each of them. On the flat west bank, opposite Kareima, was the site of the extensive Base Camp of Merawi used by the Expedition.

The first time I visited Merawi, General Jackson was still alive, and I asked if I might 'make my number'. The General had a most distinguished career in the Sudan from its earliest days and was one of the very few who were allowed to settle in the Sudan on retirement. He was very charming, in a reminiscent mood, and this was the only time that I met him.

A few miles downstream, on a concession, lived the Olsens, an elderly Danish couple. He was a relic of the early days. With the passing of the Jacksons, life became very hard for the Olsens and the Danish Government repatriated them.

Colonel Jackson, no relation to the General, also had a distinguished Sudan record, and was allowed to settle in Dongola. He had an estate at Mansurkorti and grew some wonderful citrus fruit which we could sometimes obtain in Atbara. I once visited the citrus plantations which contained some wonderful trees, one tangerine tree was carrying 10,000 fruit. The bulk was exported to Cairo.

Scattered along the Reach were several Government Pumping Stations, for example Gurier and Ghaba, providing schemes for tenant farmers with some support. These were very successful and increasing.

After passing Debba and Khandak we reached Old Dongola.

WHEELS AND PADDLES IN THE SUDAN

This historic town straddled the river. On the east bank, on high ground, was a large mud-brick building, originally a Christian church, of which the upper part was now a Mahommedan mosque presided over by a pleasant individual, who presented to me his visiting card, which proclaimed that at one time he had been the Sheikh of New York.

Midway to Dongola, at Kawa on the east bank, we visited Tutankhamen's temple. We were fortunate, after pottering for one hour, for my wife picked up a scarab and a small gold cat. My score was a gold and enamel 'Eye of Horus' and a chalcedony arrow tip.

It was only a short run of an hour or so to Dongola, which was a pleasant spot. We were met on the landing stage by Station Master Musa, one of the longest serving staff members of Sudan Railways. He radiated cheerfulness. The landing stage was crowded with sailing *gyassas,* which are the most graceful of craft. The *suk,* with some social activity, lay beneath lines of well-trimmed banyan trees, and the *merkaz* was a large brick building amidst well-tended flower beds. Dongola, now a centre of Local Administration seemed well cared for. An old friend, Sheikh Zubeir el Hamed el Melik, showed us around. After lunch we transferred from the steamer to cars, and set off on the third, and arduous, stage of our journey to Wadi Halfa, following a route along the east bank.

Immediately north of Dongola was Argo Island, 20 miles long and the home of Sheikh Zubeir, whom we visited. We spent that night at Argo Rest House, after viewing the new pumping scheme that was being built. Before retiring, as a precaution, we put all our clothes and boots on a table, 9 inches from the wall, with its legs in tins of water and paraffin. We underestimated the engineering abilities of Argo ants. They threw a bridge across the gap and devoured my wife's tussore blouse.

We spent the next day at the Defufas. These were two huge mud-brick piles about 150 feet by 66 feet, and the site of a circular grave. This was the final resting place of Prince Hepzefa, Viceroy of Ethiopia. The grave was roughly circular, say 275 feet diameter, with a central path 7 feet wide. The perimeter wall was 1 foot high and that of the central pathway was 7 feet high. The space between the centre path and the edge was divided into cells, with one large central cell on the south side for the body of the Viceroy. It was reminiscent of a wasps' nest. At the burial feast 1,000 oxen were slaughtered, and their skulls were placed to encircle the grave.

Some 300 slaves were either drugged or strangled and laid in the grave, all in the same position, with their bits and pieces. The Viceroy was laid in his special cell. After filling the whole tomb with loose earth, it was covered with a mud-brick crust. Subsequent burial of members of the Viceroy's family was by cutting a hole in the crust, and clearing a cell.

During the excavations at the Eastern Defufa some moss-agate knives were found, causing speculation as to their purpose. We were fortunate in finding one. I also picked up some *obols* (chalcedony beads), placed in the deceased's clenched fist to pay the ferryman, Charon, his charge.

The Eastern Dufufa was situated about quarter of a mile north of Hepzefs grave. The date was Middle Empire, Hyksos, about 1,700 BC and it was probably a fortified trading post. A trail to Um Nebadi gold mine started from here, and much gold would have passed through en route to Egypt. The Western Defufa lay nearer to the river. There were signs in the surrounding area of ancient manufacturing activities.

We set out to the north in the morning, passing Nuri and the 'Twin Virgins' (two breast-shaped rocks) and thence to the Kajbar Cataract. Next came Geddi and on to the Rest House at Delgo for lunch. Delgo was the centre of the Local Government area of Mahas, with the uncommon facility of a Post Office. After lunch we pushed on to Wawa Rest House, pleasantly situated on the river bank, across from Sulb Temple on the west bank; it is probably the most extensive antiquity in the Sudan and we had a boat made available for some sight-seeing.

Up betimes, we had a chilly crossing. Amenhotep's temple was very extensive, over 600 feet in length, and beautiful in the early sunlight. I noticed Slatin's name carved on one of the stones. A temple of this size suggests a city somewhere nearby. We enjoyed the return trip in the sunshine.

Then we left for Abri, passing some good rock drawings at the roadside, and had lunch at Abri Rest House. Abri was the centre of the Sukhot Local Government and noted for its production of fine dates. That afternoon we set off for Akasha, through country which had witnessed the battles of Kosha, Firket and Ginnis, during the Kitchener Expedition.

At Kosha were the ruins of the locomotive sheds where maintenance work for the locomotives on the Sudan Military Railway section to Wadi Halfa was carried out, and continued on for a while after the Kerma–Kosha section of track was picked up. It was eerie to walk amidst debris of parts and plant no longer worth the cost of transport to take them elsewhere, such as a wheel on a broken axle.

We arrived at Akasha in the early evening. The Rest House overlooked the river, and was distinguished by a toilet with a 15-foot stuffed crocodile on its roof. Five miles north of Akasha, on the west bank were the renowned hot sulphur mud springs of Ukma. These attracted clients from as far away as Cairo. The patient was immersed by his friends in a mud hole and many benefited thereby.

As we were waiting to set off next morning the 'Royal Blue' drew up. This was the only public transport through the 'Batn-el-Hajar' and it showed the ultimate in overloading. The road surface was appalling but a road service was being achieved; they had just completed the worst section, the 'Batn-el-Hajar', and this lay ahead of us! We stopped at Ambigol Well, and from here branched off to the left for the testing climb up to the forts guarding the Semna Cataract. I had brought with me my Motor Transport Superintendent, Freddie Woodall, whom I had known in the Western Desert as having had great practical experience in these circumstances. The view from the top was well worth the effort. Way down below was the torrent. The forts, dating from 2,000 BC, had never succumbed to raiders, and formed a strong offensive barrier protecting trade moving by land or water. The natural obstruction to flow was formidable. There was a middle channel 120 feet wide, and two subsidiary channels, giving an overall width of 600 feet. In the low water period all flow was confined to the central channel. Carved on the rock faces below the forts were 27 flood level marks, from which it was clear that the present flood levels were 25 feet below those in the days after the forts were built. This was largely due to the face on the west bank having been undercut and collapsing, thus opening up the western subsidiary channel and relieving the peak level of the flood. I never myself saw the range between low river and peak flood, but I guessed that it must be about 50 feet.

The three forts, Semna East and West and Uronarti, are similar in style. They have massive mud-brick walls 15–25 feet thick and reinforced with beams laid in each direction, on solid foundations of granite rubble, and up to 30 feet in height. The design shows considerable knowledge of the arts of defence towers at the corners,

WHEELS AND PADDLES IN THE SUDAN

Akasha Rest House Toilet.

Transport in the Batn-el-Hajar.

entrances protected by double gateways with parapet all round, to make it possible to deal with an enemy who had breached the outer gate. Any attack had to be uphill, making the placing of scaling ladders very precarious. All three forts had a covered stairway running from inside down to below water level, so that at no time would their water supply have been lost. How big the garrison was is speculation, but at these times, accompanying wives and even children would have been usual for such a station, and one estimate of the Semna East complement was 100 fighting men. Semna West was the larger fort and the Headquarters of the Commandant, and probably had a garrison twice as large. One curiosity of Semna West is that the river bank road went through the fort, with double gates in each of the opposite walls, providing the tightest possible control over traffic on that bank.

The return journey down the sand slope to the main track presented no difficulties. However, we then turned north for Sarras over some of the worst going so far. We took a half-hour break at the Rest House en route (whose latrine was the same as that of Akasha except it ran to three stuffed crocodiles!) Akasha would, however, still win on size of its exhibit.

We pressed on to Gemai Rest House where the view at sunset of the Rock of Abu Sir, the second cataract, repaid us for all the stress of the journey. We were now within one hour's run of Wadi Halfa. An early start was not essential, so we enjoyed a leisurely contemplation of the view over our early cup of tea.

From Gemai to Wadi Halfa the road was much easier and, once arrived, we spent an hour or two at the hotel on the river bank. This hotel, in common with the rest of Wadi Halfa, now lies beneath the waters of Lake Nasser, as I expect also do Gemai and Sarras. Such is the price of progress. For the inhabitants of Wadi Halfa a long trek resulted from the inundation; they were removed to the Butana, the area south of the bridge over the Atbara river carrying the railway line from Kassala to Gedaref.

Chapter Seven

THE WAR YEARS 1939-45

Declaration of War in September 1939 found the second eleven in charge as most of the Heads were taking late leave. I was both running the Mechanical Department and being No. 2 at Headquarters. The Chief Engineer was keeping the General Manager's chair warm as well as his own. Spirits were high, and the second eleven was quite prepared to carry on indefinitely in the absence of their seniors.

There was not much preparation before the war, except at Port Sudan, where the expansionist outlook of the Italians in Eritrea had made us realise some of our shortcomings. Our sole source of electricity was the power station in the Dock area and all our dock equipment was electrically driven. We had purchased three diesel-electric shunting engines which could be used as mobile power stations, sited as required, if the main station was damaged. We soon found that failure of the smallest component quickly immobilised these units, if the replacement part was not in Stores. A personal procurement in London, triggered by a telegram, and despatch by air solved such problems up to the outbreak of war, but thereafter we frequently had a unit out of use, for want of some small part. With steam you are not so vulnerable as anything lacking can be made. Authority felt that our crane capacity would be insufficient, and so we acquired a 15-ton crane from South Africa.

Water supply, and particularly storage, needed our attention. Our source was now Khor A'arbat with a limited rate of flow, and so the first step was to increase storage to make fullest use of our source. We planned new reservoirs at ground level in the Dock area; construction was by local Greek contractors. Cement, which dominated the bill of quantities for the job, was a precious commodity now, and had a high value on the black market. Construction was well advanced when we discovered that over 2,000 bags were missing. The Director of Police put a young Sudanese Inspector in charge of the investigation. He successfully unearthed the racket. His Director was so pleased that he asked me to allow the Inspector to handle the prosecution case as well and I agreed. Truth flew out of the window, as commonly happens in these cases, but it looked as if a conviction would be obtained. In his winding-up address to the Judge, the Inspector reminded him: 'Sir! You have in your language a saying *Let lying dogs sleep.*' A broad smile crept over the Judge's face, and in due course, I was able to write a most complimentary letter to the Director of Police upon the conviction.

Rationing soon became necessary. Sugar, which we obtained from Egypt, was one of the first shortages. It came in cones — called *ras* — 3 pounds in weight and costing equivalent to 3 shillings. The Sudanese, under British occupation, had become heavy consumers. For a Sudanese, a 'good cup of tea' was a cup filled to the brim with broken *ras* on which tea had been poured. A ration of 1 *ras* (3 pounds) per head per week was introduced. This reduction in living standards did a lot to bring the realities of war home to the Sudanese.

An early action of His Majesty's Government in the war was to requisition the Sudan cotton crop. The terms were the average selling price for the previous two years plus ½ pence per pound, and this to last for the duration plus one year. As the Scheme was running smoothly on a selling price of 9 pence per pound, and the new price was to be 11½ pence per pound, it looked as if things would run satisfactorily. This was so, until Japan came into the war, and unbleached calico, called 'greys', disappeared virtually overnight from the market. This was a terrible blow to the *nass* who required two suits made from this material per year. India was chosen as a new source of supply, but the cost was 40 piastres per metre, compared with a former price of 2½ piastres per metre, and 20–25 piastres for a suit. Negotiations to get a better price were abortive, it being pointed out that the cost of raw material supplied by His Majesty's Government was so high — cotton at no less than 25 pence per pound! It transpired that the cotton we were supplying at 11½ pence per pound was being sold and shipped direct to India — at 25 pence per pound. Remonstration to His Majesty's Government, however, produced a rebate of £500,000 per year. This enabled us to subsidise the price of imported calico, and ease the pain for the Sudanese.

Grain became another problem. After two successive poor

harvests, we asked the World Health Organisation for advice on rationing. *Dura,* that is millet, was the staple food of the *nass*. Its usual price was £E5–£E6 per ton. The World Health Organisation called for a ration of 15 pounds per month for an adult, which gave a national consumption well in excess of the country's crop in a good year. We had always suspected this. At harvest, and in the months after a good crop, *merissa* (beer) was brewed and folk ate well, so that belts had to be tightened in the weeks before the next harvest and so we must have always had rationing by scarcity. The only place from which *dura* was available was Abyssinia, where the Empress headed the consortium which had the monopoly, and the price was £84 per ton. We had to pay it, but it taught us a lesson. I became an emulator of Joseph, in a minor way. We built *mustabas,* brick-covered plinths about 1 foot high, with a brick-on-edge surround, in our Stores yard. They were about the area of a tennis court, and on these the grain was piled up to 18 feet. Grain not needed for immediate use was stored in Atbara, and issued as required.

Mustard soon disappeared from our tables and the hotels were without any. A hermetically sealed caseful of tins of Coleman's product was unexpectedly washed-up on the shore near Port Sudan. As I was Commissioner of Wrecks, I took charge and passed it to the Hotels and Catering Department who gave us in return one tin.

Early in 1940 I went to Cairo to look for any materials that would be helpful to us. There was a lot of hardware about, brought from Germany by Jews, in lieu of cash. I also discovered local manufacturers new to us. A source of high-quality rubber vacuum brake spares was one important example.

Also in 1940 the Prime Minister of Egypt, Ali Maher Pasha, visited us. We laid on a full-scale programme for him. My job was as escort, meeting him at various points and handing him on. I had passed him to the Chief Mechanical Engineer for a tour of the Works when a messenger suddenly rushed up to him with a telegram. I do not know what it contained but even if it had been a warning of a bomb waiting for him in the copper-smiths shop, which he was on the point of entering, Ali Maher could not have been more precipitate in his flight. I next had to receive him at the Egyptian Club at noon. I got there 20 minutes early but he was earlier still and very sulky. Next came an 8-mile trip, including a ferry crossing over the River Atbara, to Damer for lunch with the

Governor. Later I took the Prime Minister back to Atbara, where the Egyptian community were his hosts for the evening, and at 07.30 hours the next day saw him off at the aerodrome.

Another early visit, led by a Chief Royal Engineer, was an army delegation looking for a site for a base workshop. They had already cast a covetous eye upon our Atbara Works. I took them to see the Chief Mechanical Engineer. Within minutes they planned the use of the boiler shop for tank repairs, and the tender bay for conveyors. It took rather longer to convince them that our spare capacity was slight, and that if they wanted us to keep the railway running normally, as surely they would, then the better solution was new facilities, situated in the neighbourhood. We generously offered them land on the Port Sudan line, six miles away. A schedule of requirements was produced and in ten days time, our Chief Engineer had the scheme ready. Their first concern was what the place should be called. Our suggestion was 'Slough', and indeed it was on the drawing. The name stuck. It was an extensive scheme, calling for a wide range of facilities, including storage of up to 8,000 tons of ammunition in scattered, thatched bunkers, a rifle barrel-straightening plant, and a hospital. Much ammunition did find its way to 'Slough', and Indian troops were in the hospital by Christmas 1941. A 'spin-off' was the provision of the first length of tarmac road in Atbara; up to this point we had not aspired to such refinements but the army felt that 'Slough' must be connected to Atbara by tarmac. So, heading into the desert, eastward towards Port Sudan, was 8 miles of tarmac. I do not think it was ever extended.

When my wife came out in May 1940, I managed to be at Aswan to meet her. It was terribly hot. I was engaged there on finding out how to adapt the sluice-lifting crane on the dam for lifting tanks from or to a barge, in an emergency. With a temperature of 128 degrees in the shade the deck of the dam was so hot that one had to stand on one foot at a time, to allow the other one to cool off. My wife found it so oppressive that she finished her journey with mild heat stroke, but fortunately the steamer had a plentiful supply of ice.

All this coming and going in connection with the 'Slough' scheme, and threats of other increased activities, made us suggest to His Majesty's Government that it would be wise to supply extra locomotives and wagon stock. We were asked to state our requirements. We asked for a further batch of Pacific 4-6-2 engines, 300 steel wagons and twenty 5,000-gallon oil tanks. The locomotives were put on order, and we were told that we would get parts from the USA to assemble 300 wooden wagons. We were to supply the underframes for the tanks, but prepared plate, welding machines and welders would be sent from the USA to fabricate the tanks at Port Sudan. In due course 20 locomotives arrived, and we heard that 40 more had been put into store at Derby. There was no great demand for 3 feet 6 inch gauge locomotives. We did not much like the bits that arrived for the wagons and only assembled half of them. The tanks became one of our most expensive assets. Five welders arrived with all their gear, and I think they regarded Port Sudan as a haven of rest. Their rate of pay was more than three times my own, plus danger money and various fringe benefits. However, 20 tanks were completed and put into service, and proved very useful. Settling up the account is a later tale.

The Italians were also short of various items, notably munitions, and about ten days before declaration of hostilities intelligence found out that *SS Umbria* would leave an Italian port, loaded with 8,000 tons of bombs, torpedoes and other ammunition. The navy shadowed it to Port Said, where scrupulous attention was paid to its safety. Authority thus managed to take six days in giving 'safe' passage through the Suez Canal, leaving only 30 hours in which to get from Suez to Massawa or at least within the protection of the Italian Navy. The position was hopeless, as two British warships, waiting off Suez, shadowed the Italian ship down the Red Sea, and arrested her and brought her into Port Sudan. The captain was refused permission to anchor in the middle of the harbour, as he was judged quite capable of blowing up his ship, and flattening Port Sudan. Instead he was taken to an anchorage at Sanganeb, 4 miles out. Twenty minutes after dropping anchor, it was noticed that boats were being lowered; he had opened the sea-cocks and the vessel sank until only the funnel, masts and upper works remained above water. I saw the crew passing through Atbara en route for internment at El Obeid. I was glad that Atbara was not their destination; we had too many Italians there already and they had set up a religious establishment in a building which gave them a fine view of the railway station and goods yard. We had already requested authority to keep an eye on them.

We received aerial attention from the Italians on 9 August, 9 September and 9 October. On the first occasion they arrived at

WHEELS AND PADDLES IN THE SUDAN

08.30 hours. I was walking home to breakfast with the Assistant Chief Engineer and commenting on the irregular formation of three planes passing overhead, when two bombs landed and exploded in gardens 100 yards to our right. We dived into a slit-trench as two more bombs went off, one slightly wounding a woman in the face. Two further bombs fell, one on the lawn 5 yards from the Assistant Chief Mechanical Engineer at breakfast, but fortunately did not explode, whilst the second did so at the bottom of the garden. One of the planes circled and made a run at the Atbara Bridge, dropping two bombs quite close and killing a goat.

The next raid, on 9 September took place around noon. The alarm had sounded, and we were making for our trenches when a plane dropped a stick of high explosive across the railway station. This attack was more successful, hitting the main cross-over of the tracks at the south end of the station, and a neighbouring police post. Another plane scattered incendiaries over the offices, without much damage though a policeman did subsequently die of shock.

Our request to Khartoum for protection brought two Gloucesters with Australian crew. The night of 9 October was a full moon, and an Australian sergeant was keeping guard over the aircraft from a deckchair, with a rifle by his side. He was facing the moon, listening to the faint popping of a throttled-back engine, when he saw an aeroplane silhouetted against the moon, gliding towards him. He fired at it, and it turned to port, and unloaded anti-personnel incendiary bombs as well as two high explosives. Its course was parallel to the goods yard and directly over the packed open-air cinema. Miraculously, no-one was hurt. Some of the bombs were duds and there was much dangerous souvenir-hunting. The following morning I collected five detonators from *nass* (the local people) who had removed them from dud bombs. I did wonder if the pilot had known that there were two loaded ammunition trains in the goods yard that night. The trains were in full view of any watchers in the Italian Convent, and the attack had come in the right direction, but 150 yards to the side. Possibly the sergeant's fire had caused the pilot to turn fractionally early, or more sharply than intended. On the strength of the suspicion, the Convent was closed 'for the duration'.

The stage was set for important events, and I was summoned to Khartoum. A weighty delegation was arriving with some epoch-making scheme. We assembled in the Council Chamber in the

WHEELS AND PADDLES IN THE SUDAN

Palace and the delegation entered. It consisted of a lot of 'brass' and an official of the Irrawaddy Transport. Our deliberations were to be concerned with planning for transporting 1,000 tons per day of war materials from the mouth of the Congo to the Mediterranean. Our specific concern was to be for the section from the Congo border, near Aba, to Juba and down the Nile to Wadi Halfa, or in practice to Kosti, as the rail link from there to Wadi Halfa already existed. Two fundamental points about the scheme stood out, as far as I was concerned. Firstly, the total lift of goods from Juba was currently 2,000 tons per year: secondly, the 200 kilometre stretch between Shambe and Bor, the heart of the Sudd, was probably the most difficult main river navigation in commercial use anywhere in the world.

The Head of the Delegation, sitting as Chairman, asked my views on the proposals. I said I would wait until I had heard the experts speak. The Chairman then painted a rosy picture of what the Congo had promised to do. The Congo fleet would take over, I think, at Matadi, and carry the goods into a northern branch of the Congo River, I believe it was the Uele, to a point where an existing Decauville track pointed towards Aba, which was in road connection with Juba, our southern terminal on the Nile. He admitted that the Decauville track, apart from needing extending, might need replacing by wider and heavier gauge track, and that there were many bridges between Aba and Juba which would need reinforcing, but that neither aspect would be a great problem. He said that they were most fortunate to have an authority on river transportation, the Head of Operations of that highly successful organisation on the Irrawaddy. He was next to speak. His main troubles were sand banks and how to navigate them. I spoke next and was very blunt: 'Speaking of the Sudan section, I think that the man who thought up that scheme should have his head examined'. The Chairman was chilly: 'The Prime Minister (Churchill) is very impressed with the scheme, and is giving it his blessing'. I apologised for being so critical, but asked if anyone in the room had ever made the journey through the Sudd swamp area by water, preferably when the Sudd was running? No-one had. I asked if anyone had flown over it, in daylight and low enough to pick out the bends and waterways. One or two of the audience raised their hands. It was clear that I was the only person who had really experienced the Sudd, having been through it twice when the Sudd was running. I was bound to

WHEELS AND PADDLES IN THE SUDAN

comment that discussion would be so much easier, if a number had actually seen the Sudd. I said that it might be possible to lift 365,000 tons per year from Juba, given the right equipment and back-up facilities, but emphasised that it could not be done with the equipment described. It was proposed to use small high-speed, petrol-engined landing launches of about 200 hp capability, and wooden barges, constructed of double three-quarter-inch diagonal planking with canvas interlay.

I dealt first with their capacity to withstand impact. I sketched out what navigating 200 kilometres of the worst part involved. Many of the bends were of the sharp hair-pin variety. The tow was typically three barges ahead and one on each side of the propelling vessel. Alternatively it might be a 2-2-2 formation with propulsion between the rear pair. On coming to a left hair-pin bend the tow was run into the papyrus ahead, with a little starboard rudder and engines eased back with the hope that the stern would be carried round to 90 degrees. The bows would then be pulled out of the papyrus by the impact of the port side of the tow and the stern on the papyrus, so that the bows would be caught by the current and swung to 180 degrees, not necessarily quite in the channel, but heading in the right direction, athwart the stream on the crown of the bend. With the engines full ahead, the tow would, with luck, soon be heading down the other arm of that hair-pin, ready to tackle the next one in similar fashion, and so on for 200 kilometres, provided the tow was still in one piece. The wear and tear was heavy; lashing cables parted, bollards were pulled out, and steamer rudders got broken (at least two spares were carried). The skill and judgement of the *reis* was paramount to carry out these manoeuvres.

On the bank of the Blue Nile, opposite the Palace, was the dockyard, where our steamer fleet repairs were done. I invited the meeting to stand up and look across the river at three steel barges, with their pushing knees bent up at 90 degrees. If that happened to steel barges, what hope was there for wooden ones surviving the journey? As regards the 200 hp launches, I doubted the ability of their sides to stand up to the impacts during navigation of a bend. I feared for the safety of petrol-engined craft in the dry season, when the vegetation dried off and a raging inferno was not infrequent. We had provided sufficient petrol storage capacity at Juba for our needs, so as to avoid shipping petrol in the dry season, as we were aware of the risks. At first sight it looked as if two depots for petrol would be needed in that 200 kilometre stretch. In a few words, wooden barges and light craft with petrol engines were quite unsuitable for the job.

I was then asked what I would recommend. For a lift of 365,000 tons per year my first estimate was 240 steel 100-ton capacity barges (allowing 30 percent out of service, under repair) and 40 diesel-engined stern-wheel towing units, to a proven design. This size of fleet would require considerable expansion of repair facilities, I commented also that this scale of traffic through the Sudd added a hazard on account of what other tows were up to at any time.

I was told that what I had said was difficult, if not impossible, to realise. The material was, in fact, already on the high seas, arriving shortly. How could I help? I said I would set up an immediate building programme for barges, and I would put the launches in the river, get them into running order, and get together several crews under the best of our *reis,* and test out the theory of operation. I felt that their experts must accompany a trial run, hoping that I would be proved wrong, though I believed otherwise. The meeting agreed to give the equipment a trial.

When the barge material arrived, we promptly started building on three slipways, two barges in tandem on each. We launched three barges every third day, slipping each incomplete barge down the slipway. Getting the launches into running order was soon done, and crews assembled without serious difficulty. When all was ready, I asked the army to accompany the craft on trial. Ten barges and eight launches with crews to suit set off. They worked their way gently up to Juba, mainly towing one barge only, in line ahead. On the way back they made up a couple of tows of two launches and four lightly laden barges, keeping the remaining four launches and two barges in reserve. I do not recall the details of the trip, but half the units were lost and the remaining components limped home. We were absolved of responsibility for the losses and were told to stop building any more barges pending further decisions. The eventual verdict was: to return the launches to Port Sudan to await further instructions; to try to work any completed barges up to Alexandria; and to despatch packed barge material to Port Sudan.

Getting to Alexandria was touch and go, it depended on there being sufficient water in the Nile at the sixth and fifth cataracts at this time of year. The 40 or so barges were, however, safely worked through to Abu Hamed. Passage through the Dongola Cataracts was not possible, so a special loading way was constructed to get the barges up from the river and on to 30-ton rail trucks, with an additional flat at each end to protect the overhang. The width of a barge made it an out-of-gauge load, so all the signals in the 11 sections across the desert to Wadi Halfa had to be moved back. The trains were then worked, with especial care, to Wadi Halfa, and the barges refloated and taken through the Aswan Dam and on to Alexandria, where they were put to use in the docks.

We heard no more of the scheme *per se*, but many road bridges between Aba and Juba were strengthened, several new warehouses erected and improvements made to the quay at Juba, and indeed some hundreds of tons of goods did turn up there. The scheme was named African Forces Line of Communication (AFLOC). Our interpretation as Africa's Fantastic Line of Communication, in the absence of the official one, was certainly not correct!

There was a sequel. Two years later, I was in the Financial Secretary's office in Khartoum, when the Civil Secretary, Douglas Newbold, came in, saying: 'I heard that the General Manager was with you. I have someone here who wants to see him'. He introduced the Minister of State, who, when shaking hands said, 'I was hoping I would see you. We owe you an apology'. He added: 'You were right'. Could more be said?

With the Italian raids on Atbara came a host of other happenings. Kassala, on the line from the Makwar Dam to Port Sudan lay very near to the Eritrean frontier, and was an inviting target. The Italians soon captured Kassala, and cut the railway line 15 kilometres on each side, thus breaking the southern part of the loop. We were told not to expect outside aid until 5 October, when an Indian Division would arrive. In the meantime, at Atbara, we were highly vulnerable. The Italians had only to push forward 40 miles to the River Atbara, travel 180 miles along its bank to reach us, and put the Railway Headquarters out of action. Our protection was 200 British troops, an anti-tank trench and a small Home Guard. I had a calendar of squares on my desk, and crossed out one square every morning on arrival in the office; I was relieved to cross out the last one on 5 October.

During this period of waiting, the 8,000-strong army in the Sudan had to make the most spectacular use possible of its resources. The *Kaid* sent for me to see what help the Railways could give. He wanted to make intensive use of his locally made armoured personnel carriers, and his few small tanks. He needed, as quickly as we could make them, heavy portable ramps, strong enough to entrain or detrain them anywhere, and a lot of heavy plates, so that the vehicles could move from one flat truck to the next. The Chief Mechanical Engineer did a marvellous quick job and the *Kaid* was soon able to put his plan into action. This was to make a noisy demonstration with his armoured force at the end of the track on one side of Kassala, entrain again, and dash 1,700 kilometres round to the other side of Kassala, via Khartoum, Atbara and Haiya, to stage another noisy demonstration of fighting force. The sequence could be repeated as desired. It kept the Italians guessing, for reports captured after their capitulation showed that they had estimated our opposing forces at 110,000 strong. It used up precious fuel but it was worth it to keep the Italians static in Kassala.

The Indian Division arrived on time and prepared to advance into Eritrea. We also received some anti-aircraft units for Port Sudan, and three Royal Airforce bomber squadrons which were stationed on the Red Sea Hills, at Summit, Wadi Gezooza (named after an empty lemonade or *gezooza* bottle lying about) and Erkowit. The aerodromes were natural gravel expanses with pegs driven into the ground to mark the corners. Taking off with a heavy bomb load at an altitude of 3,000 feet gave some problems, but the Italians paid little attention to the airfields, possibly because they were still short of bombs.

Around this time, an Italian mail plane flew over Atbara every night at 02.00 hours. We used to speculate on its load. One day an aircraft carrier arrived at Port Sudan to take on board two squadrons of fighters, flown up from West Africa. This was an opportunity to intercept the mail plane, which crossed the coast just south of Port Sudan, but on the night in question, the plane did not make its trip, and the departure of the carrier to Singapore could not be delayed.

The army, now installed at 'Slough', began looking about for wider spheres of influence. The railways rather tempted them, as they had precedents to varying degrees in Persia, Iran, Syria, Palestine and Egypt. They had brought an ex-Sapper General Manager of Tanganyika Railways, Colonel Maxwell, to Khartoum, to be in charge of Communications and wanted control of Sudan Railways. I was diplomatically sounded out as to my views. I was unwilling to expose my fine team of Heads of Department to orders from outside and I was not attracted by the rank which would be offered, so I replied that I was not interested and the matter was dropped. We remained good friends with Maxwell; as General Managers of two African railway systems, we had much to talk about.

Coal supply became a problem. The bulk of it came from Natal, and, as shipping became short, stocks ran dangerously low. Danger point was reached when stocks, scattered over 100 locations, fell below 10,000 tons. Coal stocks were not necessarily where the demand was greatest, and one could hardly burn the last few tons anyway. I had great difficulty in convincing Headquarters Middle East that the railway would shortly be halted, but fortunately at the eleventh hour a shipment of coal arrived at Port Sudan. We were asked to give thought to oil-firing as an alternative to coal-burning. The Chief Mechanical Engineer and the Locomotive Running Superintendent obtained two oil-burners, and the Works Manager built oil tanks to be mounted on top of the tenders. Oil was obtained from Port Sudan and before long they were out on the road on trials. Results were quite promising, and we advised the authorities that we were ready for serious trials. The Chief Engineer produced a highly satisfactory design for concrete ground storage tanks and started making them at Atbara in vibrated concrete. Fifty-two tanks were required. We soon had locomotives on several sections running on oil. Before that stage was reached, however, we eked out our limited coal supply with wood, and even with charcoal briquettes of domestic manufacture.

The planned re-conquest of Abyssinia in early 1940 required a second railhead for the advance from the north. The first was provided by Kassala, and the second was to be in the form of a spur from Malawiya towards Tesenei, about 35 miles in length. We were to survey a route at once. Rails would come from India, and we had to find the sleepers. The rub was that we were to be assisted by a Royal Engineer Railway Company from Longmoor, UK. It had to be a fast operation and the Chief Engineer felt that British troops new to the climate would prove a terrible handicap. Preparatory work was begun, the survey made, and the route pegged out. A lot of bank work, up to 6 feet high, and small detours of banking at *khors*, was started. The Royal Engineer Company was full of enthusiasm, but the Chief Engineer decided that they should cut their teeth on laying the track for the sidings at Malawiya station. They managed only about 70 yards a day with little sign of improvement. The Indian rails were nearing Port Sudan, and time was running short so it was decided to start on the line proper, for 1 or 2 kilometres. The Royal Engineers were put on to it.

This type of work required two main parties. The 'bankhead', camped out ahead, did the earthworks, leaving in their wake a flat bed, at the correct level, on which the rails were laid. They also did the initial work at each *khor* crossing, making an earth bank diversion on which the track could be laid temporarily. Next followed the 'railhead' party, with its train of materials, consisting of open wagons of sleepers, flat trucks of rails, and wagons of components, fishplates and bolts, bearing plates and spikes. The material train was pushed to the end of the line, sleepers carried forward and dropped roughly in position. A dependable man with a regular pace walked along the track and the sleepers were adjusted in position to his pacing out. Meanwhile rails had been carried forward, and were waiting to be placed on the bearing plates on the sleepers to be followed by the insertion of spikes in previously drilled holes; the fishplates were then fitted to join on to the last rails. The *osta* sighted the rails, they were given a lift here and a push there, he gave a whistle, and the train moved on by a rail's length and the cycle was repeated time upon time.

The programme required a cycle of something better than 2 minutes. Rail-laying was an integrated process, where the slowest contributor governed the overall speed of the advance. The Assistant Chief Engineer, acting as railhead engineer, tried to incorporate the Royal Engineers into the procedure but they just could not work at the required rate. He decided therefore to keep them as a unit on 'boxing-in', which was the last stage. When the material train had passed back and forth over the newly laid track, and some lifting and straightening had been done, the track would be 'boxed-in' by adding earth, as required, to the level of the tops of the sleepers, and general tidying up. To have to use the Royal Engineers on 'boxing-in' was a sad ending to their employment but the job had to be finished on schedule. A few days later tragedy struck; the Royal Engineers Major shot himself and the unit was withdrawn. As soon as the rails arrived from Port Sudan, laying started in earnest, and the Assistant Chief Engineer finished the job with two days in hand. It was a fine piece of work.

At the next station to Malawiya I found a marooned American who had lost his party. We picked him up and gave him tea. He told us that he was one of ten civilians collected in the Middle West to give civil engineering assistance on problems arising out of the United States Army occupation. In civilian life they were mainly small builders and contractors. With their 'grub-car' they had been landed at Massawa, and proceeded to Kassala. The 'grub-car' was equipped with bunks, immense water tanks, 2 months supply of tinned bread and plenty of other food. They were under strict orders not to drink local water or to take refreshment at local cafes. They had transgressed on reaching Kassala, with resulting upset tummies, but they had recovered. We suggested that perhaps he ought not to be drinking tea with us, but he said that was quite alright, and added: 'I do like your cookies'. These were rock cakes made by my wife. We dropped him off at Kassala, and I hope he regained the comfort of his 'grub-car' without any calls en route.

In May 1941, on Cairo station platform, I was approached by a Military Attache, Major Hope, who asked my help in finding a hide-out for a man who had been involved in the installation of wireless transmitters and receivers for use by the secret service in Rumania and Yugoslavia which had gone bad on us. This was no difficulty. My Superintendent of Mechanical Transport, Woodall, was rather a recluse and also the only individual in the Sudan with a wireless-transmitting licence so he seemed like suitable company. The man was put on the train, and I wired Woodall to meet him at Atbara station and take over. He stayed for ten days calling London every hour for seven days to obtain measurements of signal strength. His transmitter was carried in the pocket of his large coat. At the time there was thought of locating a reserve high-power transmitter at Atbara, in case the Abu Zabal one near Cairo should be lost.

Depletion of coal stocks, and the consequent liberation of space under the coal transporters at Port Sudan, was probably the reason for dumping on us 70,000 tons of chrome ore. The United States obtained most of its chrome ore from Turkey, and, with deteriorating conditions in the Mediterranean, stocks were shifted to the nearest safe port that could handle it, which was Port Sudan. The event made us think. We had a hill of chrome ore of our own, close to the railway line, at Qala-el-Nahl, between Sennar and Gedaref. Could we not do something about that? As General Manager I would welcome a couple of 600-ton trains per week over that line. Our enquiries revealed that the world's requirements of chrome ore were handled by one man, who was not interested in new supplies from the Sudan. He advised us to stay clear and avoid getting hurt. As far as I know that hill still stands inviolate.

'Slough' was at least partially in operation by December 1941. As already mentioned there were Indian troops in the hospital to be remembered at Christmas time. We sought the help of the Indian doctor. All that was lacking in their diet, he said, were the sweetmeats so dear to the Indian heart. If we could find the sugar, his cooks could do the rest. Vast quantities of sugar were found, and grease-proof paper for bags. I vividly recall our chauffeur, Mohd Koko, staggering round on Christmas Day with us carrying a *tisht* piled high with sweetmeats. It was an occasion which gave a lot of pleasure.

For some months before his return to Abyssinia the Emperor lived incognito in Khartoum, in the Pink Palace, as 'Mr Smith'. He wanted ceremonial drums for his re-entry and Sudan Railways was designated to supply them. These were a suite of one Bull drum, four cows and five calves, roughly 5, 3½ and 2 feet diameter. This meant great inroads on our copper stocks, plus the problem of finding ox hides of up to 5½ feet diameter for the Bull drum. I was due to go on inspection in the south so endeavoured to find one with merchants at trading posts. I took with me some 5½ feet laths for ease of measurement on the spot. At Wang Kai I found an excellent hide, and two reserve specimens, which I despatched to Atbara right away. The finished Bull drum was magnificent, fitted with rings to be slung on poles carried by four men, marching ahead of the Emperor as he rode into his kingdom. I left a photograph of the complete set of ten drums on the wall of my office in Atbara as a memento of the minor part we had played in 'Mr Smith's' return.

Cecil Rhodes had dreamed of and worked for an overland Cape to Cairo route. Although quite long stretches of 3 feet 6 inch gauge track in the north to south direction gradually appeared, the middle section including the Sudd was so moist as to need wide detour to reach suitable terrain. With no strong commercial stimulation, and dwindling dreams of Empire, it did not seem to justify the cost.

In World War II, however, upwards of 2,000 vehicles were driven overland from South Africa to Egypt. They skirted the east edge of the Sudd, and met the River Sobat not far upstream from its junction with the White Nile, south of Malakal. Some months after, in our launch *Sobat* up Khor Filus, we went ashore to view the

WHEELS AND PADDLES IN THE SUDAN

Cape-to-Cairo road. It was the rainy season and the soil was like butter. The road was an 8-foot wide track, with 4-foot high grass on each side, and a wet mud surface on which one could barely stand upright.

There are signs of revival of the idea of a north to south railway link. Sudan Railways has now reached to Wau, on the west of the Sudd. There is talk of further extension south and east along the Nile-Congo Divide, to Juba, and on to Kenya, whose rail gauge is also 3 feet 6 inches. I have myself driven it by car and consider it quite feasible physically. An attraction of the scheme is the possibility of grain production for the Arab world market, using Arab oil money to finance the scheme, which has strong advocates in Kenya.

One Friday morning, when fishing from a dinghy at Port Sudan, a hospital ship steamed in. We noted a big dent in its bows and recalled recent wireless news of a hospital ship being involved in a bombing raid at Tobruk. An hour later a Quay Inspector hailed me from the shore saying that the Commandant of the hospital ship requested our presence at breakfast, adding: 'He says he is your cousin'. I told him to relay the message that we would be there as soon as possible. I had a cousin, a Harley Street specialist, whom I had not seen for 20 years. After breakfast we toured the ship, a Bibby liner, whilst awaiting the arrival of a hospital train with convalescents from Gebeit to be exchanged for the wounded. The train was delayed for track repairs due to heavy rain during the night and things were, therefore, at a standstill until its arrival.

The matron of the ship made her opinions clear about a railway which could not run on time! I asked about the dent on the bows; it appeared the ship had been struck by a flying chunk of quay when leaving Tobruk. The changeover went so smoothly that at 13.00 hours my cousin was sailing out of harbour instead of lunching with us.

On the subject of train delays in the Red Sea Hills I remember what the District Commissioner at Sinkat did about them; he constructed a private road from Sinkat to the coast and protected it with noticeboards. We were once invited to drive down it; it must have been after the Italians came into the war as we passed close to the wreck of one of their planes which was a cause of much interest to the Hadendowa.

We heard with shock that the battleship *Queen Elizabeth* had been attacked by Italian frogmen whilst anchored in Alexandria

WHEELS AND PADDLES IN THE SUDAN

Harbour. Temporary repairs were made at Alexandria to enable her to proceed under her own steam, but more work was needed before she could cross the Atlantic for complete repair. This work was carried out at Port Sudan under ideal conditions, warm clear water and a 2 feet clearance over a sandy bottom. These conditions were so appreciated by the divers that I felt they had a bearing on a later issue. In due course the *Queen Elizabeth* arrived safely to the USA.

Soon after this, 'The Admiral', Commander Yates, formerly in charge at Khartoum North Dockyard, visited us. He was now involved in naval repair work at Alexandria. The navy sent him to us because of his contacts, for a softening-up first round in a scheme which the navy was hatching; the possibility of using Port Sudan for repair facilities outside the Mediterranean.

'The Admiral' tested my initial reactions and, in due course, a high-powered party, including 'The Admiral', arrived at Port Sudan. Their problem, with the deterioration of conditions at Malta, was to find suitable space on land and water, including housing for 2,000 dockyard mateys. They wanted the whole of Port Sudan. We firmly defended the need for its continuance as a port, and indeed the only port for the Sudan and I felt sure that the favourable reports of the divers working on the *Queen Elizabeth* had whetted their appetite. In the circumstances that they were envisaging, the Nile route via Egypt would be of no avail to us. We also did not think that Port Sudan lent itself to the scale of development required, and we recommended instead Mohd Gul and Haleib, 100 miles to the north along the coast, with almost unlimited shore space and deep water. It had over 20 feet of water alongside a natural quay, and a small source of fresh water in the Hills, not unlike Khor Mogg at Port Sudan, but not tested as to flow. After considerable discussion the meeting broke up. As it happened, however, the evacuation of Malta never became necessary.

In 1942 we received a summons to be ready to attend in Khartoum at short notice. It was all highly secret. We subsequently learned, after a change of date, the Duke of Gloucester was to visit. We duly went to Khartoum and put our service-car in Khartoum North Dockyard opposite the palace, intending to go to the function by launch. A sandstorm, however, led instead to a long detour by car. It was rather early as we approached the palace so we waited a while 100 yards away, listening for the cathedral clock to strike. In the

WHEELS AND PADDLES IN THE SUDAN

sandstorm we missed the strike and found that it was dangerously near zero hour. We had to move quickly and climbed the marble stairs at an undignified rate to be received at the top by the Private Secretary with: 'I'm glad you made it'. We just managed to take up our position at the head of the line when the procession entered. After dinner the venue was the ballroom where, at the far end, on a dais, were two gold armchairs. His Royal Highness was led to one of them and in turn, we all occupied the other. My wife had to lead off. She kept the conversation going very well and overstayed her span. I was No. 4 and found a subject of common interest, but he was, I thought, a very tired man.

War conditions and mail delay led to the introduction of the 'aerogram'. One bought a form for sixpence and wrote a letter within boundary lines on one side and posted it. A mini-photograph was taken of the letter and the roll of film flown to a destination where the film was developed and the mini-photos enlarged and posted to the required address. It functioned very satisfactorily for some months and gave a more speedy mail service.

Following the loss of one or two mail-carrying planes another expedient was tried. This was the choice of paying a higher rate of postage — 15 piastres instead of 4½ piastres to have the letter flown by circuitous route via Accra, Natal in Brazil, and New York. It became popular for family correspondence.

There was anxiety in Egypt as to whether the line at Alamein could be held and, at this time, two train loads of residents considered to be at risk were sent to the Sudan. One individual, the widow of German doctor who had escaped from Hitler's regime became my responsibility. She was entrusted to the Governor General for special care. His Excellency asked what I could do. I made a post for her as housekeeper at the Grand Hotel, Khartoum. Madame Maria Huldchinsky accepted the post and created a wind of change. Sailing along a corridor clad in white broderie anglaise with mob cap and chatelaine bag hanging from her waist, she was an impressive sight. She proved to be a talented artist and before long His Excellency extended his patronage to an exhibition of her paintings and portrait heads at the Palace. She was launched. At His Excellency's suggestion I gave her facilities to paint in the Southern Sudan and in due course we purchased a portfolio of 40 paintings to hang in the Grand Hotel at Khartoum. She remained with us for two years before returning to Egypt. As a memento she gave me four of her paintings.

Mme Huldchinsky's paintings.

WHEELS AND PADDLES IN THE SUDAN

During World War II the Italian navy, short of munitions, caused little trouble. One of their submarines was lost on a reef down Aqiq way but I cannot recall other happenings. Air raid casualties were suffered at Port Sudan when a native cafe was hit. The final curtain at Massawa was comedy. Their Admiral in full dress uniform, being called upon to surrender, drew his sword, endeavoured to snap it across his knee, and when it bent into a U-shape he cast it into the sea.

During the war, dust storms and elementary traffic aids at Khartoum Airport sometimes forced people to break their journey at Atbara. If Service personnel, they stayed with us rather than at the Rest House. One day orders were received from Khartoum that a distinguished voyager was to be entertained and no questions asked. None were, but inquisitiveness revealed to the house-boys the gold-laced kepi and be-medalled uniform hung out in the wardrobe. The 'stranger' was General Le Gentilhomme, en route for Djibouti to enlist French Somaliland for General de Gaulle.

Another visitor was a captain in charge of Development of Hydrofoils, a subject on which I was not well informed. We learned quite a lot about these interesting craft. They were fast motor-boats — hydroplanes — with two small additional floats, one on each side, which could be wound down and cause the craft to ride on the two floats instead of on the step of the hull. In this position they make particularly poor targets for torpedoes.

Lady visitors were less frequent but we shall always remember the Colonel in command of the South African Women's Air Force, who was very charming. Married to a Lieutenant she found their respective ranks frequently an embarrassment.

We also recollect with pleasure the Dutch Ambassador to the Hedjaz, Van der Meulen, who visited the Sudan several times and came up to Atbara. He was serving at Jeddah for the war at the personal request of his Queen. Jeddah was a special post, held by an excellent Arabic scholar and normally only for one tour. Van der Meule had a wealth of stories about the country, of which he was very fond. In Sanaa, he told us, he had come across a relic of the Imperial Court of Franz Joseph functioning as a Foreign Secretary and surrounded by a miniature version of the court at Vienna. It was as if time had stood still. Van der Meulen's name was an absolute talisman if you wanted something done in Dutch official circles as my wife was subsequently to find out when returning home on my retirement in 1946.

With the World Health Organisation looking ahead to the problem of feeding the increasing world population; the idea of mechanised agriculture required attention. We, particularly in the Gedaref area, had wide open space and suitable soil, though lack of irrigation was a risk. A trial area gave encouraging results. More machinery was moved in and the next year a larger area was planted. Bird damage to the first crop was no greater than usual, but to the second it was enormous; it seemed as if all the yellow sparrows in Africa were gathered there, and it caused serious thought to be given to the viability of mechanised agriculture in Africa. I never heard how it progressed after my time but the idea is still current and the Wau area was recently mentioned. Perhaps improved earlier ripening seed has been discovered.

Every six months during the war, our Financial Secretary, Louis Rugman, visited the Hedjaz to 'inspect the books'. Few, if any, books were in fact kept but interest lay in the cash position. The Hedjaz still largely depended on the takings of the Pilgrimage. Every pilgrim had to pay a basic 40 sovereigns to land at Jeddah and for that the whole tour was laid on in basic form, 'lorry to Mecca, food and sleeping space for so many days, lorry to Medina, and after a day or two back to Jeddah. For improved transport and accommodation at the various sites you could pay up to £2,000 in sovereigns. The number of pilgrims, particularly wealthy ones, was falling and the cash position needed watching. King Ibn Saud was still sitting on his treasury — a huge locked chest — and anyone in the Government seeking cash had first to prise him off his seat. This was not easy. I would have liked to be present at the 'auditor's inspection'.

Oil was not yet flowing considerably. The royalty was $1 per barrel, but drilling was proceeding with success. It was, however, a time of drill and cap. I mentioned to the Financial Secretary that one of my staff, Woodall, listened daily to Shell Oil of California reporting to Head Office. The Financial Secretary was interested and asked for a copy for his office and so Woodall got an extra job as offical monitor.

Everywhere at this time money was being collected for war charities and my wife felt that Atbara, too, must play its part. She made her opinion felt and the idea caught on in all communities. It was to be a united effort in which each community would play its part. My wife had a committee of 40 which used to meet in a great circle of chairs on our lawn. With her Arabic tutor sitting with her as secretary, she presided as chairman and all proceedings were in Arabic; it was a great talking shop. In general, there were four representatives from each community. Speakers would come to the middle of the circle and declaim their views which would bring a lively response. They accomplished quite a lot whilst imbibing much coffee and lemonade. The target was £E1,000 in a one-day sale. It was to be called 'Suk el Kheiri' and be staged on the Atbara Sports Club ground. The main stalls, run by each community, were booths of palm trunks and matting in a semi-circle, filling the whole of the playing field, with fringe activities around and in the Club buildings. The Governor came over from Damer to open it and a hectic five hours followed. One of the greatest successes was tea on the tennis courts, served by the British wives. All our servants lined up to partake of tea served to them by *'El sittat el Englezi'*. At the end of the day the total raised stood at £E920 and the final total was £E1060. The goods left over passed through our house for final disposal. One of the most amazing items was 11 black cotton, very large bathing costumes, such as are occasionally seen on the French stage. Their history might have been quite interesting. One of the charities to benefit in the distribution was Mrs Churchill's 'Aid to Russia' fund; her letter of acknowledgement reads as follows:

10 Downing St.
Whitehall
23 May, 1944

Dear Mrs Williams

Thank you so much for your letter.

I am so glad you told me about the Victory Fair which was held in Atbara, by which the splendid sum of £1,000 was raised. I am much moved that the members of your committee decided to allocate £225 to my Red Cross 'Aid to Russia' fund.

I send to you and your Members my grateful thanks for this welcome gift.

I am most interested that Atbara adjoins the mud village which my husband knew forty-six years ago as Dakhla. I shall tell this to him, and where your generous contribution to my Russian Fund was collected.

With my thoughts and wishes,
    Yours sincerely
        Clementine S. Churchill

WHEELS AND PADDLES IN THE SUDAN

The success of 'Suk el Kheiri' led the proprietors of our local cinema to suggest that a Gala Performance would similarly raise much money. Would my wife obtain a suitable film? In the Arab world 'suitable', among other qualities, calls for length; about five hours duration is desired. The proprietor of the 'Cinema Bramble' in Omdurman was an acquaintance of ours; Gaddis Abdel Sayed was a very interesting character. When Lord Kitchener left Wadi Halfa for the front on 30 September 1897 he took with him as personal telegraphist Gaddis Abdel Sayed. After the fighting was over he stayed on in the Postal Service, eventually retiring as Postmaster, Khartoum. In retirement he ran his cinema, the 'Cinema Bramble' in Omdurman and was willing to help. He said he had just the film for the occasion. It was 'The Bleeding Heart' and had very appropriate posters. The Atbara Cinema management was delighted. It was essential, they said, that my wife should be present at the performance and make a speech, in Arabic, of course. On the night a flower-bedecked box awaited her and it was a complete sell-out. With regard to the speech, I remembered the great success of a speech by 'The Spoo' at a New College Bump Supper in which he ended almost every sentence with 'Head-of-the-River' to mounting applause at each repetition. We thought we would try the same method with 'The Bleeding Heart'. There was help available for the Arabic and a suitable version was written out. At the appropriate moment, with the script discreetly reposing behind the decorations, my wife started her speech. The magic worked quite well and each time it was punctuated with applause, and voted a great success. After two hours my wife was permitted to withdraw whilst the audience continued to wallow. Some hundreds of pounds were raised by that one performance and devoted to Sudan war charities.

Among our last visitors at Atbara was a financial mission to settle for the locomotives which His Majesty's Government had provided and the wooden wagons and petrol tanks which had come from the USA. The mission consisted of two British officers and two Americans, a Colonel and a civilian financial expert. The Financial Secretary gave me freedom to negotiate without his staff being present, subject to his final veto on any agreement reached. I told him also that my figure for the locomotives would err in favour of His Majesty's Government but I would pay as little as practicable for unwanted wooden wagons and a figure for the tanks in line with their value and not with the excessive book cost.

The price for the locomotives was complicated; there was the cost of £9,000, monthly hire, and a rebate connected with the period of hire. I calculated that £8,200 was a fair figure. The British officers, however, were quite unaware of any hire charge or rebate. They asked £6,900 per locomotive, neither more nor less. I had agreed with the Financial Secretary that we should pay the fair price and, after difficulty, it was settled at £8,100 per locomotive.

The Americans were very amused by all this, and, when we started on the wagons, the Colonel announced: 'I want a gen-u-ine Bed-ou-ine deal!' I think he got it! He said he did not want to take away 200 wagons erected and 100 yet in crates, and we were not particularly keen on them in the long term. We quickly agreed a knock-down price. Next came the large petrol tanks for which we had provided underframes. The book price was colossal, five welders and their gear, each paid nearly three times my salary, had spent months at Port Sudan welding them up. They had cost six times their proper price and the solution proved painful to both sides. we finally settled for £10,000 per tank. In a little over 1½ hours I had spent, subject to the Financial Secretary's final approval, just on half a million of Government money. It was a wonderful feeling!

The British officers then suggested to me that we buy three more locomotives that were in the Middle East. Apparently at least three of the 40 locomotives lying spare in the UK had been dismantled, packed and shipped to the Middle East. Parts were lying at Suez and at Haifa and we could pick the bits out and arrange shipment to Port Sudan. The pre-war price of these locomotives was £4,000. I could see trouble ahead if they accepted any offer from me. I said I would take them at £4,000 per locomotive, all pieces to be delivered to Port Sudan and any shortages in excess of £100 per locomotive to be to their account. No deal was ever agreed.

It was a trait of the Political Service to send short and brilliant telegrams and also to burst into poetry. Douglas Newbold, Civil Secretary, during most of my time at Headquarters, frequently did so. On one occasion, when the water flush of his saloon regrettably did not function to his satisfaction, he sent me a five-verse gem. It took us rather longer to prepare the reply than to mend the defect, but then we were more at home with the repair. It was not easy to obtain copies of these verses. There were two I wanted to obtain but I never managed it. The Financial Secretary, Louis Rugman, commemorated the slave-raid near Daga Post, which was debated at Westminster, in 'The Pillage of Pill' and Douglas Newbold wrote a famous poem 'Aboud with me'. However, a burst watermain in Khartoum evoked the following ditty:

'Was none who would be formost
to check the water's drop?
For Khartoum shouted 'Forwood!'
and Forwood yelled out 'Stop!'
And backward now and forward
Wavered each silly plan
And while they talked their half-baked tripe
Well guaranteed our souls to gripe,
the nearly empty water pipe
Each day less freely ran.'

Forwood was Director of Public Works at the time. In the archives of the Civil Secretary's Office was an interesting book of sketches by R. K. Winter in his early days, Douglas Newbold loaned me the book to make some tracings, more particular including scenes of special interest to Sudan Railways. I found several drawings highlighting our shortcomings. One was of a typical foreign dignitary, Prince Fortunatus XXV, Hereditary Prince of Parvacivitate arriving on time (*fortunatus sine dubio*, as it is a very rare occasion) and being met by the railway staff. The Prince with an aide-de-camp carrying a basket of decorations is shown presenting one to the last of a line of four railway chiefs and a dog. Another is of various railway officials at Port Sudan. A third sketch depicts a frequent occurence at a wayside station, when a passenger, tired of the delay, asks when they will be moving on. The caption reads 'Train (mixed), already four hours late, stops at Station No. 42':

Passenger (leaning out of window of train):
'Khubr ay, ya akhie? El wabar yasafir emta?'
'Any news, my brother? When is the engine going to start'?
Railway official (a wheel-tapper in baggy trousers):
'Badein, ya Bey, Hadret el Nazir awiz yiktib gawab li familia bita hu wal commissari rah yishrib gahwa wi el telephongi'.
'Presently, your excellency. The station master wants to write a letter to his family and the guard has gone off to drink a cup of coffee with the telephone clerk'.

WHEELS AND PADDLES IN THE SUDAN

I kept a record of a fourth sheet, a delightful series entitled 'Political Service Levee Dress — Modes in the more remote provinces'. I remember another telegram. Arrivals from, and departures on, two leave periods, early and late, had to be advised by telegram to the Civil Secretary's Office. Serving at Kassala, at the same time, were a vet called John Going and a District Commissioner called Cumming. They were on opposite leave periods with, as it happened, coincident date. The telegram read: 'Going coming and Cumming going'.

Chapter Eight

KHARTOUM TO JUBA – August 1945
FIRST TRIP OF *M.L. MELIKA*

With transfer from the Mechanical Department to Headquarters I had to take a lively interest in the waterways of the Sudan. I made the journey Khartoum to Juba, up the main Nile, several times, and I here use my notes for a journey in 1945 as a basis for this chapter.

At 15.15 hours on 23 August 1945, *Melika* set off from Khartoum North Dockyard on her first voyage. Work on her commenced in November 1944 and progress was slow till April 1945 but with a great spurt she was completed on time for 15 August 1945 and on trial attained the speed of 15 kilometres per hour. She was a nice-looking craft and of particular interest to us as we had been involved in the design (and my wife launched her).

We got away smartly and dropped down to the source of the Nile, Mogren Point, where the Blue and White Niles meet. We turned southward to await the bridge opening. Omdurman Bridge opened daily at 5.40 and 15.40 for 20 minutes to allow river traffic to pass through. At the junction of the rivers their characteristic colourings were very noticeably the chocolate colour of the Blue Nile laden with silt and the milky discolouration of the White Nile.

The bridge opened on time and we passed through whilst the *Gordon Pasha* was getting into position to make the downstream passage. On the east bank lay the sunt forest opposite the southern-most buildings of Omdurman. Also on the east bank were the remains of 'Gordon's Tree' just to the north of the Egyptian Irrigation Dockyard, which was an extensive and well-found organisation for the maintenance of dredging equipment and inspection steamers.

Close by on the same bank was the British Overseas Airways landing stage with 'Gordon's Tree' Aerodrome behind it. A flying boat was riding at its mooring with one of its engines under repair.

From this point until Gebel Aulia was little of note, just flat sandy banks and an occasional tree. After 29 miles (all distances were noted in miles from Khartoum) we came to the Gebel Aulia Dam, completed in 1937 with an Egyptian Irrigation Department cantonment sited on the north side of the gebel and the east bank. Bronze plates on the dam gave particulars of its leading features in English and Arabic.

GEBEL AULIA DAM

Messrs Goode, Wilson, Mitchell & Vaughan Lee	Consulting Engineers
Abdel Kawi Bey Ahmed	Resident Engineer
Messrs Gibson & Pauling (Foreign) Ltd	Contractors

Total Length	5,000 metres
Length of Masonry Dam	1,693 metres
Length of Embankment Dam	3,307 metres

GEBEL AULIA DAM

Messrs Goode, Wilson, Mitchell & Vaughan Lee	Consulting Engineers
Abdel Kawi Bey Ahmed	Resident Engineer
Messrs Gibson & Pauling (Foreign) Ltd	Contractors

Total Length	5,000 metres
Length of Masonry Dam	1,693 metres
Length of Embankment Dam	3,307 metres
Greatest height of masonry	22 metres
Approximate total cube of structure	1,000,000 cu. metres
Reservoir Level	R.L.377.20
Low Summer Level	R.L.370.75
Length of Reservoir	300 kilometres
Quantity of water stored	3,000 million cu. metres

GEBEL AULIA DAM
This dam was begun in 1933 during the reign of
HIS MAJESTY KING FOUAD I
and completed in 1937 during the
reign of
HIS MAJESTY KING FAROUK I

The dam was a popular centre for fishing and Khartoum anglers spent much time there. At certain times of the year the turbulent waters on the downstream side of the dam were alive with fish and turtles.

The lock was closed for repairs for three weeks every year and for that period navigation was interrupted. The lock was opened on demand at any time between dawn and dark.

On this journey darkness fell just as the dam came in sight but was brilliantly lit by electric light which allowed us to approach with caution and tie up for the night to the downstream approach wall of the lock.

Soon after 05.30 hours the next morning preparations commenced to pass us through the lock. An old Sudan Railways Steamers *reis*, Mohamed Mahmoud, was in charge of the lock and gave a cheery welcome. The lock having been emptied, the great gates were slowly wound back into recesses in the masonry walls of the lock. We were then ordered to enter with care and were moored to bollards. The gates behind us closed and the sluice gates opened to allow the water in the lock to rise to the level of the reservoir upstream of the dam. When the lock was full, the upstream gates could be opened in the same way as the downstream and we were free to pass out as soon as the bascule bridge (like the Sudan Railways Bridge at Port Sudan), which carried the road across the dam, was raised. Passage through the dam took about three quarters of an hour.

The dam policeman noted that there were three of us enjoying early morning tea in our dressing gowns on deck, the wife of the doctor at Malakai being our passenger. Returning two months later, my wife was straightly interrogated by the policeman as to what had happened to my other wife. He had noted that I had two wives when going upstream. He accepted my wife's explanation as to identity somewhat grudgingly.

The river above the dam was very wide when the reservoir was filled. Filling commenced in July and the dam was filled by October. The reservoir when full, contained 3 milliard cubic metres. The emptying period was from January to March. When full the reservoir was a vast expanse of water as the country on either side of the river bank was flat and navigation was not easy as what were formerly islands became shallows. As a consequence many trees died from prolonged immersion in the water and marked the higher ground.

WHEELS AND PADDLES IN THE SUDAN

Through the winter and when the reservoir was empty the Reach teamed with bird life, but during the summer little was seen. On a previous trip when we were broken down at Shabasha Island we counted over 20 different species.

The first town of importance was Geteina, situated on the east bank at mile 58. Its mosque was conspicuous against the skyline from some distance. On the same bank came the first of the Government pump schemes, Gemelab. There were a number of these on the Reach, mainly, if not entirely, as Alternative Livelihood Schemes to settle persons displaced by the reservoir.

The country throughout was flat, with occasional sand dunes on the east bank. The only hill was Jebel Araskhol on the west bank. Wad-el-Zaki was a considerable village on the east bank and next came Hashaba Pump Scheme. So flat was the country that with field glasses the telegraph line could be traced for miles along the east bank.

The reservoir continued very wide, several miles across. Dubasi Pump Scheme lay on the east bank upstream of the village of that name. Shabasha with its gubba and island were next passed on the west bank.

Bakht-er-Ruda, the Sudan's outstanding educational experiment, soon came into sight on the west bank. A few miles further on we reached, on the same side of the river, Dueim, at mile 128 which used to be the capital of the White Nile Province, but was now the seat of two District Commissioners and one Assistant District Commissioner. The Sudan Railways maintained an office on the river-front and a pontoon landing stage. There was a power-driven ferry for motor cars to maintain road connection between Dueim and Medani. Upstream of Dueim, also on the west bank, was Dueim Pump Scheme.

After Dueim the reservoir became narrower and more clearly defined. The banks were less flat. Um Gerr, on the west bank, was the next Pump Scheme and then at mile 152 we passed Kawa on the east bank. Kawa shipped a considerable quantity of agricultural commodities in the season.

Opposite Shawal, another Pump Scheme on the east bank, was the commencement of Aba Island which extended nearly to Kosti. On Aba Island was Sir Sayed Abd el Rahman el Mahdi Pasha's large agricultural undertaking with numerous pumps scattered the whole length of the island.

On the downstream journey we lunched with the Sayed, a spectacular figure, and his son, Sadik. The house and grounds were attractive. The former contained some fine antique English oak furniture, including the marvellous bulbous leg refectory table from the Welcome House at Jebel Moiya. After lunch we toured his estate. We drove through his cotton which looked very promising, and visited several pumping stations (the engines of one of them had led to much correspondence between us). In the museum we saw the ancient Fung throne. In the up-to-date dairy a Sudanese dairymaid demonstrated her complete competence; unfortunately she refused to train any other Sudanese. Lastly we visited the stables of his stud of 70 racing horses. When we regained our launch we found it heavily laden; a crested crane to grace our garden, two sheep, two turkeys and vast quantities of every kind of farm and garden produce. Royal largesse indeed. At 3.45 p.m. we bade farewell and continued on our journey. At many of the river stations along this Reach there were two *meshras*, one for high river and the other for low. Fashashoya was a large village on the west bank and then came Wad Nimr, the last of the Pump Schemes before Kosti was reached at mile 198.

M.L. *Melika* in Gebel Aulia Dam.

Sir Sayed Abd el Rahman el Mahdi.

The town of Kosti owed its existence to chance. When Lord Kitchener sailed south in 1898, his boats were passing this spot when a light on the bank was noticed. Lord Kitchener instructed his telegraphist (Gaddis Eff. Abdel Sayed) and a sergeant to go ashore and investigate. They found a Greek merchant, Kosti, in a little bush shop. Lord Kitchener on being told remarked: 'Turn a stone in Africa and you find a Greek'. The spot was given the name of Kosti. When, in course of time, a railway was laid to El Obeid it had to touch Kosti. If that Greek had not had his lamp alight that night in 1898 quite a different point of crossing the White Nile might have been chosen!

In 1945 Kosti was a flourishing town and almost a river port. River craft accosted a masonry quay wall served by steam cranes at all reservoir levels. Storage was provided in the quay area by two goods sheds. As Kosti was the terminal for the passenger services to Juba there were special facilities, like sidings and ticket office. Maintenance and repair to steamers were carried out in floating or shore workshops and there was a Locomotive Running Shed. With the heightened river levels due to the dam, Kosti town had recently been rebuilt on higher ground. It had a Town Council of which Assistant Engineer Abdel Sayed Abdel Gaddous and Senior Traffic Inspector Mohamed Sadik Fareed were members, and a pleasantly situated hospital of 150 beds.

Like most other ports Kosti also had a sinister reputation, though the District Commissioner had really sharpened up the police.

Some 9 miles upstream of Kosti the railway line to El Obeid crossed the White Nile by a 9-span bridge. The centre span, the largest, could be rotated by hand through a quarter of a circle to give passage to steamers and sailing boats. The bridge was built in 1910 by the Cleveland Bridge Co. of Darlington. All material was brought to the site by river and when the railhead reached the river they found the bridge quite ready and so there was no delay. Trouble was experienced during construction from water pythons of very considerable size which used to climb from stranded *sudd* islands into the timbers supporting the bridge. The Bridge carried a roadway on each side, suitable for light motor traffic, animals and pedestrians.

KOSTI TO MALAKAL

From Kosti onwards the scenery became luxuriant green with grass and trees. *Toiches* became prominent features. A *toich* is a flat river bank slightly above water level at low river which quickly floods on a rising river. It carries an abundance of coarse high grass which grows during the flood. As the river slowly falls this coarse growth dies off sufficiently to be burned and the new young growth springs up and makes excellent grazing for animals. The *toiches* were the winter grazing ground of all tribes living near the river.

The telegraph line to Malakal and the south could be seen away on the east bank. The banks were flat and it was 50 miles to the first *jebel*. The river was 600 to 800 yards wide. There were few people to be seen on the bank.

After 20 miles we came to Abu Zeid Ford, two gravel bars which caused trouble to navigation during the low river period. In 1940 a cut was dredged through the shallower bar to give the same depth of water over each, which improved matters. Eleven miles further upstream was another obstruction in the form of Zuleit Rocks, a shelf with a narrow way round at the west end which caused trouble at low river. The twin peaks of Jebelein were in view on the east bank. In 1942, in connection with military requirements, a branch line was laid from Rabak to Jebelein but with change in the military situation it was picked up at the end of 1944.

Floating grass and 'cabbages' became common. South of Jebelein was an island 7 miles long and after another 7 miles Keri Kera Khor took off to the west and extended 3½ miles. This *khor* was for some years blocked up and was opened by dredging in 1944, when we saw an Egyptian Irrigation Department dredger at work.

Rejoining the main stream from Keri Kera Khor we passed through beautifully green and wooded flat country. The first place of importance was Geigar on the east bank at mile 288, which exported agricultural produce. Next, at mile 306, and also on the east bank came Renk with a small concrete quay, which was an unusual facility. Renk used to be the seat of a District Commissioner (Upper Nile Province). The *suk*, Post Office and other Government buildings lay about a mile back from the river.

Eight miles south of Renk was Dinka's Ford, another shallow shelf which gave trouble at low river and then required a pilot *reis*. The river was 400 yards wide and a *tauf* (small ambatch canoe) could occasionally be seen. Soon after Dinka's Ford on the east bank was one of the few stands of decent timber, extending for about one mile.

WHEELS AND PADDLES IN THE SUDAN

At mile 333, on the east bank, was the Sudan Interior Mission Station of Banjang, one of the few we had never managed to visit. There were tiresome shallows and a narrow channel at Tomat Island at mile 340 and 2 miles further on lay the wreck of the stern-wheel steamer *Amara* towards the west side of the channel. *Amara* was blown away from her mooring in 1917 and sank.

By now Jebel Ahmed Agha, named after an early Governor of the district was in sight. The hill, shaped like a recumbent animal, was about 340 feet high and lay several miles back from the river on the east bank. Before we reached it we passed Galhak, at mile 354 and also on the east bank, a settlement which had much declined in importance.

From Jebelein onwards we had many unwelcome passengers in the form of serut flies. They are large flies about an inch long with the capacity to make the most perfect landings and announce their arrival by a sting like a red-hot needle. Fortunately there are no after effects, but their numbers made them very tiresome. They required swatting with a heavy hand and an accurate eye.

Jebel Ahmed Agha, mile 359, was the first hill after Jebelein and the only one until after Malakal. It was covered with boulders, bushes and a few trees and had small caves populated by wild pig. On the river bank was one of the larger wood stations of the Agriculture and Forests.

The country on either side of the river was now a wide stretch of *toich* with trees behind, presenting a picture of luxuriant growth. Um Barbit wood station was passed on the west bank and there was little change in the scenery for the next 40 miles. At mile 405 we came to Kaka on the west bank. It had declined in importance over the years. Sudan Railways used to have a goods shed here but early in the war it was removed to Juba as the trade from the Nuba Mountains had almost entirely ceased. As you approach Kaka you will always see a number of Shilluk lads sitting on the bank intent over fishing rods. They are among the most colourful specimens you will meet along the Nile bank.

Above Kaka the river took a long bend to the left to reach Melut 16 miles away. The east bank of the bend was lined with trees and a new wood station had been opened at Abu Haraz just past Kaka.

Melut lay on the east bank at mile 421, serving the rich grain-growing area around Paloich, 22 miles inland. There was also a Sudan Interior Mission Station here.

WHEELS AND PADDLES IN THE SUDAN

At Aradeiba, mile 447 east bank, there were some shallows and a recently opened wood station. Three miles further upstream, on the west bank was Detwok, a Roman Catholic Mission Station of the Mill Hill Fathers and then at mile 468, also on the west bank, came Fashoda, now know as Kodok.

Fashoda used to be the capital of the Upper Nile. Seized by Major Marchand in June 1898, it was the site of 'The Fashoda Incident' — an occupation lasting six months, terminated by Lord Kitchener, whose tact persuaded Major Marchand to withdraw to Tchad on 11 December 1898. Fashoda was then renamed Kodok.

This was the home of a District Commissioner and the centre for the administration of the Shilluk. There were a few shops, a productive garden and it also exported some cattle. Once in *Sobat* we ran over a hippopotamus when leaving Kodok whilst we were having breakfast. The result was an avalanche into our laps. From Kodok onwards the banks were in general green but bare, with some Shilluk villages in the distance. At mile 486, west bank, there was the extensive Mill Hill Fathers Mission Station of Lul which had sisters on the staff. The first groups of Doleib palms appeared. Their upright trunks and characteristic swelling were a feature of the landscape for the next 30 miles and they made a picturesque setting for the village of Wau, at mile 498, west bank. From here it was not far to Malakal, the most advanced community on the Nile south of Khartoum.

Malakal, the capital of Upper Nile Province, was situated on the east bank 41 miles from Kodok at mile 509. The Egyptian Irrigation Department had Headquarters here with their own cantonment which included dockyard offices, houses for officials and all utilities such as electric light, water and ice. There was a large aerodrome with long runways whose construction was a major undertaking, a flying-boat landing area, and an anti-amaryl Rest House. There was also a large hospital and an United Church used by many denominations of Christians.

The mosque had a minaret made from the frame of an aeroplane. There was an extensive *suk* and the Sudan Railways maintained a river station. Malakal lay in an area of heavy rainfall and its disparagers were inclined to say that it was hardly above flood level. Such a statement is an exaggeration, though it certainly did rain at Malakal! The *suk* has the unusual adornment of two zebras, by name Kenya and Uganda, who roamed at large.

Proceeding upstream one passed the water and electric light plants of the Public Works Department, the police lines, dairy and radio station. Then the river forked at a long island. We took the west channel. On either bank well inland were compact Shilluk villages, generally with a few dom palms among the *tukls*. A Shilluk village was clean and tidy. The west bank was a wide grassy plain, with a frieze-like horizon of *tukls*, palms and trees. Amid many *taufs* we noted one bringing home the breakfast — two fine *aigl* around the 100 pounds mark. After a few miles Yedu Island was reached extending to beyond Sobat Mouth. The channel to the west of the island was known as Bahr Harami and was the haunt of many crocodiles. Its west bank was lined with Shilluk villages.

The river was very dirty with grass and myriads of *sudd* cabbages. On the east bank for a while *toich* gave way to scrub as the land rose a little and then 10 miles from Malakal lay Taufikia which was originally settled by Sir William Baker in 1870. At this time the Bahr-el-Jebel was completely blocked by *Sudd* and the only possible route was by the Bahr-el-Zeraf. Baker, who had been delayed in starting from Khartoum, found himself unable to force the passage of the Bahr-el-Zeraf and had to return to the main river. He selected as a site for his camp during the rains of 1870 the spot which he named and we knew as Taufikia. Today Taufikia is an agricultural station of the Agriculture and Forests and for some months in the year supplied Malakal with vegetables.

Six miles further on at mile 525 was Sobat Mouth, a favourite haunt of the inhabitants of Malakal who liked *aigl* fishing. The Sobat rose in Abyssinia and was a considerable though seasonal river. It was at its lowest in April when its discharge was 8 million cubic metres per day and at its highest in November when its discharge figure was 67. Its great value to the Nile system was that it was the first river to rise and produce extra water in the very difficult period immediately before the Blue Nile flood. In May and June the Sobat produced 28 percent and 45 percent respectively of the net amount of water available at Wadi Halfa. It was navigable to Gambeila from June to October in a normal year. Its water was red-brown and it was a silt-carrying stream.

A mile or so upstream of Sobat Mouth, Bahr Harami joined the main stream on the north bank and was the short cut to Malakal for small steamers. A little further on, Khor Lolle took off the north bank and ran parallel to the White Nile right up to Lake No. Nine miles from Sobat Mouth on the south bank was the mouth of Khor Atar where the first Government Intermediate School in Upper Nile Province was to be built. The south bank in this area had many Dinka villages but the north was all *toich* with Shilluk villages a couple of miles back beyond Khor Lolle. At mile 553 the Bahr-el-Zeraf joined the White Nile.

Occasionally one passed a 'tow', a steamer with a cluster of barges. The steamer would be at the rear with a barge lashed on each side; it would be pushing passenger and goods barges ahead of it, probably seven or eight in all, in tiers of three. It included a Post Office and a considerable complement of animals — a veritable floating village.

On an earlier trip, in 1942, we passed a very large tow, loaded with army lorries, driven up from South Africa to Juba and then loaded onto barges. The tow was being pushed by a large powerful dredger that we had hired from the Egyptian Irrigation Department.

From Zeraf Mouth to Lake No both banks were Game Reserve, that on the north being a small one but the other bank formed the north edge of the big area known as Zeraf Island, bounded on the east by the Bahr-el-Zeraf from the Mouth to the Cut, on the west by the Bahr-el-Jebel from the Cut to Lake No and on the north by the White Nile from Lake No to Zeraf Mouth.

The banks were low and flat. To the south could be seen, 15 kilometres away, the small granite knob of Jebel Zeraf and to the north, in the distance, the Nuba Mountains. As far as Tonga we were in Shilluk country and villages were fairly numerous.

Half an hour after leaving Zeraf Mouth we came to two tree-lined Egyptian Irrigation Department banks at right angles to the stream. On the south was the Abu Tonj Tie Bank and on the north was the Abu Tonj Cut. The latter joined Khor Lolle, which ran parallel to the White Nile, to the main stream. Just upstream on the south bank was the tail of Maiya Barboi, a long sheet of water which was often overgrown with grass. Half-way up the *maiya* on the south side was Barboi Wood Station, but the tail was too shallow to allow entrance to the *maiya* by steamers at all states of the river so an old cut, opposite the wood station, was re-dredged in 1944, and steamers could now enter the *maiya* to wood without serious difficulty.

At mile 562 we came to Tonga, a station of the Mill Hill Fathers, on the telegraph line to the Nuba Mountains. At this point the

WHEELS AND PADDLES IN THE SUDAN

A typical Tow.

A Tow loaded with army lorries.

country changed and stretches of papyrus and elephant grass were seen along the bank. The vegetation changed from about 4 feet in height to 10 feet, although there were still short stretches of dry ground and low trees. This section was the transition stage from *toich* to the swamps of the *sudd* area. At Wath Kec on the south bank there was some dry land and as a result a merchant's hut, the remnants of a garden, and a track into the middle of Zeraf Island. On both banks there were trees about a mile back from the river. A little further on there was another *maiya* carrying the intriguing name of Maiya Seignora. There is romance behind it; it was named after the Seignora, Miss Tinne, a stout-hearted, young and beautiful explorer.

Alexandrine Petronella Francina Tinne was born at the Hague in 1839. Her father died when she was five years old, leaving her the richest heiress in Holland. In 1859 she made her first Nile journey, reaching Gondokoro. In 1862 she bought a steam boat in Khartoum, set off up the Nile, and got nearly as far as Gondokoro and returned via the Sobat.

In 1863 she prepared her great expedition to reach the sources of the Nile, taking one steamer, two dahabeyas and two nuggars, her mother, aunt, two European maids, the scientist Von Heuglin, an Italian interpreter, 200 soldiers and servants, and ammunition and provisions for ten months, with 30 mules or donkeys, four camels, and one saddle horse. She paused awhile at Maiya Seignora, and set out for Meshra. There, everything went wrong. Most of the animals died. Both Steudner and Von Heuglin suffered much from fever and Steudner died. Von Heuglin obtained 150 porters in Bongo country and took them to Meshra.

She set out, crossed the Jur and reached Biselli but fate was against her. Famine was rife, her medicines were exhausted and her mother died. She abandoned the expedition and returned to Khartoum losing on her way her aunt, two European maids, Contarini, the Italian interpreter, a German gardener and many of her servants. The Seignora and Von Heuglin survived to get out via Suakin. In 1869, on an expedition to Lake Tchad she was murdered by the Tuwarek. In 30 years she had travelled greatly!

From Tonga there was hardly a habitation within half a mile of the river, but as one approached Lake No there was a stretch of some miles of dry land on the north bank studded with small trees and bushes. Lake No was situated at mile 601 and just short of its entrance on the north bank was Meshra Bagardoum which gave access to the main river for the trade which would otherwise have had to come out by the Bahr-el-Ghazal service.

From Lake No radiated the Reference Poles of the Egyptian Irrigation Department at five kilometre intervals along the rivers, up the Bahr-el-Jebel to Juba and the Bahr-el-Ghazal to Meshra and down the White Nile to Rabak. The RPs as they were called, were invaluable for locating one's position, particularly in the swamp areas where landmarks were virtually non-existent.

We continued up the Bahr-el-Jebel. This section of the river was regarded by many people as something to be endured but not enjoyed. For the first ten Reference Poles the country was swampy, particularly on the west bank. On the east bank, which was Zeraf Island and the Game Reserve, there were short lengths of small trees and wooded country on the horizon. Drier ground was found on both sides, particularly the east at RP 10 where Buffalo Cape wood station was situated. From here the postboats would pick up a barge loaded with wood fuel to take them through the Sudd. The river was about 100 yards wide and flowed along straight reaches and easy bends. The nature of the bank could be judged by the type of vegetation. If papyrus, it meant that there was earth on or close to the water level. *Um-souf,* on the other hand, had its roots floating in water and gave no indication of soil. Elephant grass denoted a soil level slightly higher than the surrounding level. Contrary to some people's belief, the Nile throughout the Sudd region flows in a channel defined by earth banks which are for miles overflowed during the flood. Nevertheless the earth bank was there, even if masked by vegetation, and all the Reference Poles and Name Plates stood on fairly firm ground. Near RP 21 on the west bank was the small trading post of Ryer, dealing mainly in cattle and hides. There was little change in the scenery. A definite clump of trees and a palm tree stood about 2 miles from the river to the East at RP 25 making a landmark. Round about RP 28 the papyrus border on the west bank became very narrow and for a while one passed bushes in grass, with a long belt of trees, some 3 miles back to the west and 5 miles away to the east on Zeraf Island.

Thar Jath at RP 29 on the west bank was a small trading post with hides as the main activity. At RP 42, on the west bank, was another trading post Adok, with the possibility of growth as work had begun on a road to connect with Tonj. I intended to travel over it on one visit and brought my transport with me, but the weather would not permit. Hides were the main export.

Entrance to the Zeraf was obtained through either No. 2 Cut at RP 58 or by No. 1 Cut at RP 59 on the east bank. For the next 60 Reference Poles (300 kilometres) there was a wide expanse of lakes and channels in the Sudd and these two 'cuts' were originally dredged to improve the flow into the Bahr-el-Zeraf. They were apt to be blocked by *sudd*, which, contrary to what was expected, improved flow in the Bahr-el-Zeraf. It was tiresome, however, to come up the Bahr-el-Zeraf and find both cuts sudded up at the same time.

The scenery was constant here, a wide expanse of green, with numerous channels such as Drury's Channel and Baker's Channel all posted and mainly on the east bank. They marked exploratory work done by pioneers, when the main stream of the Jebel was sudded up. If you were not involved with navigating bends or contending with *sudd*, the scene was very placid but calm can quickly be broken. Once, when in *Sobat,* crusing along, perhaps 3 yards from the papyrus, we came across in a gap a fine bull elephant, standing about 15 yards from the edge with three females just behind him. We were sitting in line with his knees. He was not at all pleased to see us. He extended his ears, raised his trunk aloft and sounded a warning to his females. For a couple of seconds we wondered which way he would move. When he decided to stand his ground and guard his harem, we were very relieved.

At RP 81 on the west bank was Shambe, standing on its *maiya.* It was on firm ground 3 feet above water level and accordingly was better provided with facilities, and presided over by Gregorio, a Greek trader of over 30 years standing who baked very palatable brown bread. It was the river terminus of a road linking Yirol, Rumbek, Tonj and Wau. There were two merchants, with sheds, and a Post Office. Shambe was a station for Egyptian Irrigation Department work with a Nile Gauge and an Evaporation Tank, which was made of iron and measured 15 feet × 10 feet × 3 feet at the water's edge, filled with growing papyrus and supplied with water to a constant level in order to measure the rate of transpiration.

The artist and big-game hunter, J. G. Millais, was once marooned in Shambe Rest House for a week in the 1920s and decorated it with fine murals of Sudan wild life — elephant, lion and giraffe with buffalo.

WHEELS AND PADDLES IN THE SUDAN

Murals by J. G. Millais in Shambe Rest House.

WHEELS AND PADDLES IN THE SUDAN

As we arrived on one occasion Gregorio found that a large python had swallowed one of his kids and wrapped itself around a palm. I was immediately taken off to inspect the crime and suggested that the python should be speared to prevent repetition. On my next visit to Shambe, I was presented with a fine python's skin, complete with spear hole.

Another time five natives met us, each carrying a young ostrich. I think they were expecting a soft sale as the price was only 5 piastres for each bird. I had to disappoint them, as I will not willingly collect ostriches as pets. One could generally count on seeing something of interest when calling at Shambe.

We were now well into the *sudd* area and if the *sudd* was running we saw a lot of it, floating down in islands, up to 100 feet in length, perhaps even giving passage to a family. I once kept watch at Awei Tail 1B, near RP 86 and in one hour 42 'islands' averaging 75 feet long were discharged into the main stream and this was only one of many 'tails' discharging. Navigation, even when the *sudd* was running was easier going upstream. In a launch, however, one would not experience the stress of navigating the bends which I mentioned in connection with AFLOC which was unavoidable on a downstream journey with a heavily laden tow.

Every now and then, mainly on the west bank, we passed little groups of Dinkas, living in two or three *tukls*, on a patch of wet ground, to be measured in square yards, perhaps 4 inches above flood level. They had water and fish but little else except canoes in which to escape when the vegetation was burning.

A superior site with, say, one foot of freeboard above the surrounding swamp, was likely to be used as a site for an Egyptian Irrigation Department River Gauging Station which measured the flow of the river. To do this a wire was stretched across the river and readings taken along it at regular distances. Those unlucky enough to arrive at the spot while they were busy on the job had to tie up and patiently await completion.

In this area I once saw, ahead, bodies sailing through the air. I asked the *reis* what was happening. *Timsah* (crocodiles), he replied. Shortly we drew level with the scene, two crocodiles of about 12 feet, turning cartwheels in their efforts for sole possession of the bloated carcase of a bull. I shot one of them; perhaps the other had a two-course meal!

At RP 118, Atem Head 1B, one could, with guidance, get away

WHEELS AND PADDLES IN THE SUDAN

Dinka hut in Sudd.

River Gauging Station.

into the swamp to visit Jongelei. This was the point from which it was proposed to cut a canal to discharge into the White Nile between Bahr-el-Zeraf Mouth and Sobat Mouth, thereby delivering to the north a vast quantity of water of which much would otherwise be lost by evaporation in the *sudd*. It was a scheme which would have considerable repercussion on the lives of the Dinka and other cattle-owning tribes with a life-cycle attuned to the cycle of the vegetation caused by the periodic overflow of the Bahr-el-Jebel. A second repercussion would be the behaviour of the Bahr-el-Jebel with reduced flow. I had arranged to visit Jongelei on this trip and to borrow the second *reis* of *Walad*, the Egyptian Irrigation Department tug, to act as pilot. We tied up for the night at RP 118 and entered Atem Head No. 1B at 05.30 hours under expert guidance. In 4½ hours we reached Jongelei. Some years ago when this scheme was first proposed a dredger was brought in by the Egyptian Irrigation Department and a short distance was dredged into the solid edge of the swamp to enable the nature of the soil to be determined. I landed and walked round but all one could see was this entry and two small steel buildings. I left Jongelei and rejoined the Bahr-el-Jebel at RP 86 without difficulty. The whole trip took just over 8 hours.

Dinka cattle camp.

WHEELS AND PADDLES IN THE SUDAN

The Jongelei Cut has been under discussion for more than 60 years. A documentary film on the BBC in, I think, 1981 showed a large secondhand digger, released from a completed job in Pakistan, at work on the start of the Cut from the northern end, so it must be assumed that the scheme in some form, possibly ending at Bor, rather than Jongelei, has been decided upon. Another use to which these side-channels could be put is to provide a possible alternative route in the event of a serious *sudd* block on the Bahr-el-Jebel. There is an even shorter and easier route by entry near RP 93 and out at RP 86 but it requires more frequent use and every year.

Approaching *toich* country around Bor you will, at certain times of year, pass extensive cattle camps. These have some spectacular animals in them. The Dinka, at low river, bring their cattle right down to the Bahr-el-Jebel to provide them with food and water; most of the families remain behind in the 'summer' camps. The humans at these cattle camps will consist almost entirely of males accompanied by a few boys, just a few families and a handful of girls to do the milking (which is very definitely a woman's job). The lasses are expert, and are keen that you should acknowledge it too. They normally milk into a gourd with a 1½-inch neck, a skill which calls for very accurate aim. When we wanted to buy milk, we would offer a 10-inch diameter white enamel bowl to contain it. The lass would be peeved, to put it mildly; it required no skill to hit that size of target and its cleanliness was an insult. It also contained no additives, such as urine or blood, which were considered highly desirable. It took at least 20 minutes persuasion to get her to comply with the request. I rather think that the cows appreciated the skill of the girls as I never saw any refusal by a cow to co-operate. On the one occasion when I saw a man try his hand, however, we had to wait a very long time for our milk! The cattle camp on this occasion was a small one. We could see a few cows, a man and a boy so we stopped and our boys went ashore with a bowl to buy some milk. There was lots of talk but no sign of action, apparently as there were no milkmaids no milk could be produced. One of the crew had a fair smattering of Dinka and he was instructed to beguile the man into having a go. At long last, as there were no adults present, he said he would try. The cow was not amused! She refused to co-operate. After a long time the boy was instructed to lift the cow's tail and blow hard into its rear end. I asked for what purpose and I was told 'to make the milk drop'. It worked. We got a basin of milk, before any adults returned to camp, but the pictorial decoration on the boy's face required a new 'make-up'.

Bor, RP 129 on the east bank, was one of the bigger stations on the river. It was the Headquarters for the District of the Bor Dinka, with a senior District Commissioner, as they were something of a problem. The station looked rather pretty from the river but the mosquito were pernicious. It was a productive spot and except at the top of the flood the steamers were able to obtain fresh fruit and vegetables from the *Merkaz* gardens which were situated on the west bank. Hippos in this part of the river frequently disputed the right of canoes to cross and so the ferry to the garden was by steel *felucca*. On more than one occasion the District Commissioner went into the brook! The *suk* had recently been rebuilt and was tidy without being attractive. Bor was a collecting centre for Khartoum Zoo and a red-hussar monkey, Bakheit, was well known to many travellers.

The quay made an imposing river front and behind it were vast stacks of firewood for the steamers, which on occasion had been known to take as much as 1,000 cubic metres at a visit! The firewood was loaded by Dinkas, each Dinka carrying one piece of wood, and so one was likely to stay at Bor for a long time. The Egyptian Irrigation Department had an office at Bor and a shallow-draft tug, and the *tahteeb* or plan for much of the gauge reading on the Bahr-el-Jebel was worked from here. Bor also boasted a wireless telegraphy installation. Its export trade was mainly hides, hippo hide, dom rope and to Juba, cattle and sheep.

With Bor, the *sudd* virtually ended, though there were still stretches of *toich*, and some trees. On the east bank we soon came to the first 'cliff' since Malakal. Along the east bank ran the telegraph line to Juba. As the flood began to fall there was a lot of narrow strip cultivation on the river bank by the Dinkas. Just before reaching Malek, RP 128, was an island and then *tukls* and *luaks* became numerous on the east bank, as we approached the station. Malek was one of the earliest stations of the Church Missionary Society in the Southern Sudan and the centre for work among the Dinkas. For many years it was presided over by Archdeacon Shaw between whom and the Steamer Department a state of war generally existed. His successors experienced some of the repercussions and there were *reis* who considered it almost their duty to take a rise out of the *gassis bita Kanisa Malek* (the clergyman in charge of Malek church).

The Archdeacon was a great killer of elephants. Elephants damaging crops could be destroyed without accounting on your licence. The area of influence of the mission was large, and calls from the flock for aid in these circumstances were numerous. The quantity of good ivory sent to the *merkaz* for stamping under this category indicated his good fortune and his skill. He also shot lions. Once, when driving after dark to Juba Hotel, he shot two lions and hoisted them on to the front mudguards of his model 'T' Ford. A heated argument was taking place in the lounge as to whether there were any lion near Juba. His verdict was conclusive.

When he retired in 1938, he left behind an ordained Dinka priest and another, Gordon, his secretary and a language expert. On his way home he stayed a night with me in Atbara, I felt he was loath to leave Africa but it was not for long as he was soon serving as Chaplain to the Forces in East Africa.

Beyond Malek the east bank was for a while fairly well wooded. At RP 130 the river divided into two channels which ran, with several cross connections, for 30 kilometres. At this point the telegraph line crossed from east to west bank by means of special masts. The RPs were along the east channel but at RP 131 the river had made a *kassa* (breakthrough) from the east to the west channel through a narrow neck 50 yards wide. The usual route was via the west channel to the *kassa* and through to the east channel. It was possible to go all the way by the east channel but not so by the west. Sheikh Tombe could only be reached from the upstream end as the west channel north of Sheikh Tombe was sudded up. The country on both sides was *toich* with trees on the horizon which approached closer at RP 133 soon after which there was a stiff 'S' bend. The two channels re-united at RP 136.

Soon after RP 138 we came to Gemmeiza, an old wood station. Round here after the peak of the flood there was quite a lot of cultivation in small plots along the river edge. At RP 140 the *toich* was about 5 miles wide on each side with thick woods beyond. Soon after this came the troubles with sand banks at low river.

Terakekka stood at RP 144 on the west bank and was quite an important spot. It was connected by road to Amadi and was in many ways the natural port of Western Equatoria; it was also an important wooding station for our steamers. In the dry weather there was a direct road to Juba available across the Lado, 54 miles or less than two hours. It stood well above flood level and had a natural landing stage with deep water. Recently the Rest House has been rebuilt in brick and thatched but fortunately the garden still remains.

The river curved away upstream of Terakeka and on the west bank there was a cliff beloved of kingfishers. After some kilometres was Kadule wood station, one of the largest and tidiest on the river. Next the river forked round an island about 7½ miles long. The west channel was the prettier as it was alongside the trees, but most boats took the east channel. For several years part of the Juba Bridge, which was carried away in 1943, was resting at the downstream end of this island. The two channels united at Simsima, on the west bank, an old wood station and the site of Keiro, one of the stations the Belgians built in the Lado Enclave.

At RP 149 were the tiresome shallows of Ashong, a wood station on the east bank, and here transhipment frequently had to take place in the low river season. Mongalla, one of the numerous capitals of Equatoria, was situated also on the east bank, at RP 150. (This frequent change of capital is a point on which 'officials' are very touchy. Equatoria has been ruled from Lado, Keiro, Gondokoro, Mongalla, Rejaf and Juba and a better site than Juba could easily have been found, but a wise man keeps quiet on the subject). A fairly substantial station was built at Mongalla in brick but eventually a move was made to Rejaf. Some of the buildings still stand like gaunt skeletons. A post boat once had the interesting experience of making its way through a herd of elephants intent on fording the river at this spot (probably to reach the extensive fruit and vegetable garden which was still visible on the west bank). The days of Mongalla are, however, past and the few remaining inhabitants do little more than hawk hashish to steamers forced to tie up there for the night.

I once had an interesting experience myself with hashish at Mongalla. I was heading downstream from Juba and had completed correspondence which I wished to return to Atbara by airmail from Juba the next day. I knew that a steamer bound upstream could be contacted at Mongalla, so I tied up and waited for it to arrive. It was about 19.00 hours and I was standing on the bridge of the launch looking downstream. One of the crew who had been ashore was coming on board carrying a sack which, on seeing me, he dropped down an open hatch and scuttled away. I asked the engineer for the sack and he tried to persuade me that there was no sack. Eventually I discovered that it was, as suspected, hashish. I told the engineer to get the dinghy ready and signal the on-coming postboat to stop. I watched the fireman throw the sack into the boiler firebox amidst general grief at such a waste! The crew of my launch were subdued for the rest of the journey back to Khartoum wondering what would happen to them. Subsequently investigation showed that the crop had been grown in the middle of the District Commissioner's garden, which, like my launch, was regarded as 'safe'.

After Mongalla the river divided into a number of channels and at RP 154 on a western branch was Old Lado and then the modern village. Shortly after RP 156 we came to the point where the shallows finished and the Gondokoro channel took off to the east. This channel passed Gondokoro and rejoined upstream of Juba; it was a good waterway.

By now the goal of our journey, the capital, Juba, was in sight, sprawling along a low spur of Jebel Kuruk on the west bank at RP 158, 1,090 miles from Khartoum. It was quite modern. On the river front were quays and warehouses of the southern terminal of the steamer service.

BY THE BAHR-EL-ZERAF

The Bahr-el-Zeraf was the alternative and shorter route to the south. It entailed traversing one side of a triangle instead of two and the triangle was Zeraf Island, a large game reserve.

On my first trip south I awoke one morning at Zeraf Mouth. We had arrived during the night and were moored alongside a post bearing the legend 'Astronomical Point'. This meant that the point at the confluence of the two rivers, the Bahr-el-Zeraf and the White Nile, had been fixed by astronomical observation and was part of the major triangulation of the country. Zeraf Mouth was a very convenient wooding station for our steamers with supplies from a number of cutting areas on the Bahr-el-Zeraf.

The river was about 40 yards wide and flowing faster than the main river. As it was just before the 'Rains' the river had only a narrow bordering of rushes. With shade trees of rounded, rather than the more usual flat-topped profile of the Sudan, the whole prospect was strangely reminiscent of a slow-moving English stream. After 6 kilometres, habitation became more scattered and trees more numerous. Bird life was well represented and flocks of guinea-fowl were scampering along the banks. A dug-out containing a hunting party crossed the river just ahead of us.

WHEELS AND PADDLES IN THE SUDAN

Soon after kilometre 6 the wreck of the stern-wheel steamer *Hafir* appeared. This steamer was mysteriously sunk whilst in Province Service in 1941. Whatever the cause the District Commissioner had to swim for it and the craft remained there, sitting on the bottom of the river with water covering the upper deck and little more than a finely camouflaged funnel and wheel-house showing above the water-level. The whole was tastefully adorned with reed and papyrus growing in position, rather like a large window-box.

At about kilometre 12 there was, on the east bank, a small dredged basin made to provide handling facilities for barges used when transporting stone to Malakal for construction of the aerodrome's runways. The stone was obtained from Jebel Zeraf which was clearly visible some 4 miles inland and brought down to the basin on a specially laid rail track. As a reminder of this activity there still remained on the river bank six old 25-ton steel wagons and one steam locomotive, bought from, and still showing the markings of Egyptian State Railways.

On the next section the Zeraf was quite wooded with *Acacia arabica* (the gum tree) and the river was seldom narrower than 35 yards. Passing here on our first journey we saw a lion on top of a 5-foot high anthill at 60 yards. We paused to watch him. He took no notice of us and after about ten minutes his mate joined him. For about five minutes they observed us. We never knew if there were any cubs as the grass was 4 feet high. The lioness then dropped out of view, joined 5 minutes later by her mate, and we got underway. That was our first view of lion in the wild.

On another trip, about 5 kilometres further on, we came upon a pride of lions, resting under a large spreading tree, at a distance of about 40 yards. The one lion and three lionesses were well-grown. Their coats appeared to be very greyish, possibly due to having rolled in ash as the grass had all been burned off. They remained quite still, lying down facing the river for some seconds but they appeared to be a bit worried. Whether it was the sound of the engine room telegraph at the stop signal, or the flapping of the flags on the launch in the breeze, I do not know but the females got up and padded off into the trees. The lion remained for perhaps 15 seconds and then he too got up quite leisurely, and followed his mates. I have to admit that in the suddeness of their appearance and the general excitement I quite forgot until too late, to take a photograph.

In this area buck in wide variety are plentiful. At kilometre 66, on the east bank is Fanjak, the Zeraf Merkaz, but one seldom found the District Commissioner 'at home' as he travelled a lot.

At kilometre 87 on Zeraf Island, was Khor Nyazbjel, or Khor Bertram as it is presently known. There was a Church Missionary Society station at Jaibor in the interior of the island and this *khor* at some seasons gave access, though I never managed to make it by that route on account of the number of fish traps and weirs.

Once when coming downstream we had a game with a crocodile. As we passed an 8-foot high anthill, the engineer told me I had missed a good crocodile reposing in its shade. I told him to turn round and as we approached I saw the crocodile slide round to the upstream side, and, as I passed the anthill, he returned to the downstream side. Crocodiles are used to the noise of a boat passing and take little notice of it; it is almost always a one-off occurrence. If, however, the noise is repeated they are on the alert and quickly react. I went on upstream for a half mile, turned, started off downstream, switched off both engines and dynamo and floated down quietly. The crocodile was quite worried to see me a third time, but as he started to move to the other side of the anthill I put two rounds into him; I stopped him and we thought he was dead as both shots were between the eyes. We pulled him out straight and fetched the sounding rod, marked in feet; as I wanted to measure him fairly accurately because I was trying to establish what fraction of the total length of a crocodile was represented by the distance one could see when a crocodile was swimming, from his eye-ridge to the tip of his nose. We wanted four measurements; eye-ridge to tip of nose, eye-ridge to hip, hip to tip of tail and total length. I had come to the conclusion that the fraction was about one-eighth of the total length, and this specimen, with a total length of 12 feet, approximated to that fraction. When measurement had been completed Yassein, the engineer, was standing on the crocodile for his photo to be taken. At this point the crocodile, apparently he was only stunned, came to life, and endeavoured to unship his jockey. I dashed to the launch to get the rifle which I had left on board. The crocodile made for the river and I just had time to put two rounds into him and stop him for good. We then put a rope round him and towed him out into the stream to provide a tasty morsel for another of his kind.

You expected interesting happenings in this Game Reserve. It

WHEELS AND PADDLES IN THE SUDAN

Yasein on crocodile

was my habit to kill off as many large crocodiles as possible and my rifle was generally within arms reach as I sat on deck. We also had trouble with a swarm of bees. On day, half a mile ahead, we saw *Nekheila*, a small stern-wheeler, zig-zagging all over the river and made derogatory remarks about the sobriety of the *reis*. The real cause, however, was bees and we too got well stung as we sat on top of the water tank on the roof of the bridge. Getting down a rickety ladder and two companion ways, enshrouded in angry bees was not easy. I called for 'Flit' and Yassein appeared with two cans which he poured over us. As we drew level with *Nekheila* we hove-to and enquired what had happened. Apparently it was the drumming of her engines, diesels, that had upset a large swarm. Their crew had quickly retreated into the mosquito house, leaving the *reis* on the unprotected bridge, and we saw with what result. We removed over 200 stings from my wife.

At around kilometre 170 was a 'hippo meat factory'. These factories functioned at a special period in the year, when a co-operative effort was made by the *nass* of an area to go to a spot, hallowed by custom, where hippo are plentiful, and by concerted effort produce a supply of dried hippo meat to last them for some months. It is one of the few activities in which the *nass* involved themselves in sustained effort. There was also hippo-hide for whips as a by-product.

From kilometre 177 there were very few habitations. However, cattle *luaks* were visible on both banks at a distance, indicating some habitations inland. From about kilometre 200 we saw no game other than hippos and crocodiles. Apart from the plentiful dom-palms, few other trees were to be seen. However, at kilometre 227 the horizon on the island became well wooded and continued so for 15 kilometres.

Khor Gurr at kilometre 242 on the east bank was a considerable opening, about 200 yards wide. At kilometre 272 was Dom Island, proclaimed by a notice plate. It had a width of 40 yards and was probably Baker's camping site during his advance to Equatoria. In the last 50 kilometres the Bahr-el-Zeraf had many *maiyas* and channels, particularly on the east bank, and at kilometre 289 was the tail of No. 2 Cut whilst the tail of No. 1 Cut appeared at kilometre 293. One always hoped that one or the other would be free enough of *sudd* to allow passage into the Bahr-el-Jebel.

WHEELS AND PADDLES IN THE SUDAN

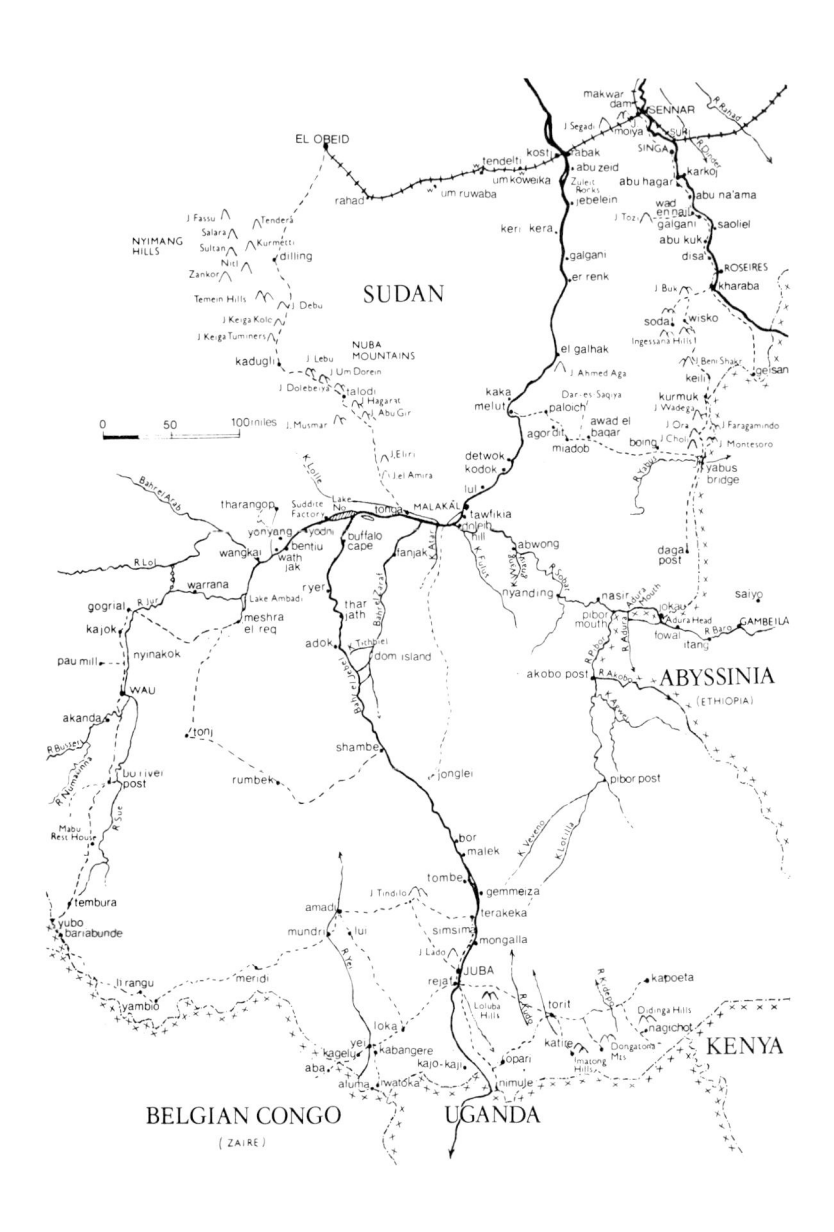

Chapter Nine

DOWN SOUTH

The southern province of the Sudan, Equatoria, is a vast tract of country, extending from Nagichot in the east to Sources Yubo in the west and Wau and Aweil in the north. My first visit was when Martin Parr was Governor and Equatoria was known to us as 'Martin Parr's Empire'. I do not think it would be unfair to say that he himself regarded it that way. Its area was, after all, considerably greater than that of the UK. The distance of more than 1,000 miles between Khartoum and Juba encouraged that idea and the Government discouraged contact (the southerners were not to be contaminated). I seem to remember being told that one only visited Juba after obtaining permission of the Governor. I personally never went that far, but would write and tell him of my intention to visit. Except on the question of the employment of northern labour as cargo-handlers at Juba during a time of stress, we got on well together. He certainly was the power in the land with his fine house and its magnificent Persian rugs. I remember one outstanding brown background Bokhara.

Juba, as I knew it, was very young, the latest in the succession of capitals of Equatoria. It was a centre of communications; by road south to Uganda at Nimule and south-west to Aba in the Congo, an airport and the southern terminus of the steamers. The volume of freight carried was, however, not very large. Before World War II it was about 2,000 tons per year which did not require extensive facilities. The quay was not a great expanse of concrete; there was grass, gravel and trees. Military demands increased the number of goods sheds but we were spared the enormous increases threatened by the AFLOC scheme. Access to the east bank and the road to Nimule used to be by a ferry but in anticipation of the growth to come the Royal Engineers arrived and built a bridge on wooden trestles. It was not an easy site; the current was strong and I think the length of the bridge was in excess of 400 feet. I only crossed it twice and was glad to reach the far side. It had an ominous bend in it and was restrained by a heavy wire cable upstream with numerous smaller cables from it to trestles in the centre of the bridge. It looked rather like a suspension bridge laid on its side. Its life was not long (a flood carried it away) and then the ferry came back into action.

Several merchants had bases in Juba and had quite extensive enterprises, involving transport and pioneering. We got to know one of them, George Haggar, a Syrian, quite well and eventually visited him on his concession at Iwatoka. Among his interests was the development of an asbestos deposit close to the Nimule road. I used to visit Nimule whenever I came to Juba as Sudan Railways ran a motor-transport link of 120 miles to Nimule on the Uganda border where it met the Kenya Uganda Railways steamer link coming down the Nile. If there was a problem of mutual interest we would meet and discuss at Nimule.

It was a pleasant run and I remember one trip in particular. Colonel Cave who commanded the Equitorial Battalion offered to take us as passengers in his truck as he had some work to do at Nimule. Colonel Cave was a great authority on the birds of the south, with many other interests which included a private aeroplane, kept at Torit. We gratefully accepted. This journey was at the time the ferry was in use. We landed on a flat bank with grass extending back for 5 miles, beloved of game including rhino. At mile 7 was the Rejaf turn. By this time the road was running through open woodland and at mile 15 was the Torit turn which took off to the east. At mile 19 we crossed the River Leifero by a girder bridge and saw the first mahogany and passed a pair of giant hornbills. We breakfasted at a magnificently sited Rest House in the Loluba Hills. My wife has an additional memory — of being escorted to the toilet, for her safety, by an armed policeman, who remained discreetly nearby throughout.

The road continued through wooded undulating country with plenty of evidence of elephant. It reached a summit at mile 55 and was an area with many interesting flowers. On another trip, when collecting some plants, we found a patch of dark pink trumpet flowers, rather like a streptocarpus hybrid. Our agent at Juba, who was travelling with us, suggested that a suitable name might be *Rodum sidum,* and we adopted that name. I have already told of the repercussions with Mrs Tothill.

At mile 66 came the bridge over the River Kit and at mile 77 the asbestos concession. There was a hole 40 feet across and 30 feet deep, and considerable optimism at the prospects. The rising road wound ahead, with magnificent views over the next undulating section, and then sloped gently down to mile 90 where a road on the right led off to Shukoli. At Shukoli was a ferry across the Nile by which one could reach Kajo-Kaji. My notebook had an entry 'Stigand's house at Kajo-Kaji is pure Cotswold'. I wanted to see it but a walk of four hours on the other side was involved and that was not possible.

At mile 76, on the left, was the turn-off for Opari and some fine views. Next we crossed the Assua bridge of four spans at mile 108. It is the largest bridge I know of in the south. Proceeding to the summit at mile 114 we were rewarded by a magnificent view. From this point was a long curving descent from which roads branched off, left to Gulu and Uganda and right to the Fula Rapids and the Grass Bridge.

The facilities at Nimule were not extensive and activity was slight except when a Kenya Uganda Railways steamer was tied up. The day I arrived was quiet and I soon completed my work. Colonel Cave arranged lunch at the Rest House a couple of miles back from where I managed to photograph the Nile snaking away for a great many miles in Uganda. For the return trip we had an 18.00 hour deadline to meet for the ferry. About half-way on the journey a cheetah walked out on to the road about 100 yards ahead and the policeman picked up his rifle. It watched us for a second or two, continued to cross the road then dropped into the open road-side drain; for a quarter of a mile we were travelling together, the cheetah being about 15 yards ahead of us, and then it decided to continue its journey and bounded away to the left. We made good time, despite a burst tyre about 40 miles from home, and arrived at the ferry with five minutes in hand.

KATIRE AND GILOGILOPILILI

War shortages caused me to visit timber production in the Imatong Mountains. We had some good trees growing in the Southern Sudan and felt we might be able to help ourselves. To get to the site we left Juba by the Nimule road, and crossed the 5 miles of flat grassland where charging rhino, weighing 1½ tons were an

WHEELS AND PADDLES IN THE SUDAN

occasional risk. It had happened to our agent when travelling with the District Commissioner. A rhino near the road, on their beam, spotted them, disliked them and immediately charged. The question was whether the somewhat elderly boxcar in which they were travelling could accelerate sufficiently; it did and the rhino passed the tail-board with a gap of 10 yards. Such a liability in the south was an added reason for a good standard of vehicle maintenance.

Having safely covered these 5 miles we continued down the Nimule road and then branched off to the east at mile 15. The road was fairly flat and skirted a number of ranges of hills. At mile 32 we passed Jebel Nyangala at the end of the Loluba Hills and at mile 40 touched the Lyrian Hills. The River Kudo was crossed at mile 55 by a long causeway and 3 miles after crossing the Kinyeti Bridge at mile 81 we reached Torit. The Equatorial Battalion base and workshops were at Torit.

Here we met the Forestry Officer in charge of the project, Vidal Hall, who was to be our guide and host in the Imatongs. The distance from Torit to Katire, at the foot of the mountains, was 36 miles but it took us four and a half hours to reach our destination. At Ngarama, mile 6, at the near end of the Imatongs, the road forked to skirt the two sides and our road took the western side. We soon ran into heavy rain and got stuck once. We had carburettor and petrol-pump trouble with Vidal Hall's car. On the way we passed through remnants of gallery forest and shortly before we reached Katire we were joined by the road from Talanga Forest.

Katire was tucked in at the foot of the Imatongs. It obtained its water from the Kinyeti and was the site of two saw-mills for converting logs to sawn timber. The timber which was being sought was an alternative to British Columbian Pine which Sudan Railways rated very highly for railway coach-building and which under war conditions had become difficult to find. We had obtained a small consignment of podocarpus from Kenya, which seemed to offer possibilities, and so we asked our Forestry Department about the likelihood of finding it in the Southern Sudan. Podocarpus grew at 6,500 feet in the Imatongs but very little below that level and so it was decided to try to win some from the top of the Imatongs and convert it at existing saw-mills at Katire. These mills had been set up to convert timber from the lower slopes of the Imatongs and mahogany from Talanga Forest.

WHEELS AND PADDLES IN THE SUDAN

The next day we took a strenuous walk, climbing from savannah at 3,500 feet to high forest at 6,500 feet. Everything was carried by a long string of Lakota porters, which I think cost us 4 piastres each for the round trip. The walk was full of interest with frequent change of view of the slides and other means of bringing down the logs. We stopped for refreshment at the pond into which the top slide delivered logs with a great splash, rather like the old Earl's Court water chute. For the last hour the path passed through high forest, where the trees were festooned with moss, ferns and orchids, we reached Gilogilopilpili in time for late lunch.

The name of the spot sounds intriguing. My Headquarters had lost touch and wired Governor Juba, 'Where is the General Manager?' On my return, the Governor showed me his reply, which was: 'Gone to Gilogilopilili', and added with a smile, 'That made 'em think!'

We stepped out of the forest on to 75 yards of gently rising short grass leading to a thatched log cabin with a back-cloth of podocarpus. It was a beautiful sight. The wall of the centre living room folded back to give access to a large paved sitting-out area beyond which was a big dish for a log fire, and a fine view.

We had arrived at the high forest. The podocarpus stand was very fine, with trees rising to 120 feet with straight boles and 20–24 inch butts. The problem was to get logs down to Katire in sufficiently long sections. Transport was complicated. Rubber-wheeled carts were used over the level sections, heavy timber barrows over the easier slopes and two slides over the steep ones. In descending the 3,000 feet seven changes had to be made. Most of the logs being handled were 8–10 feet long. I was told that logs of up to 20 feet had been obtained but I saw nothing over 14 feet. The problem requiring solution was how to transport 20–30-foot logs. The present production was a triumph of improvisation deserving the greatest credit. What available means, if any, could be used to enable longer logs to be handled?

In the afternoon we walked to Itabol Rest House, mainly through high forest. In the open were many 6-foot high white proteas with beautiful scented blooms 5 inches in diameter.

On our return to the log cabin we found fires lit, inside and out, and in the setting sun, the warmth was quite acceptable. After tea, as we sat over a great log fire, someone noticed, at the side of the fire, a black line 2 feet wide, unrolling like a carpet. It was an invasion of soldier ants! Fortunately one of our boys knew the drill in such circumstances. He fetched a frying pan, filled it with hot ashes from the dining-room and dumped it on the leading ranks. Other boys quickly followed his example and there was plenty of hot ash. The column quickly went into reverse and set off in another direction.

We had to make an early start next morning and I was sitting on the side of my *angareeb*, when the two dogs dashed in. Disappointed that I was up, they jumped onto my wife's *angareeb*, effectively shunting her to the far edge and compelling her to get up. After breakfast we bade farewell to Gilogilopilili with much regret — we could have enjoyed a few days up there very much.

On the return journey we descended by a different track which kept close to the longer of the two log slides and I was always glad when a log safely passed us on its headlong course. We were back at Katire by 11.00 hours and I was shown round the two saw-mills. I noticed an old friend from Atbara — a frame saw — being installed. After lunch we left for Torit to spend the night with the District Commissioner and on to Juba in the morning.

NAGICHOT

The following year, on our next trip to Juba, we visited Nagichot, a station in the Didinga Hills which had recently been opened. The initial run to Torit was not uneventful, even though we knew that section well. Travelling over a section of gravel road, we ran into a heavy rain storm. Great pools of water developed on the road surface and in pressing through one of them we threw up a stone which hit a blade of the cooling fan and bent it to form a cutting edge which very neatly described an 8-inch circle in our radiator. It brought us to a standstill. Fortunately we had a second car with us and were only about seven miles away from Torit Camp and the Equatorial Battalions Base Workshop. Having requested help from the Equats for the stricken car we drove on to Torit where the District Commissioner lent us his house for the night. We were further in luck when we found that the Equats had a spare radiator.

From Torit to Nagichot was a run of 93 miles. The last 17-mile climb up to Nagichot was by a one-way road, down in the morning and up in the afternoon, and the second car had to catch us up, so we went on ahead to stop a night at a Rest House near the foot of the climb. It was a pleasant run, mainly on the flat as the road wound from hill to hill, with a succession of Rest Houses. We stopped for lunch at mile 46 and Murukuren Rest House, which was delightfully situated under trees at the foot of the Dongatona Mountains.

The Kidepo River was crossed by a girder bridge at mile 54. We drove on and at a mass of Tigrida lillies and mile 64 the road branched left to Kapoeta and right to Nagichot, turning into the Didinga Hills at mile 76. We drove on another 5 miles to Chukudum Rest House and camped for the night to await our second car.

Before 1913 the Didinga Hills and the Toposa country belonged to Uganda. In that year the area was transferred to the Sudan. There was no profit to the Sudan from the extra territory gained. No attempts were made by the Sudan to administer the area during World War I and the effects of this on neighbouring areas were such that the Ugandan Government occupied the Didinga Hills again in 1921. The troops were under the command of Captain King with Dryberg as Political Officer. Civil Administration started in 1922–23 with Dryberg as District Commissioner but his tenure of the post ceased as the result of his unorthodox, but successful solution of an invasion problem which I have already mentioned. Captain King returned to the district as District Commissioner in 1929 — and we were going up to visit him.

The Didinga Hills rose from open rolling country. They were intersected by ravines or gullies, carrying good timber, with some perennial water. Nagichot stood at 6,500 feet, and was approached by the motor road wide enough for one-way traffic. The climb was achieved in 17 miles, a very creditable piece of work. The station itself was in a park of open grassland with trees dotted about and the buildings were widely separated, constructed in stone and brick with thatched roofs. The site of the station and the old Rest House had been selected on Saint Andrew's Day 1921 for future development as a station if one should be required. The first sod for permanent buildings was cut 20 years later, on Saint Andrew's Day 1941, and the station was occupied from November 1942. The District Commissioner had an attractive house with a magnificent view and there was a Rest House, *Merkaz,* police station and staff quarters. A Post Office and an Assistant District Commissioner's house were under construction. Water of excellent quality was drawn from two springs and abundant firewood was obtained from nearby woods. On the first morning I asked the District Commissioner about obtaining meat; I was issued with one sheep at a cost of 10 piastres, and I still have the receipt! It was disposed of at the going rate as being part of a fine paid in kind.

On the open grassland the trees were poor specimens, handicapped by frequent burning of the grass, but in the ravines there were many large trees of varied species, not to mention wild flowers, butterflies and monkeys.

In the morning we set off from the Rest House. The path led downhill towards some bigger trees which indicated a stream. We saw the first hints of small pockets of gallery forest in the deep gullies on these hills. The path led over open land to a larger gully also with remnants of gallery forest and some large trees, though no very fine specimens. There were many half-grown podocarpus up to about 15-inch butts and some olives. The whole was entwined with creepers and trailing moss.

Coming out of the gully and the trees the path sloped upwards over open grassland with small groups of misshapen trees and red-brown soil. Eventually we reached the crest of the ridge with its wonderful view. Behind us, stretching to within about 150 yards of the edge of the ridge, lay thick wood. It was easily penetrable, with trees rising to 40–50 feet. We continued along the ridge to the top of the valley and at the end of the high ground we sat down for lunch.

On the way back we passed an old *merkaz* garden, with pineapple plants, marvellous clumps of plumbago and strawberries. The path led on past a potato garden. The soil on all sides, in fact, appeared very fertile, composed very largely of decayed vegetable matter, with good sub-soil drainage. We arrived home pleasantly tired.

On our Sunday morning walk we arrived at a small quarry from which the building stone for all the houses was obtained. The only building in sight was the Sudan Defence Force Rest House, 2 or 3 miles away to the south-west. A lorry arrived to load stone and we enquired if there was a path leading to the Sudan Defence Force lines, but all agreed that the only way round was by the road. On our return we collected some interesting botanical specimens.

A pleasant Sunday afternoon, known as PSA, for many in Nagichot followed a morning of mild drinking of *merissa* (beer). Sunday was not a working day and soon after 14.00 hours ornate individuals, both male and female, mainly Latuka, would pass the

Rest House heading eastwards. Many stopped to give a 'preview' of what was to be seen on the dancing floor. The most ornate party consisted of six Latuka, three men and three women. Two men wore highly polished brass helmets, brass collars, thick ivory arm bangles and carried big spears. The third was the band, his instrument being an enormous post-horn, 10 feet long, blown like a flute, and built of cane. The women wore brown skin skirts finishing in a bead belt. One had her back covered with wales nearly one inch high, another wore a short red tarboosh and the third had a large key suspended round her neck. Two Acholi males gave a display of mock fighting as they passed; they were a study in white-washed bodies with white feathers in their hair.

Lobeito, our interpreter, said that the dance would take place in the army lines. Our drivers and staff were all out to lunch so we sent Lobeito to request their presence as soon as the ceremony was over. They turned up in half an hour and taking Lobeito and Yassein in the car we soon covered the 3 miles to the 'dance'. The guard turned out as we entered the lines, much to our embarassment, and as we

Latuka dancers with horn.

parked the car at the mens' married quarters we saw ahead of us the dancing floor.

The ornate party of Latuka held the floor. The orchestra had been augmented by a small drum and a youth with metal castanets and one of the women wore an anklet of iron bells. In the dance the men and the women faced each other, the women taking the more active part, advancing with considerable 'black-bottoming'. Meanwhile the men were taking short steps and brandishing their weapons, all the movements being in marked rhythm.

As soon as this dance was completed, a 'chorus' came on from the wings — or more correctly from between the *tukls* — composed of about 40 Latuka soldiers, almost without exception naked, with their bodies and faces picked out in various designs and colours. One had white shorts, with a futuristic design on them, and mushroom-coloured leggings. Another was completely covered with white stars and had a necklace of flowers. Another had a breast-plate of colobus monkey skin. They carried sticks, knob-kerries, spears, brass bound korbags and short wands with a tuft of hair on the end of lion's mane or colobus monkey. The most frequently performed element in these dances consisted of variations of the chorus moving in a circle with short rhythmic steps whilst the 'stars', the Latuka party, performed in the centre. In another variant, which occurred often, the chorus formed columns of six wheeling round in the centre of the circle with the 'stars' at the head of each column. After a while the chorus would retire to have a wild follow-my-leader round the adjoining *tukls* leaving the floor to the 'stars' who would do a variation on their opening number.

We were very impressed by the good nature of all taking part; everyone enjoyed himself immensely, yet there was little horseplay. They delighted in just avoiding treading on one's toes, and invariably were successful. An admiring crowd stood watching, composed largely of soldiers of the Equats, more staid matrons and small children, most of them keeping time with their little bodies. Several 'belles' were exchanging bandinage with the spectators. An unusual sight was to see boys aged seven or eight carrying babes about on their backs in very efficient carrier slings. Many of the dancers had various mission badges hung round their necks and I wonder if their harmless exertions would be regarded as grievous back-sliding.

A sergeant, over 6-feet tall, stood in the front row of onlookers, holding his son, perhaps aged two, by the hand. The sturdy little lad was thoroughly enjoying the proceedings. The dancing which took place every Sunday up to 19.00 hours, and formed an important 'release'. As we got up to go, a soldier of the Equats asked us to take a photo of him with his bugle. We agreed and he dashed off to turn out the guard and post himself on the right where he was immediately joined by a dancer and a soldier in mufti. A more irregular guard could hardly be imagined! He asked us to be sure to let him have a copy.

After enjoying the local weekend festivities at Nagichot we resumed the business of surveying the timber. From the furthest point previously reached, we descended the *col* forming the end of the Naperatong valley and climbed up to Lauda on the far side. It took us 1¾ hours. There was extensive timber and a magnificent view. Turning back I decided to endeavour to reach the plateau behind the Sudan Defence Force lines across country. It was slow-going across four thickly timbered ravines, three of them without paths which meant under or over thick undergrowth and fallen trees. The hours slipped by quickly and we were not always headed in the right direction, so I was grateful, at around 19.00 hours, to run into a policeman and a rescue party who led us back to Nagichot.

Talking the matter over with Captain King afterwards, he said it was very easy to lose one's bearings in these hills; they were all so similar and landmarks so few. When marking out the trace for the road he frequently found himself proceeding in the wrong direction — though not lost! It had certainly been an eventful last day at Nagichot, and with regret we set off down the hill the next morning.

WESTWARDS FROM JUBA

The main road to the west out of Juba was the Aba road, heading directly for the Congo, passing through Yei. From this road there were turnings northward to Amadi, Meridi and Wau, and southwards to Kajo-Kaji. There were many bridges along it, built to carry up to 3-ton lorries. In 1942 they were in process of being rebuilt to carry wider and heavier vehicles in connection with AFLOC, and when I was there in August 1942, traffic of 5,000 tons per month was imminent, so bridge-building activities were much in evidence.

WHEELS AND PADDLES IN THE SUDAN

The road skirted the hill at the foot of which Juba stood. Its name was Jebel Kuruk and the road rose a little. Looking back one had a good view of the hills on the east bank of the river, and of Rejaf Cathedral. It was Sunday morning, and the mail lorries were setting off. The road surface was rough for a main road, and I wondered how it would stand up to the anticipated traffic load. In summer it was necessary to adjust tyre pressures every 25 miles or so. We passed a number of nicely wooded hills, skirting some quite closely.

At mile 62 we came to the Lalyo turn off for Amadi, where the Inspector of Education for the South lived, and where, perched on a small hilltop, was the habitation of the local Sultan. Just away to the north were the Loka Hills, Gumbiri and Longoli, 5,605 feet high and a fine sight. Around Loka, at mile 68, there were forestry activities and also a Church Missionary Society Station.

As I have said it was Sunday morning, and as we neared Loka we were met by a band of lads and lasses engaged in a Church Parade. The lasses' 'Sunday Best' was mainly large bunches of leaves fore and aft. Why one of them was additionally balancing an upturned black beer bottle in her palm was not discoverable! Anyhow they were all in the best of spirits and accompanied us to the Mission Station.

The activity of the Church Missionary Society was mainly educational, the Nugent School which produced clerical staff for the South, and a Trade School complete with dormitories and playing fields. We met the de Sarums who were in charge and showed us round the establishments, which were a splendid undertaking.

It was not long before we came upon evidence of the AFLOC Scheme in operation. We saw a convoy of loaded army lorries en route for Juba from Aba in the Congo, parked for a roadside halt. Shortly before reaching Yei were two sawmills busy cutting sleepers from vuba timber for the Sudan Railways. In 1917 Fawkes and Storrar had come looking for suitable timber to help out our supplies in World War I for Mechanical and Engineering Department needs. They had looked at Vuba, before going on to the Aluma area in quest of mahogany. As a result a certain amount of vuba was cut and sent to Khartoum. I do not think, however, that any sustained timber production arose directly from their visit and investigation.

The sawmills were quite busy, and I met Marshall, the local Inspector of Forests, and discussed the quality of sleeper being produced, it left a lot to be desired, and a closer adherence to our specification was promised.

It was 100 miles from Juba to Yei, another picturesque spot. On the south side of the village green were the *merkaz* and the Rest House, facing them the police station and the modern prison. I remember magnificent mango trees and strutting bronze-coloured turkeys. The District Commissioner controlled a pineapple plantation producing delicious golden fruit. The Church Missionary Society on the north side of the road offered us hospitality.

Our host was Janson Smith of the Education Department and his establishment was dominated by 'Susie', a recently acquired young chimpanzee. My wife took Susie in hand, and equipped her with nappies and bedded her down in a folding work-basket, which certainly dealt with a lot of the nuisance. On arrival of the two Church Missionary Society ladies for tea the following day, the tea party was not without surprises, as Susie came too. However she survived domestication, and accompanied her master on many treks, and certainly was alive two years later, although I don't know what was her eventual fate.

Janson Smith was very enthusiastic about educational work in the South, enjoying the quick responsiveness and keen power of observation that he found amongst the youth of the South, even if it sometimes led to awkward situations. He instanced the experience of his Chief at a recent inspection of a Catholic Girls School. The girls were lined up, the Sister brought in the Inspector, and introduced him by a short speech. There was some tittering whilst she spoke, and at the end the girls burst into song in the local dialect. The Sister became increasingly embarassed, and the Inspector, ignorant of the local dialect, unwisely sought translation from the Sister, who eventually yielded to his insistence. Against a background of ever increasing joyful singing of the girls, he got his translation, whuch was very freely rendered into English as: 'Mr--- we are so very pleased to see you, and your buttons are undone'. I think this story well illustrated the point. Janson Smith was a very entertaining host, and he filled me in with a lot of background about Kagelu, and also Iwatoka, where we were going later.

An early start next morning was needed as there was much to see at our next stop, which was Kagelu Experimental Station. We left Yei along an avenue of cedrillas and mangos, flanking plantations of young teak. Our guide was Ferguson, the Inspector in charge, and he had much of interest to show us, including the tapping of the mature rubber trees, and processing of the latex, which was particularly valuable to the economy since the loss of Malaya, and the making of string and rope from the locally grown sisal. The processing of cassava to make tapioca was new to me. Basket work of a high standard was also being done, and there was some most attractive pottery. A blacksmith with bellows of a type dating back many centuries was an interesting survival. In the afternoon we visited plantations of coffee, rubber, teak and palmoil palms, and an extensive plant nursery, winding up with plantations of sugar cane and pineapple.

IWATOKA

Our next destination was George Haggar's concession at Iwatoka, taking up an invitation made when we had met him on one of our trips to Juba. We left Yei in the morning via the Aba road, turning south just short of Kagelu along an avenue of rubber trees in the Kagelu Rubber Forest. Some very large mango trees were seen amongst their abounding distribution here. At mile 16 we turned off at the school, crossing the River Yei to Kabangere Coffee Plantation, which was George's earlier venture. It occupied 375 acres, of which 140 acres were planted, at an average height of 3,100 feet. The concession ran for 30 years from 1936 and was concentrated on 'robusta' coffee, with only 5 acres of 'arabica'. Chillies, castor seed, pineapples and cassava, which takes 14 to 15 months to mature, were all under cultivation. The labour force ranged from 200 to 400 according to the season. It was a well-run enterprise, and Dr Myers considered it the the finest coffee plantation he had seen when he visited it before the drought of 1941–43. The citrus trees were bearing well, and there were experimental plantings of 'American nut', sapota for chewing gum and *casa maroa* (Brazilian apple).

After a couple of miles we made another detour to the left to visit the Aga Falls on the River Yei. This involved a 1½-mile walk as the road was out of repair and the bridge was down, but the grass had been cut for us, and we were able to negotiate the river by stepping stones. On the far side we climbed up the hill and came to a cast-iron notice, 'Private AGA FALLS Welcome', and then to the site of a Rest House, built as a weekend retreat by Tracey, our

Governor at Damer, when he was District Commissioner at Yei. It had been burned down in a grass fire, but its immediate surround had been marked out by four small white marble corner pillars, inscribed Matthew, Mark, Luke and John. It was a wonderful site with a fine view of the Falls, which were in two sections with a total drop of about 130 feet. The River Yei formed a pool at the top of the escarpment, and the falls were the result of its overflow. The vegetation all around was gorgeous with the orange-red of the spathodeas in full flower. There was a local belief that if you tossed a piastre into the stream you would ensure no rain falling on that day; we paid our tribute, and made our way back over the stepping stones, to our car.

We continued the climb up the escarpment through pleasant country, and after 7 miles the circular road was left at the signpost for Iwatoka, at a group of buildings. These were a school, and merchant's shop, not a common sight in these parts. We were within 2 miles of our destination. The road crossed the River Yei near a low waterfall which was the location of a ram for local water supply, and we passed along an avenue of cedrillas lining the coffee plantations on each side. The houses of Iwatoka were on the right. The word Iwatoka means 'the place that the elephants cannot penetrate'.

The background to this 'estate' was the granting of a 30 year concession in 1931 to two retiring officials who had spent a long period of service in the South. It ran to 600 acres, of which they had planted up half with Arabica coffee. At the commencement both were bachelors but soon after one got married, the partnership broke up and George Haggar took over the concession in May 1939.

One of the first things we were shown was the reason for Iwatoka's name. About 100 yards from the houses was a cleft in the rock. The narrow path dropped down quickly some 30 feet and extended perhaps 50 yards. The width of the cleft at the bottom was 10 feet with steep walls giving a width across the top of 25 feet. At the bottom was a tiny stream with pools, in a very moist atmosphere, with water dripping from the ferns and vegetation clothing the side walls, and a profusion of small trees and flowers. It was the epitome of the kind of habitat that Botanical Gardens strive to create in their tropical houses — quite superb. Why no elephants penetrated it was self-evident — we found it difficult enough ourselves to negotiate an entry!

The site was land cleared from gallery forest, with a rich soil from decayed vegetation. At an altitude of 4,000 feet it was bounded on one side by the River Yei and enjoyed plentiful rainfall, falling mainly between March and November with lesser falls in the December to February period.

George Haggar had changed the cultivation over to robusta coffee but ran into a three-year drought lasting till 1943, both types suffered equally.

We also saw crops in annual yield of castor seed, chillies, potatoes, cassava and pineapples. Other crops on a commercial scale but not yet yielding included paw-paw for papaine, tea, tung and cashew, and he had experimental plantings of Derris root, sugar cane, tobacco, cinnamon, peach, apricot, plum, apple, avocado, fig, vine, pear, sapota for chewing gum, *casa maroa*, kaki, loquat and kola.

A surprise awaited us at the end of our afternoon tour; we found ourselves at a pool at the bottom of a cascade. My wife promptly took off her shoes, sat down on the grass verge and dangled her feet in the pool for a delightful five minutes or so, when two house-boys appeared bearing tea ceremonially served on silver trays, and including what we had glimpsed but not mentioned — strawberries piled high in a bowl. It was a memorable tea party.

The following morning we visited the Aluma Plateau, which I was keen to see, as Fawkes, my first boss, had told me of his visit there in 1917. Aluma's Jebel, as the natives call it, is another layer on the escarpment, shaped rather like a sphinx without a head. We met Chief Aluma, a descendant of the Aluma that Fawkes had met, and caught him when sober — the first time in many years, so we were told. He came with us to the top of the plateau, from where the prospect was marvellous, stretching right away into the Congo. The old chap described to us all the points of interest.

In the afternoon we visited the gold workings at Aloto. Between the wars two prospectors, called Caley and Forbes, sought gold in the streams between Juba and Yei with what success we do not know. They went home in 1938.

The Aloto was a wide gently sloping stony stream bottom, with, at that time of year, a little water trickling down. It was being worked by sluicing. Each sluice was a sloping wooden trough, with a board on top pierced by a number of 1½ inch holes, spaced at 3-inch centres, whilst the bottom of the trough was fitted with wooden slats. Two pans of soil, sand and stone were put at the top end of the board, and a boy bailed up water and tipped it over the pile, and two men then scrubbed the soil over the top board with wooden scrapers; the larger stones fell off the end. Small stones were removed from the holes with a nail, and there was a weekly clean-up which was panned. Each sluice had a gang of nine men, with a headman, paid a daily wage plus a bonus reckoned on the amount of gold produced. I was shown the fruits of a week's work; it filled two-thirds of a one pound jam jar, which at present day prices for gold would be worth quite a lot of money.

We had a long chat with George Haggar about concessions. He wanted to expand, having been involved agriculturally in this area for seven years and not without success. He asked me if I was interested in taking over the concession from him when I retired. Life at Iwatoka certainly had Shangri-la qualities, but I declined for family reasons. It proved to be a right decision, as the Revolt in the South in later years brought much violence in Yei, and life at Iwatoka would in fact have been very hazardous.

Chapter Ten

UP THE BAHR-EL-GHAZAL

The east end of Lake No had a narrow exit 50 yards wide, between firm banks, into the White Nile. This was regarded, according to the RPs, as the commencement of the Bahr-el-Ghazal. In describing the river it is convenient to take distances mainly from the Egyptian Irrigation Department Reference Poles situated 5 kilometres apart.

The stream was sluggish, with a drop of only 12 feet in the 144 miles from Meshra-el-Req to the Lake No exit. This averaged 1 inch per mile. It was at its maximum height in December, when the floods of the Jur and the Bahr-el-Arab, which peak in September, have percolated through the swamps to reach the Bahr-el-Ghazal. It had dry land on its south bank or reasonably close to the river edge from RP 7, and was therefore the catchment drain. As a result of the slow current, navigation was at times much hindered by blocks of *sudd*.

The first 10 kilometres up to RP 2 lay through Lake No, which was wide and fairly shallow, harbouring a number of large islands of *sudd*, which shifted position with strong winds. In the lake, and particularly at the mouth, some fine aigl fishing was to be had. My wife caught her record fish here, 56 inches long, 48 inches girth and weighing 95 pounds and she brought it to boat. I had some tussles with big fellows, but failed to get them to boat. There were also good *cass* (tiger fish) to be caught, and many hippo, who were not always content to mind their own business. It was common to see 'ma' swimming along with a baby hippo perched on her back; in such a case it was wise to keep at least 100 yards clear.

At the west end of the lake, on the northern shore, were the remnants of the Suddite Factory. The main steel girders had been removed to leave only the boilers and engines in pieces. The Suddite enterprise was designed to convert *sudd* into briquettes for steam-raising. Successful trials in 1911 led to the formation of the Sudan

WHEELS AND PADDLES IN THE SUDAN

E.W.W's record fish.

Fuel (Suddite) Co. Ltd, with a nominal capital of £250,000. Only a small quantity of briquettes was produced, and the factory ceased production shortly after the outbreak of World War I. I doubt if the heavy machinery was ever erected. Formal notice of revocation of the concession was given in 1921 and the company went into liquidation. In 1919 Sir Howard Spicer and Mr John Wells toured the Southern Sudan and were also interested in the possibilities of converting *sudd* into a useful product. As a result a company called Sudan Cotton and Industrial Development (1919) Ltd. was floated with nominal capital of £250,000, it failed to attract sufficient additional capital, and also went into liquidation, with termination of the concession finally in August 1923. Interest in using *sudd* revived just before the last war, when a Glasgow firm, John Watson and Co., thought of using *sudd* for making newsprint, I do not know whether anything practical came of it.

The idea may revive yet again. In 1983 the media revealed that oil had been found at Bentiu in the Bahr-el-Ghazal, 87 kilometres upstream from the Suddite Factory site. There is already talk of a pipe-line to Khartoum. Which route it will follow is not yet disclosed, but a strike of oil means the availability of crude oil and, quite likely, natural gas. This fact of close availability might well, at a time when newsprint is scarce and costly and environmentalists call loudly for timber conservation, encourage in some entrepreneur the idea of converting *sudd* freely available in large quantities.

The river proper started at RP 2, at the west end of Lake No. The channel here was over 100 yards wide, with swamps on either side. These were the home of the shoebill stork, one of the unique products of the Sudan, for which zoos all over the world would pay a great deal. He is a phlegmatic fellow, standing his ground when you pass, seldom even moving. In September you would see them paired off, standing on top of a low shrub or ant-hill, and making a very quaint picture.

Near RP 7, Khor Doleib took off to the south and ran nearly parallel with the main stream. Its mouth was another good fishing spot for *aigl* and *cass*, and usually carried a good complement of hippos as well. From here on, until beyond Wankai, swamps became less prevalent, but the river generally had its edging of papyrus and *um-souf* backed with bushes and low trees on the land.

The amount of animal life seen depended largely on the time of year. Up until May, grass and reeds had largely been burned off, so spotting game was much easier. The south bank was lion country, and on the north bank, especially from RP 9 to RP 11, giraffe could be seen throughout the year. Waterbuck and white-eared kob were plentiful, as were hippo, especially in the lakes, and crocodiles. Mixed groups of animals were often seen. Bird varieties included fish-eagles, cormorants, greater and lesser egrets, saddle-bill storks, black ibis, lily trotters, geese and ducks, and occasionally a bateleur eagle.

Between RP 11 and 12, the sizeable Khor Loich took off to the north, and between it and RP 11 on the south bank was a memorial to a Hungarian sportsman, Baron Hanyadi, who was badly mauled by a wounded lion when big-game shooting. He died within sight of Khartoum.

The next steamer stop was at Yodni, a small trading post on the south bank between RP 14 and 15. Like all trading posts along the river it had some specimen trees. These were planted by Captain Fergusson, a former District Commissioner, who was murdered at Lake Jur about 1929. At Yodni there was a fine *Ficus nitida* and some golden mohurs, several merchants, and the remnants of a garden.

The clear width of the river was about 20 yards, and passing another steamer called for care as well as choosing the best spot. The papyrus and rushes, however, provided a yielding cushion.

The next station was Yonyang on the north bank, where the Mill Hill Fathers were working among the Nuer. Father Moran, a cheery Irishman, was in charge of the work, with Father Keegan, a Dutchman, working from a floating church, named Saint Martinus, in which he toured the neighbourhood. The church was self-propelled and most ingeniously fitted-out.

I walked to the station to make Father Moran's acquaintance. He had been at Yonyang since the Mill Hill Fathers took over from their predecessors, the Verona Fathers, in 1938. The approach to the populace was mainly educationally based, though at that time only nine boys were in school. The Nuer desired neither religion nor education, nor indeed medicine. Father Moran showed me his workshop, garden, and a flourishing dairy. He was speared by a mad Nuer in August 1942. In the next 36 hours he was rushed by launch to Malakal, where he made a good recovery. Awarded the fine of 70 cows, he sold half of them to pay hospital bills and the rest caused milk and cream to abound at Yonyang.

Normally Yonyang was visited twice monthly by the postboat, and, from the conversation, we realised just how much a break in the service meant to them. Half a mile upstream was another, deserted, *meshra*, connected back to the station by a tree-lined avenue. It had been built by the Verona Fathers.

A few miles further on was Bentiu on the south bank. There were several merchants, and an excellent Province garden with mango and other fruit. We always picked up a good supply of fruit and fresh vegetables.

From here on the clear river width was 15 yards, with the banks 100 yards apart. It was a section prone to frequent *sudd* blocks in September and October. In May the papyrus and rushes were dry and could be burned, and the fires were extensive. Some were started on purpose, to spear more easily the fish lurking beneath.

Near here, in March 1935, Bob Gordon, the Assistant Superintendent Engineer at Khartoum North, had an interesting experience. Coming downstream in *Sobat*, a herd of 12 elephant crossed the river ahead of him. A mother and calf got separated, and the mother bolted, leaving the calf in fairly shallow water. Bob readied four of the crew to drop in to the water with ropes. *Sobat* drew 22 inches forward, but successfully got alongside the youngster without running aground. The crew then slipped ropes under its tummy, got a pair of gangplanks over the side, made a sloping ramp up to the sitting-out deck of the launch, secured one end of the ropes to the rails, and hauled away on the free ends. The calf was brought on board to the railed sitting-out deck. A male elephant decided some action was needed and dashed back into the river. There was a moment of suspense before the engine responded and got *Sobat* safely off from the shallows, once everybody had scrambled aboard. As *Sobat* slid into the stream and away, the protesting herd followed along the bank for a couple of kilometres.

The milk aboard was totally insufficient for the calf's needs, and on arrival at Tonga, the crew took on all milk available and Bob telegraphed the doctor at Malakal for a supply of condensed milk to be ready on arrival in 12 hours' time. After consultation a feeding plan was agreed, and they headed off on the three-day journey to Khartoum. Of course, the news of bringing back an elephant preceded them, and a committee of welcome was waiting at Khartoum North Dockyard. For the next ten days Jumbo and Bob saw a lot of each other but eventually Bob bowed to advice and deposited Jumbo in the zoo, where he died four nights later, probably of a broken heart.

There are many such 'animal stories' connected with our trips. Near RP 24, for example, we saw a fine full-grown male waterbuck being collected by a crocodile. We tried to prod the crocodile beneath the surface with a *midra*, but manoeuvring the launch was not easy, and within a couple minutes the crocodile had the buck completely submerged. The female had retreated and when we passed again three days later, she was about 100 yards upstream of the corpse of the buck. The crocodile was on guard between it and the bank, and swam out to meet the launch but he must have concluded that we were bigger as, 6 yards from the boat, he dived and swam away.

At RP 25, on the north bank, under a clump of trees, was the *meshra* of Wath Jak with its one merchant's hut. A little beyond, on the same bank, was the sudded-up entrance to Khor Nyang. One struggled through this for a quarter of a mile before reaching a fine sheet of open water. In January 1944 we made this passage and went on the 7 miles up to Tharangop, where a Chiefs' meeting of Leik and Jekaing Nuer was in progress. We met Nyinger Rih, the Chief of Leik, which was a territory to the north of the Bahr-el-Ghazal and to the east of the Bahr-el-Arab. To mark the auspicious occasion he tried to give me a bull, which would have been somewhat of an encumbrance on board *Sobat*! I said it would be more fitting that I gave him one. It was quickly produced by the District Commissioner and everyone seemed pleased. We then met Gar Kek Luop, the Chief of the Jekaing, whose territory was south of the Bahr-el-Ghazal, extending from the Bahr-el-Jebel to Wangkai. He had recently received a Sword of Honour, and exhibited it with great pride. A local sight at Tharangop was its prison, consisting of four *tukls* and a sketchy surrounding croton hedge. There was no guard, and the prisoners proposed themselves for leave when they thought fit. There was no incentive to run away because the food in prison was decidedly better than at home!

From Wath Jak to Wangkai the river was much wider in most places with 40 yards of clear water. For much of the way there were meadows with small trees and euphorbias, always growing up in the protection of other trees. On the south bank there was a half-mile deep belt of trees in grass backed by an expanse of grassy plain up to 10 miles wide leading to the higher ground, speckled with trees and *luaks*.

WHEELS AND PADDLES IN THE SUDAN

I have mentioned the nuisance of *sudd* generally, and proceeding upstream once, in *Melika*, I had much trouble with it. Our only advantage was that we were attacking the blocks from their downstream face, but, being screw-propelled, we lacked the efficiency of a stern-wheeler. My diary reads: 'In *sudd* block at RP 10 from 13.40 to 14.30 hours; helped by *Stack* and some Nuer in a dug-out. Called it a day at 00.45 hours in a block of over 100 yards. Commenced work at 05.45 hours; cleared block — RP 23 — at 07.00 hours. Passed Khor Nyang, RP 26, heavily sudded, at 11.03 hours. Into further block of 70 yards, RP 26, at 11.08 hours and cleared at 12.03 hours. Into further block at 12.18 hours and clear at 12.38 hours. Passed RP 27 at 13.00 hours. Into block 13.20 hours and out at 13.40 hours. Passed RP 28 at 13.50 hours. Into block 13.57 hours and clear at 15.00 hours. Arrived Wangkai 15.20 hours'. The days work was thus — travelling time 2 hours 52 minutes. Clearing *sudd* 6 hours 53 minutes. Distance covered approximately 25 kilometres.

Wangkai, at RP 30, lay on the north bank; it had a number of small merchants, and the trade was in hides. An ox hide here used to cost 1½ to 3 piastres, and until quite recently could be bought for 5 piastres, so it was a profitable trade for the merchant. It was here that I found the hides required to cover the Emperor's ceremonial 'bull' drum. Wangkai was a useful spot as it had a flat open site well above flood level, used for stacking the sleepers and timber brought down from the upper waters of the Jur. Since the Jur River season was short, it was worth the double-handling to off-load at Wangkai and stack, freeing the barges to get back up for the next load, leaving onward transport to Kosti and Khartoum for later in the year when the Jur was closed.

Trade at Wangkai was carried on by barter, as is common in this part of the world. The Nuer had little use for money, and his needs were covered by spearheads, iron for knives, beads, grain and an occasional yard of cloth. One day a young Nuer, who spoke Arabic asked if *Sobat* was an aeroplane, and stated that all the local people believed it so to be! A number of the Nuer worked as wood-cutters for the Forestry Section, using donkeys for conveying themselves as well as the wood. To cross the 75 yard width of the Bahr-el-Ghazal, they got into a dug-out, one paddling and the other grasping the ear of a donkey swimming along on each side of the craft.

The District Commissioner's Nuer servant had recently asked if he could have a few words. The District Commissioner agreed, and instead of asking for a loan to buy cattle, the boy wanted to know whether at that time the Government was eating the Nuer or vice-versa. The District Commissioner had to admit that with shortage of staff the Government was eating the Nuer — which rather shows that the non-educated Southerner was beginning to think.

A few miles further on, and still on the north bank, was the mouth of the Bahr-el-Arab. It was usually well sudded up but the confluence itself was a fine sheet of open water 300 yards across. We once had an unpleasant experience here. It was 15.00 hours, and a storm was blowing up. We decided to anchor in the middle, on a long cable, giving ourselves enough room to ride out anything — but not so! We dragged our anchor but going full ahead managed to pick it up, and tried to get our head into the wind, but the blow had developed into a miniature circular storm centred on this span of open water opposite the Bahr-el-Arab. All we could do was to execute tight circles and chase it, but always a bit behind. I feared that we could be rolled over at any moment, and so after the third circuit, I told the *reis* to desist and head off for the nearest rushes trusting to luck that we could thrust the bows into them; this we managed to do and then heaved a heartfelt sight of relief!

A few hundred yards from the mouth on the east bank was the wood station and police post of Ghabat-el-Arab. It was well patronised by Nuer prisoners from the Bul section on the west of the Bahr-el-Arab. In January 1944, together with District Commissioners Wilson and Kennett, we attempted to penetrate the Bahr-el-Arab with *Metemeh, Nekheila* and *Sobat*. Wilson was keen on opening it up as he had been working on clearing the channel with prison labour since 1940. The first 500 yards was through thick *um-souf* along a passage which had been forced by *Metemeh*. The next 1,300 yards was reasonably clear water and had been excavated by the prisoners. Next came the real problem. It was said that 3 miles ahead lay clear water, and *Nekheila* made a start, but found it heavy going, so we brought *Sobat* alongside to make a combined assault on the thick weed, we had little success. We then tried towing *Sobat* astern, to profit by the breaking up of the weed by *Nekheila's* stern wheel. Progress was slow as the latter was in contact with the river bed. Decayed vegetation was only 2 feet from the surface but our tramping around soon increased the water depth to 3½ feet. In this way we advanced a mere 150 yards before settling down for the night.

The following morning we started early, and soon decided to leave *Nekheila* and go ahead with *Sobat*. We relied on assistance for towing and vegetation clearance from 35 Nuer prisoners, subsequently increased to 60, and in this fashion we advanced 450 yards by noon. There were still 2 miles to go, which at this pace would take us five or six days. We did not have this sort of time so the attempt was called off. It was interesting that these Bul Nuer were keen to open up the river, and their Chief, Tegjiek Dwaldong, was waiting for me at Wangkai to offer help. It would be far less trouble in future, he said, to come in by canoe than to walk for three days. To mark the occasion I presented him with a bull and in return received a bull-name, and am thus called Tutniel in Nuer hierarchy. My wife was accorded the name of Nyagenna, meaning the daughter of the Genna, their name for the lower reaches of the Bahr-el-Arab.

The Nuer language contains a wealth of words to describe in intricate detail shape and marking of their cattle. It is said that a Nuer can describe to another, albeit a stranger to the herd, one animal out of, say, a couple of hundred, so that he can select it without difficulty.

Clearing the Bahr-el-Arab.

WHEELS AND PADDLES IN THE SUDAN

In September 1944, with District Commissioner Wedderburn-Maxwell, I had another shot at opening up the passage of the Bahr-el-Arab with four craft, the *Marabout,* a large steel *felucca* manned by 17 Nuer prisoners, the *felucca* belonging to *Sobat* and a dug-out with four prisoners. We harnessed the 17 prisoners to *Marabout* and the four to the *felucca* from *Sobat*. Weed made the going difficult, and we also narrowly escaped attack by hornets. By the time we got to Withateir, about 4½ miles away, the prisoners had been in the water for three hours and were beginning to get cramp, so we put them in the *felucca,* and proceeded by poling, with intermittent help from the engine on *Marabout*. We carried on till 14.00 hours and then pushed the boat into the papyrus, leaving it under guard, whilst the prisoners cut a path through the 8-foot tall grass. After nearly a mile we struck the cattle track to Wangkai just before 15.00 hours, and then had a 4-mile walk back through the 9-inch deep mud of the track.

Next day we set out on horse, donkey and foot at 08.00 hours to rejoin our craft. The start was delayed by various problems. It took us 1½ hours to reach our hacked-out path, and we sent the horses and donkeys on to await us at Mantong, 4½ miles ahead by water. We got afloat by 10.00 hours, with a corporal and 12 prisoners in the *felucca,* and Wedderburn-Maxwell, myself, Yassein, the launch boy and a police sergeant on board *Marabout*. Conditions had not been improved by an invasion of red ants during the night. For the next two hours we awaited patiently the co-operation of the engine whose pump was recalcitrant, making what progress we could by poling. By noon we had made about one mile, and I decided to send *Marabout* home with ten of the prisoners plus corporal and launch boy. The rest of us pushed on in the *felucca*. The going continued difficult with the channel reduced to 8 feet in places; we encountered four or five blocks of *um-souf* and the water was full of yonyang moss, but there was good depth of water, 7 feet or more in spots. We used the outboard when we could in the patches of clear water, but as we advanced the water generally became less clear, and eventually the cooling system got choked. We were then left only with poling in water often inconveniently deep and full of moss. It was only the thought of our mounts waiting ahead that kept us going. The sight of the ugly face of one of the donkey-men peering through the papyrus at 16.45 hours was welcome indeed, and he confirmed that our mounts were not far distant. The last half mile was relatively open water in a channel 100 feet wide, with no worse obstructions than water lilies. Mantong was reached at 17.05 hours.

The 8-mile journey back over the cattle track was in rain and mud up to a foot deep. My pony fell so I plodded ahead on foot before taking Wedderburn-Maxwell's abandoned mount. We lost the track temporarily many times but a mile from base were met by a search party. We sent them on to look for the donkey-borne remnants of the party. I got back to Wangkai at 20.00 hours, ten minutes behind Wedderburn-Maxwell. I was the luckier in that *Sobat* was moored to the bank, whilst *Wingate* was reposing on a lump of *sudd* at the mouth of the river, and he had to wade out to her up to his neck in water. The donkey party had lost their way, despite professional guides, and only got back at 22.30 hours. It is ironic that in 1905 the first 19 miles of the river were open to navigation by steamers.

Whilst we were away on this expedition, my wife stayed aboard *Sobat* at the wood station. A large party came down to the boat at mid-morning, stopping some distance away. One who spoke some Arabic came forward and engaged the *reis* in discussion. They wanted to know if they could perform a dance for Nyagenna, and my wife agreed. For half an hour they danced near the boat, and then the spokesman came forward again to say it was rather warm, and they were getting tired, they would now like to stop. My wife thanked them for the performance, and after a farewell chant they broke up and trooped away.

The lower, overgrown reaches of the Bahr-el-Arab were rich in bird life. With the water surface covered with moss and lilies, it was a paradise for lily-trotters, birds which pay little attention to man, and just get on with their business. They nest on a mat of this surface growth, right out in the open, laying four eggs. The little chicks soon learn to scurry about after the mother bird, and families of between one and four chicks are a common sight in September. As the launch approached one mother with but a single chick, she became very worried, and squatted down on top of it; we feared that in her desperation she was going to drown it. Half a minute later she got up and trotted away with breast feathers somewhat puffed out, and two little black legs hanging down from it. She had simply tucked it away safely until she could go off to a safer spot. The papyrus and rivers edge plants were one mass of weaver bird's nests, providing us with the perfect chance of observing their craft at close range. In the early morning light the white and pale mauve flowers of the water lilies were a superb sight.

The open water at the mouth of the Bahr-el-Arab was also a great place for hippo. We used to moor there and it was far from restful, as the hippo found the keel of *Sobat* an excellent back-scratcher, which meant a constant succession of vibrations, grunts and blowing as they enjoyed themselves!

Continuing up the Bahr-el-Ghazal the next 5 kilometres were wide and shallow, with lines of *ambatch* growing on each side. The channel then became more sharply defined; 12 yards or so in width of clear water, with an edging of *um-souf*. It was at its lowest level, and in its most interesting state, in May, when the hunting season was on. Large groups of canoes would pass en route to participate. Along the southern bank there was for some distance higher ground, with trees and frequent habitations. The north bank was miles and miles of *toich*, a flat green expanse. After 10 kilometres *toich* began to appear on the south bank with the higher ground receding from the river.

The river in May was full of fish called *weir* by the natives which made long low jumps from the water. Weighing up to 15 pounds, they would dart in all directions, hitting the launch with a resounding thud, and paying no attention to the 'dolly' trailed behind us. Hippo and crocodile were also common, the latter 6 to 8 footers and tending to keep to the safety of the water on account of the Nuer hunters.

At RP 33 was the first hippo meat factory, it worked on a substantial scale to satisfy the demand from a general migration to the upper waters of the river to obtain supplies of meat to last some months. There were two main hunting methods: driving the animals out of the *ambatch* thickets on shore or hunting them in the river, from a floating raft or a dug-out.

The factory was a sandy *meshra* to which the carcase was hauled, and first the hide was cut off and stretched on a frame of two posts and cross members erected vertically. The meat was then cut off into strips, rather like good sized strings of sausages, and hung up in the sun to dry. A crowd of marabout storks and vultures attended to pick the bones clean, and eat up any discarded trifles, and they worked most efficiently. Very little smell was noticeable. Sometimes factories might be one unit with up to eight or ten men. Others could be as many as eight or so units working alongside each other. We witnessed most stages of the business, including bringing a hippo to the bank.

The hippos themselves do not seem to resent being hunted and will sunbathe not 150 yards from a factory hard at work. They seemed totally indifferent to the likelihood of it being their turn next!

The river in September was by contrast, much less interesting, the mud-flats had disappeared, the hippo hunters had gone home, most of the bird life had migrated and peace reigned.

However, a journey in May would probably get no further than the entrance to Lake Ambadi. We managed to push a little way in, after sticking at RP 40, near the mouth. Tiger fish were leaping into the engine room, and into the *felucca* alongside. The largest weighed 9 pounds and they were rapidly filleted and stowed away in the refrigerator. Yassein, our engineer, rowed ashore to a factory at the mouth of the lake to buy fowls. These were cheap enough at four for 6 piastres, though what they really wanted was an old shirt!

Lake Ambadi was about 10 kilometres long, with the Jur River joining it 2 kilometres from its west end. The lake changed its shape from year to year. It was really little more than an open piece of shallow swamp, full of fish, with some of the best *aigl* fishing in the Sudan to be had in the vicinity of RP 40. For several years running we had an annual fishing contest with Wedderburn-Maxwell, District Comissioner Western Nuer, and the Forestry Inspector. Start was at daybreak in two *feluccas* and fishing went on till 10.00 hours with a total catch of nearly half a ton. I am afraid that our regular challenge never succeeded against the home team, who invariably won, but we did have some good catches.

From Lake Ambadi the river narrowed down somewhat, but was still wide and shallow. Between RP 43 and 45 we dredged lengths to give depth equal to the lake. Between RP 44 and 45, on the north bank, was the mouth of Khor Toor, dredged in 1922 to improve access to Meshra-el-Req, but now heavily sudded, and we have reverted to the alternative approach via the east side of Toor Island. On the island was situated 'Ocean Quay, an inspired naming of the last point of access to Meshra when the river level falls. From here ran a road across the length of Toor Island and an Irish bridge through the bed of Khor Toor.

Five kilometres straight ahead was the sudded-up entrance of the Tonj River, so called, although whether the fine stream that ran

Our catch at Ambadi Lake.

through Tonj in the Rains actually got to this part of the swamps was not certainly known. Here the river turned sharply to the right for its last few kilometres to Meshra. In the winter of 1944–45 the channel from Tonj mouth to the Meshra Gauge was dredged, with the hope that vessels would be able to get right through to Meshra — if they could get across Lake Ambadi.

There were no permanent settlements on these upper reaches of the Bahr-el-Ghazal between Wangkai and Meshra. We saw few people beyond an occasional canoe out after crocodiles. Custom here was to cut two small glands from the crocodiles for sale as a source of musk (Arabic *misik*). This was dried and sold in the merchants' shops in Meshra.

Meshra had few attractions, being humid and full of mosquitos, The Rest House was infested with bats. In its grounds was a large steel rowing boat, left by the French garrison when they withdrew in 1898. A merchant, Mubarak, had represented Sudan Railways for over 20 years, and despite its drawbacks remained cheerful, perhaps encouraged by the fact that the Bahr-el-Ghazal went no further. Meshra was, however, the port of Wau, and could be reached for at least six of the nine months of the year when Wau was out of direct communication by water. The later extension of the railway to Wau probably altered the situation considerably and brought change to life on the Bahr-el-Ghazal.

Chapter Eleven

INTO THE JUR

Just past RP 41, some 126 miles from Lake No Mouth and well along the length of Lake Ambadi was a right-handed turn into the Jur. The entrance was through swamp. It varied in width from year to year according to the growth of grass but it was more than 15 feet deep. There was little to be seen but a wide stretch of swamp with *um-souf* and other similar vegetation and occasional thickets of *ambatch*. The exception was a horizon of trees to the south of Lake Ambadi. Here and there in the swamp were dry patches showing signs of having been inhabited during the dry weather.

The word Jur is Arabic and means 'oppression'. It refers to the bad transport facilities and hard working conditions experienced by the Egyptian Army during the advance to Wau in 1900 when very long *sudd* blocks had to be opened. Conditions in my time were still hard.

The first port of call, situated about 10 miles from the mouth, was Depot Lake. The Jur River Service was complicated and the various sections of the route called for different modes of working to meet their individual peculiarities. As far as Depot Lake the barges were arranged in the normal way, which was at the side or ahead of the steamer. For the next sections they were towed cross-coupled in line.

DEPOT LAKE TO MAIYA GASSIS: The channel flowed through grass and was about 10 yards wide. Current was slow as the water was flowing nearly as easily outside the channel as inside. The train, or *gattr,* was towed in line ahead by a tug, in each direction.

MAIYA GASSIS TO MAIYA NAMAK: (upstream of Bolos Island): The channel was confined between banks and was narrow. Current was fairly slow. The *gattr* was towed in line ahead, in each direction.

MAIYA NAMAK TO A POINT DOWNSTREAM OF MAIYA GRINTI: This was the Howata Section. The channel was confined between banks and was very narrow. Current was strong. The *gattr* floated downstream with a tug at each end, the tug at the upstream end was pointing upstream. The *gattr* was towed in line ahead upstream.

POINT DOWNSTREAM OF MAIYA GRINTI TO WARRANA: The river was wide running between banks. Current was strong. Barges floated down lashed in pairs. The *gattr* was towed in line ahead upstream.

WARRANA TO WAU: A wide river with normal assemblies for barges and tugs in each direction.

Wear and tear on this service was very considerable, and so it was necessary to maintain at Depot Lake stocks of spare parts, stores, repair facilities and accommodation barges for crews to give them some protection against mosquitoes. On this Depot were generally based a steamer and tug working to Wangkai and three small tugs, 'W' Class, handling all traffic in the Narrows. There was also a steamer and two tugs to handle the traffic between Warrana and Wau.

The working was intensive during two or three months to transport everything from the Wau area northwards. Commercial cargo travelled all the way and timber went to Wangkai for stacking and on-transport at a later date.

All that could be seen around Depot Lake was a flat expanse of green vegetation. The story that only one tree was visible and that its constant shifting to every point of the compass made one want to cut it down is not correct! One large tree, however, was visible all the time at Lower Howata though there were always other trees visible as well. These trees and the small *maiyas* were the reference points of the route.

The first one was Abu Shanab, with both *maiya* and a single tree, about 10 miles further on. The *maiya* was quite large and the tree was situated on a mound at the far end. Round the tree was a small permanent settlement of Dinkas. The *maiya* took its name of Abu Shanab from a sailor who had a long moustache and who died near the spot and was buried under the shade of the tree.

We once came up as far as this in January and, after spending the night a couple of miles short of the *maiya*, visited it shortly after daybreak. The water was covered with thousands of young pelicans.

The Dinkas came out to meet *Sobat* in seven canoes, and made a fine sight as they punted along with double-ended poles, silhouetted against the rising sun. They could equal our speed of 11 kilometres per hour. Their purpose was to sell dried hippo meat. They took a poor view of our lack of interest and, as they had not left their spears at home and the site was seldom, if ever, visited by a District Commissioner, we decided not to tarry!

The next landmark was Lower Howata. This was the already-mentioned large tree with three small ones alongside. It lay a little away to the left and was also inhabited, even in the flood season.

The third landmark was away to the east and was visible the whole time one was in the Narrows. To the naked eye it looked like a bunch of palm trees, but field glasses showed them to be of some other kind. This clump of trees too was inhabited, but one never came very close to them.

From Maiya Abu Shanab the channel varied from 8 to 10 yards in width with extra on the bends. The bends were frequent and sometimes very sharp. It was difficult for a launch like *Melika,* which was 85 feet long, to proceed by herself and most of the bends called for some reversing.

Before reaching Lower Howata there were two *maiyas* which were used as crossing places. The first was Maiya Sabil. This was named after *reis* Sabil who was a first *reis* in the Sudan Railways Steamers and was in charge at this *maiya* many years ago when it was used as Depot Lake.

The next convenient crossing place, and for spending the night, was Maiya Gassis. There was a certain British Engineer, whose nickname among the Sudanese staff was 'El Gassis', who served many seasons on the Jur River. One year when taking a postboat upstream he decided that there was insufficient water ahead to proceed and moored the tow in this *maiya.* Questioned by the passengers as to why he had stopped he told them that they must wait for the river to rise another 6 inches. So that there should be no mistake he ordered a wooden stake to be made with two lines marked on it, 6 inches apart, and drove it into the river bed until the bottom line was at water level. Each day after breakfast the post was solemnly inspected but the river would not oblige. The passengers endured for three days before one of them during the night gave the stake a few hits with a hammer and sent it into the ground the required distance. The next morning's inspection brought general satisfaction and the tow proceeded without untoward incident. The name of the individual has passed into history.

WHEELS AND PADDLES IN THE SUDAN

In 1945 we spent a night here. It was most musical; a chorus of frogs and then at 01.00 hours beautiful birdsong despite the lack of trees. At daybreak canoes began to arrive and we had to stay put because we could see that the section ahead was occupied. There was little opportunity for passing a train of barges in section. One canoe brought reed mats and a sheep. We bought the sheep for 25 piastres but did not want any mats. Another was a racing craft selling fish which we bought for the cat. Business in mats was better in our escort and eventually the mats changed hands for some old rags!

The canoes were composed of three pieces. Two lengths of doleib palm, hollowed out, formed the body and were stitched together at the middle. One end, the bows, was closed by a section of gourd also sewn into position. The after-end was open or had a low wall of mud. A bailer was a prominent item of equipment and the sides were kept apart by several stretchers.

The *gattr*, which we had been watching for nearly three hours, eventually arrived. It consisted of the tug *Witch* and five barges, the last with its pushing knees folded right up like a butterfly collar. Conversation finished with a request that they should give our escort *Warden* one of several sheep which were tethered on a barge. By the time that agreement was reached the train was round the next bend and they were requested to throw the sheep into the grass and *Warden* would pick it up. This was done but it took a few minutes. When the tug arrived the sheep could not immediately be found because it had swum to the other side. I was told that accidents frequently occurred during this type of transfer, with animals almost thrown into the jaws of a crocodile.

From this point *Melika* was taken in tow. *Warden* had so far only acted as escort and cleared *sudd* blocks for us. Our *reis* was relieved; he had asked to be taken in tow from the first bend after Depot Lake but the instructions were that *Melika* should proceed under her own power as far as Maiya Gassis. Our performance to date had been poor. We had proceeded by cannoning off one bank on to the other and had taken 7½ hours to travel a distance which on a previous occasion had taken *Sobat* four hours.

Warden, which was about 50 feet long and for the occasion was carrying a crew of 16, was most efficient despite its unorthodox appearance. One of these tugs in use on the Jur River defied adequate description. There was almost no accommodation; it was

'W' Class Tug.

all boiler, engines and bridge. Four or five *angareebs* (native beds) were lashed one on top of the other in front of the bridge with mosquito nets hanging from the underside of each. The top floor did the best it could and a piece of canvas surrounded the edifice for protection against rain. Two beds were carried lashed to the diminutive bridge and were laid over the rails at night. The most sheltered spot was under the bridge and at least two were here. There was a solid roof abaft the funnel, over the engine room hatch where the men would sit for meals. One or two beds were lashed upside down to the underside of this roof and used in that position. A sheep or two was usually carried as food was not easy to obtain. Some skins and the washing were usually hanging between the funnel and the bridge. Firewood stuck out from every available space, as fuel was needed for the round trip to supplement the 3 to 5 tons of coal allowed for each journey. These ships, however, were marvellous. They were handled with consummate skill and came up year after year despite terribly hard knocking about. Most had been sunk on the job and raised during low water to work the next season before going to Khartoum for repairs. Only those who have travelled behind them have any idea of the splendid job these gallant little ships did. Their crews were rewarded by an extra ration of tea and sugar; 1 pound of tea and 4 pounds of sugar per month, as against one-eighth pound of tea and 2 pounds of sugar for the land-lubber.

In charge was Abdel Rasoul, a typical Sudanese of the old school. He was smiling, resourceful and for a number of years the general handyman and king-pin of getting the work done on the Jur; he was excellent. We were connected to *Warden* by crossed hemp ropes and towed about 10 feet in rear. In this way we travelled much faster than by ourselves, giving only an occasional turn on our engines. Abdel Rasoul stood on the roof abaft the funnel and gave instructions to the tug and *Melika*.

Soon after Maiya Gassis was the point nearest to Lower Howata. The channel was about 8 yards wide and the next landmark was Upper Howata, with a clump of bushes and trees, away to the west. It was also inhabited. Curiously, the area of these two landmarks was not the section generally known as the Howata Section, which was further up the Narrows. Howata was an Arabic word meaning fishers and referred to the Dinka who, between February and April, separated this part into sections with wooden barriers in order to catch great quantities of fish which, when dried, provided food to be eaten the whole year round. At that time of year the water was very shallow and the fish passed through narrow openings in the barriers.

At Upper Howata one could see trees on the horizon through 270 degrees and in the other 90 degrees was situated Lower Howata, 'palm trees' and Abu Shanab.

Not far ahead was one of the easily distinguished landmarks. It was referred to as Bolos Tree but incorrectly so, as Bolos Island lay a short distance ahead. This tree was a nuisance. It had an arm overhanging the river which damaged the barges and steamers every year. Its proper name was Shagirat-el-Tagir, referring to the fact that a merchant once ran a canteen there. It was of particular interest to our crew as a barge sailor was buried there; he had been killed while standing at the door of his cabin when a bollard broke and a piece of iron crashed through his skull. The tree was infested with snakes, said to be King Cobras, and was now often called Shagirat-el-Dabib. On the west bank, a little further on, was Bolos Island, 50 yards in diameter and with small trees and bushes. It took its name from a Quarter Master Sergeant of the Egyptian Army who camped there for a while in the early days. I once landed on

Bolos Island and found a large nest of curious-shaped crocodile eggs in a hollow.

Less than a mile further on was another island to the west with some good-sized trees on it. It was known as Abloong, which means fish eagles, which used to nest there. This bird formed the badge of the Sudan Fighter Squadron of World War II. The stream here was fast running and in 1944 navigation was made even more precarious by three cuts in the banks made by Dinkas to allow the water and fish more easily to come near their villages. A large volume of water left the channel by the cuts and barges were actually sucked into them, making extraction a real problem. The cuts have since been filled in.

The next named point was Maiya Namak. This was a convenient stopping place for the night or when the section ahead was occupied. The name was derived from the Arabic for lentils. Close by was an island with some trees. In the re-opening of the Bahr-el-Ghazal Province in 1901, an Egyptian Army Unit camped on this island for 22 days and ran out of all food except their main staple, *namak*. It is thus remembered as the place where there was nothing to eat but lentils. We spent an hour here one afternoon waiting for the section ahead to be cleared and I fished with meat as a bait. I caught a weird monstrosity. The nass called it *bamsakir*. It was over 110 centimetres in length and weighed about 40 pounds. It had a great flat head on which one could stand, large protruding eyes, and eight long whiskers! It gave our cats plenty of masticatory exercise!

Maiya Namak was at the downstream end of the fast-flowing section between banks, to which the *gattr* floated down with a tug at the upstream end, pointing upstream. It was a marvellous sight to see it progressing, frequently going in three directions simultaneously. The 'guard' stood on the middle barge, armed with a megaphone. When the first, or any other, barge got stuck on a bend and the rest began to make a concertina he called for 'turn-ahead' on the tug and the *gattr* was straightened out ready for another attempt to negotiate the bend. Critics called it a crude method but it worked and, although hard on bollards and cables, it caused surprisingly little damage.

Between Maiya Namak and Maiya Grinti were some spots given names by the crews working this section but not easy to locate. There was Dorat Witch, a bend at where *Witch* was once sunk. El Gannatier was a spot with ant-hills. Shagarat-el-Sim was a poison tree and Dorat Welcome was where *Welcome* was sunk. At this last bend, on our downstream journey in 1945, when our navigation left much to be desired, the engineer put his head over the side and called down to us that this bend was where the *Welcome* sank. The *reis'* evolutions during the next two minutes caused us to expect that a similar fate would overtake *Melika*. However, we were spared.

Maiya Grinti was a large expanse of water constantly varying in shape. As its name implied it was well stocked with hippos. Broadly speaking it was regarded as the top of the Narrows.

About a mile further on was Dorat Hannak. It was a sharp, full right-angle bend with a strong current swirling round. It took its name from an accident to *Hannak*, which many years before came round the corner out of control, struck the bank and rebounded to crash into a prominent tree. It lost a great part of its cabin work. *Hannak* came to an unfortunate end; it was sunk and lost a little north of Roseires on the Blue Nile.

From this point trees became plentiful and the scenery was very pleasant. There were park-like meadows with trees and both banks were for a while tree-lined and filled with the nests of cormorants and weaver birds. Maiya Grinti extended in the background to the north. From now the sky line at least was almost always composed of trees. After a mile or so there was a stretch of meadow on both banks. In September a mass of lemon-yellow mallow-like flowers stood 4 feet high. The river was now about 30 yards wide and fast flowing. For the next 10 miles its width steadily increased to 50 or 60 yards with some slackening of pace. In a good river it was bank high and overflowing, flooding out the myriads of kingfishers. In the meadows were abandoned, dry-weather Dinka camps. During the flood nearly all *khors* drank from the river, feeding *maiyas*, in the lower lying areas, and, as the river fell they fed back into the stream.

Fifteen miles from Grinti was Warrana Wood Station. It was conspicuous from some distance on account of a large tree. The tugs handed over here on the upstream journey. It was said, though I never verified it, that the original purpose of the station was to supply wood for a tug called *Warrana* working for a mission on a *khor* about 20 miles upstream of the station. During the working season a barge was kept here to provide accommodation for crews at the changeover spot, and frequently there was a unit of the Wau/Warrana section awaiting barges, or barges waiting for a towing unit. There was a very tidy little settlement of the Forests Section with a Ranger in charge. By now the river had reached a width of 80 yards and trees on both banks made a pretty picture. Several gangs of wood cutters were at work as we passed and there were many rows of freshly stacked timber on each bank.

Bird life was conspicuous on the Jur. There were enormous colonies of weaver birds adorning the rushes with their handiwork. Any dry bank was thickly tenanted by kingfishers which frequently flew about in threes. There was a midget kingfisher of great beauty, with scarlet beak, black crest, fawn neck and chest, and deep royal blue wings. I noted a hole from which two of these flew, and stopped the launch to watch. The bird frequently returned to a little dry twig near the hole and was occasionally joined by its mate; it allowed me to walk up to within 15 yards and photograph it. I wanted something better so I cut two sheaves of grass which I erected as an inverted V, not more than 3 yards from the twig. I then lay down behind this screen and pointed the camera thorough the opening. Within 20 minutes I had several good photos of the single specimen but could not get one of the pair. There was a larger kingfisher called the malachite. Fish eagles, cuckoos, greater egrets, crested cranes, shoebills, and great herons were all there in varying numbers.

Up the Jur one was among the Dinka again. These splendid specimens of humanity thought of little except cows, but it perhaps explains why women were more important here than among many other tribes in the Sudan! And by that I mean that if the men spent their time with the cattle, the rest of the work fell on the wives.

The Dinkas paid a lot of attention to their hairdressing. Their hair was done up in blue cloth, often with feathers, beads or coins at the corners. It achieved a bleached, crinkled mass, rather like a melon, standing half an inch proud from the head. They were fond of necklaces, composed of beads and tassels symmetrically arranged. The Dinka disliked work. A District Commissioner wished to open up Khor Maleit during the dry season. He offered lashings of meat and milk, commodities to which the Dinka were very partial, but they made an excuse and declined. There were too many snakes and crocodiles.

Canoes along the Jur were scarce and no-one seemed to want to swim the river. There were certainly some of the biggest crocodiles in any of the rivers here. I once asked the doctor at Wau if crocodiles were the cause of many patients and he replied that in that area lions did far more damage to human beings than crocodiles. It is not difficult to accept that statement when one recollects that a District Commissioner in Dinka-land, Thesiger, was reputed to have a score of well over 100 lions with a best bag of 7 — all walked up and killed in one morning before breakfast!

We ferried some small parties of Dinka across the river by launch at various spots. It was interesting to watch their reactions; most would wash before coming on board and were careful with their small spears and often asked for them to be laid on the upper deck. Most Dinka carried three or four spears with shafts decorated with iron or brass wire binding.

The stretch of river to Marjak Nyom, near the mouth of Khor Maleit, was mainly meadow. Through it a number of *khors* took off, drinking very hard. Very few natives were seen and no habitations. Through the grass on the banks, which the river was breasting, there were small channels cut and cleaned of grass to allow water and fish to get back into lagoons against the dry weather. Gradually the bends became easier and the reaches lengthened out. Large trees lined the banks for a stretch with meadows, and some trees behind. It was a pretty scene and the passing of a boat still interested the few natives around.

Just over 20 miles from Warrana was Khor Maleit. It was known as Khor Shak-Shak to many of our sailors. It was 50 yards wide at its mouth and 18 feet deep and drew off a lot of water. Some 3 miles up this *khor* and lying between it and the main river was the village of Marjak Nyom. This *khor* interested me as it offered a natural waterway to the Lol which flowed into the Bahr-el-Arab to come out at Wangkai. At that time the whole system was derelict. The Bahr-el-Arab was sudded up for much of the distance from where the Lol joined. The Lol banks were for many miles broken and it was sudded up for 14 miles downstream of the point at which it was joined by Khor Maleit. Khor Maleit itself, which carried a steamer nearly to the Lol in 1913, was by now very hard going in a *felucca* 10 miles from its mouth, so great had been the deterioration of our minor waterways! Should it be decided that it would be a good thing to bring the Lol–Arab system back into working order, then Khor Maleit — also cleared out — would provide a means of using surplus Jur flood water to increase the flow in the lower reaches of the Lol and Arab.

WHEELS AND PADDLES IN THE SUDAN

In 1944 I took *Sobat* 6½ miles up this *khor*, which was 25 miles long, including the five lakes which it joined together. The next 3½ miles, including the circumnavigation of the first lake, Lake Dig-Dig, was done by *felucca* and outboard motor with a considerable amount of shoving. It was hoped to do better in 1945 with a shallow-draft, cone-propelled launch and preparations were made for a joint expedition with the District Commissioner and Dinka assistance. At the last moment the District Commissioner was unable to come but did all he could to assist. His letter on the subject read, in part, as follows:

'I am instructing Sergeant in charge of Gogrial to send you Corporal Wol Kuot, who should have brought you this letter, to help you in every way he can. Please keep him as along as you want. I think you'll find him a reliable old thing and his Arabic not entirely unintelligible. He knows all that country thoroughly and is pretty good at managing the 'locals'. Afraid you are not likely to find any head or sub-chiefs about there at this time of year; but there is an old elder, Aduol Atem, who will probably come and say 'how d'you do' as representing the lads. He acts as a sort of *wakil* for the head chief for that area, is greatly respected by the Dinka, and if there is any question of getting canoes or chaps to cut grass or pull ropes, I think you'll find him, for all his decrepit appearance, energetic and helpful. If the Dinka run away when called on to work — a thing not unheard of in the past! — The answer is, of course, to impound their cattle till they come back. Wol and Aduol can be pretty well relied on to seize the right people's cows!'

When I arrived at Marjak Nyom I found the launch *Marabout* there and Corporal Wol Kuot and Aduol Atem quickly appeared. I embarked them without delay and took the launch in tow. We set off for the point in the *khor* which was nearest to the village. It was about an hour's journey. I told them that I planned to investigate the section I already knew that afternoon and if conditions looked favourable make a longer expedition the next day. My initial requirements were four men but I might want more. I was told there would be no difficulty as 30 men had been warned to stand-by. On arrival at the landing place for the village we were met by a shouting crowd. They were called to order by Aduol and then chanted a welcome. Aduol and Wol selected five men to join them on the launch. They came on board with their *afsh* (luggage), which was mutton, and fowl in their travelling cases, glorified bottle straws with ends, sleeping mats, tea pots, hurricane lamps, and all. All were aboard by 14.00 hours. We dropped down the *khor* and after a couple of miles turned round and went the rest of the way stern first. We could not take *Melika* as far as we took *Sobat* the previous year. Since we took over the launch the engine room staff and the launch boy had been trying to get the engine to work but with little success. After waiting another hour I set off in the *felucca* with outboard motor, leaving the engine room staff to get the motor running satisfactorily for use the following day. Strangely enough, although there was at least 1 foot 6 inches more water than in the previous year the going was more difficult. I took with me my engineer, Yassein, Wol, two sailors and one Dinka. The *felucca* was smaller and lighter than that used in the previous year, which was just as well as the vegetation was far thicker. We progressed to within 100 yards of the first lake, Dig-Dig, before it was time to return if we were to be back before dark. The outboard motor took us along at a fine pace in the stretches of open water and we got back on time. Depression reigned on *Melika* as the engine of *Marabout* could not be made to function and so, regretfully, I had to call the longer expedition off. Wol, Aduol and his henchmen were very disappointed but it was impracticable to set out in a canoe which would carry not more than six persons without any gear. I felt that something was due to the *nass* who had been laid on specially. Aduol was instructed to provide two bulls at a total cost of 240 piastres and a dance. We returned for the night to the spot at which we had embarked the *nass*.

The next morning drums started beating at 04.00 hours and our first visitors arrived about 06.00 hours bearing milk and eggs. We cast off at about 07.00 hours to tow *Marabout* round to the main river. On arrival we were met by Aduol who told us they would be ready for the dance any time. We set off at 08.45 hours. The first 100 yards was by canoe through waist-deep water, it was a precarious adventure as I was perched on a camp stool! We then did a section on foot along a narrow causeway to be followed by another ride in a dug-out through deeper water. We arrived safely, however, at the far bank and then started the walk. We were soon met by the Master of Ceremonies in a black ostrich feather coned busby and a wand with a red handkerchief at the end. He and the reception committee sang and then the dancing commenced. The men were mostly naked except for the lads with loins decked in cheetah skin, or else a piece of red hussar monkey with a short length of tail naturally placed. Most were painted in wood ash or ochre. The good-looking Dinka women wore skirts of two skins, the edge adorned with beads. Their accessories were coloured bead necklaces and cow tails hanging down a foot from elbow bracelets and, at the waist, in the middle of the back, most carried a bunch of small iron bells.

Spears were not allowed on the floor and a Chief's policeman quickly collected the few that were brought on — light wands only were carried. The dances followed each other in quick succession, lasting little more than a minute each, with a short pause in between and very little repetition. There were separate items by lads and by lasses and mixed numbers. Groups of lasses continued to arrive with small girls carrying their bells, though the presence of a white woman onlooker caused some deliberation before joining in.

After 1½ hours of dancing I signified that I would like to be moving, because we wanted to reach Gogrial in daylight and deposit Corporal Wol Kuot back at his station, whereupon Aduol lined the

Dinka dance at Kh. Shak-Shak.

dancers up four deep and conducted a grand final chant. At an appropriate moment I called Aduol to me and told him how pleased we were with the whole show and gave him 240 piastres as the price of two bulls so that all should have a good feed. We set off for the boat accompanied by a bodyguard in song. Our journey back by canoe caused much merriment but was accomplished without mishap. A big crowd saw us off, with final hand touching. A pleasant time had been had by all!

But back to work! The section from Khor Maleit to Gogrial was one of the most beautiful on the Jur. The width of the river was 150 to 200 yards. The meadows were sprinkled with trees. Short lengths of forest appeared on one bank or the other but more often simultaneously on both banks. In the distance were *luaks* and dura plantations but there were few *tukls* near the river. On the crest of the flood the river was bank high and the meadows were very moist. The forest on the south bank carried any game that was about during flood. Giraffe and baboons were frequent and one section had immense crocodiles. There were generally four to six on view but I never killed a second one. Some 10 miles before Gogrial there was on the north bank a brick-built Rest House with a large shady tree in front. It had been built by the District Commissioner as a weekend retreat when Gogrial was a District Headquarters.

Gogrial lay back from the river about 1½ miles and was studded with doleib palms. We stayed here in January 1944. The section of river from Gogrial to Nyin Akok was even wider than the last section, with sweeping bends and one tiresome 'S' bend. The banks were meadow with scattered trees and occasional stretches of forest. The only place to which a name could be given was Kajok, which was a station of the Italian Catholic Mission in Wau. It lay on the north bank, about 3 miles from the river. At its nearest point on the river bank was a derelict two-storey brick building, once a retreat, from which the Fathers could enjoy the view. Small groups of *nass* invited us to purchase a sheep, goat, fowls or milk. We saw their large basket fish traps, 7 feet long and 4½ feet diameter tied to posts near the edge of the bank.

Nyin Akok, or the 'deep pool of Akok', was on the south bank. It was the first and largest sawmill of the Forests Section and cut up mahogany. There was a large log pool in which the logs were kept, for 90 days at least. In 1944, on a short ration of logs, it was producing about 3,000 tons of sawn timber per year. Pre-war timber was kept for 3 years in store sheds to season but insistent demands reduced that to one year. There were fine fruit and vegetable gardens and forest nurseries raising seedlings for reafforestation. It is, however, regrettable that little had been done to replace the high quality mahogany and bu trees cut.

The officials' houses and gardens were charming with some fine specimen trees. A poinsettia, in particular, was remarkable for size and colour. Many of the logs for the mill had to come from cutting camps situated upstream of Wau and, as mahogany would not float, it was rafted down in rafts composed of three logs and some empty 40-gallon drums with two men in charge. They were not always under control. On one occasion, when moored for the night upstream of Nyin Akok, we were heavily bumped by a raft floating along on its own. (It was a disturbing night altogether as a hippo was trying to impress his friends with the excellence of *Sobat's* bottom as a back scratcher!). On the bank opposite the mill was a *tukl* which housed a herd of pigs. The abnormally high river of 1945 flooded them out and they took to the woods but I was told that they would soon return when their food *tisht* was banged as a gong.

The last section to Wau was very pretty. The high ground here was all ironstone country and was covered with forest. Where the forest did not come down to the river the meadows continued, with forest behind them. For the first two miles after leaving Nyin Akok the south bank was thick forest. The river in this section was very fast flowing and there were two dangerous bends with the outer curve a wall of rock. The first was at an old wood station, Gorinti, 8 miles from Wau. The 1945 flood severely affected the meadows and the doleib palms were sticking out of water.

Wau itself was 305 miles from Lake No. Most passengers sighed with relief when it came in sight as the journey was slow and change of craft for the section up the Narrows was a nuisance. The original Wau was a small native settlement on the north bank where the Busseri River joined the Jur some 4 miles upstream of the present town, which started life as the French Military settlement of Fort Dessaix. In the time of the Mahdia the French invaded the Sudan from Wadai culminating in the occupation of Fashoda in 1898. The French established a number of posts in the Bahr-el-Ghazal Province including Fort Hossinger near Khogali and Meshra-el-Req. The re-occupation of the Bahr-el-Ghazal by the British was begun in 1901; the expedition was commanded by Colonel W. S.

Sparkes, later the first Governor of the Bahr-el-Ghazal Province, with Major W. Boulnois and Lieutenant Commander Fell who spent the greater part of 1900–1904 cutting the *sudd* out of the Jur.

An important institution at Wau was the cheerful Italian Catholic Mission of Saint Joseph. It covered the Bahr-el-Ghazal with some out stations including Busseri, which was the main educational centre, and Kajok. One of the main activities was the Trade School where lads underwent a five year course as carpenters or mechanics. They worked seven hours a day, divided between workshops and classrooms, on general education and drawing, for nine months in the year. The workshops turned out fine mahogany furniture. The mechanics worked mainly on cars and internal combustion engine repairing and blacksmithing. During the war the Mission was very badly off for funds and depended largely on sale of products and cutting up timber for the Forests Section. Yet the staff were always smiling and never complained and their cheery outlook always made a visit to them a pleasure. We were also impressed with the Girls School. There were four classes in the Elementary and an interesting practical class in Domestic Science which brought in older girls from outside. The Mission also ran three-year elementary school for boys.

We invited Bishop Ohler, who was in charge of the Mission, and the Mother Superior to bring the staff to tea on *Melika*. The Bishop pleaded ill health but Mother Superior and three sisters accepted and an hour later two more arrived with 40 boarders from the Girls School to see over the boat. It was quite an adventure for all. The crew explained the ship, the *reis* described the bridge and the engineers talked about their engine room. The first sight of themselves in a mirror thrilled the grils and I very much doubt if the Sister would have run to the wheel, which was nearly as high as herself, and spun it round if the Bishop had been present!

Wau believed in making the most of itself. All the roads carried their names on white boards. That by the river was styled 'Governor's Walk'. The ferry on the road leading to Tonj was self-propelled by means of a flying pulley on a cable which could be lowered to allow craft to proceed upstream if required. All was constructed in accordance with the handbook of military engineering and worked most efficiently although the Assistant Conservator of Forests from Nyin Akok was once stranded in the middle of the river because the Public Works Department allowed a worn pulley to remain in service!

Another interesting sight at Wau was the temporary zoo. The area was a good centre for game and the natives were instructed to bring in any young animals they found. They were sometimes given 5 or 10 piastres reward but they do not bring them in simply for reward. The animals were not always very young. That year the Dinkas brought in a 14-foot python! They had observed its haunts and obliged with a goat. When the meal had been swallowed a stalwart went in with a forked stick and pinned the snake to the ground just behind its head. Each time as it lashed out at him he jumped and avoided its tail without loosening the grip on its neck. At length it grew tired and coiled itself up. That was the moment for the stalwart's pals to run in and bundle him into a bamboo cage which they had ready. It was all achieved without damage on either side though I expect the python had a stiff neck for a while.

The animals accumulated during the year and most were sent out on the first postboat on the Jur River. The period of loading lasted about three days and gave a lot of fun. One year a half-grown giraffe needed loading and as his box was too big to get off the barge it was decided to box him up on board. All sorts of ties were put on him for restraint but he gave no trouble at all. He just walked straight into his box and put his head out of the top window. Not so the wart-hogs! They escaped and generally ran amok! Other animals collected included situtunga, besides all the usual types of antelope, shoebills, saddlebills and young buffalo.

The natives of Wau were very mixed. The Gurs formed a considerable portion of the population. Milk, eggs, fish and meat were difficult to obtain in Wau although there was a Government dairy. Fruit and vegetables were plentiful.

In 1945 the *nass* in this part of the world were much better off for food than their neighbours, the Dinka. There were many Dinka families about looking for food and offering to undertake agricultural work in return.

Folk had a nice habit in these parts of always dropping their spear or other weapon as you passed when out walking; it was rather comforting. If the individual did not do so he was probably a bit mentally deranged, which was very common, and it paid to keep a weather eye open.

Once at Meshra-el-Req I experienced an awkward encounter of that type. I had left Mubarak, our Agent, at his house and was returning to my launch when I became aware that I was being followed. I turned round and saw I was being stalked by a very old Nuer with a spear at the ready. Fortunately for me, Mubarak had come out of his house, saw what was happening and yelled at the old chap, who was a local character, and called him off. Mubarak came running, apologised for the old man's behaviour, saying he was *magnun* (mad), and took him off. The guardian angel was certainly on duty that day!

On the outskirts of Wau there was a smithy making spears. It was presided over by a Jew, Bagdadi; it was an interesting speculation as to how he came to Wau.

The remaining sights of Wau were the aerodrome and the quay. The former consisted of two runways at right angles, largely composed of flat ironstone, one level along a ridge and the other slightly falling in each direction. It was said to be excellent. The same adjective also applied to the little quay complete with timber fendering and bollards which had been provided for us by the District Commissioner.

The return journey down the Narrows, except when in tow, was hair-raising for a launch; the bends were numerous and acute, the waterway was fast-flowing in places and our helmsman lacked local knowledge. Depot Lake was generally sighted with relief.

On one return journey in September, when arriving at Depot Lake, I learned that the Bahr-el-Ghazal was heavily sudded beyond Wangkai and delay was certain. I had some work to do at Wangkai in connection with sleepers so I went ahead leaving the staff at Depot Lake to organise a clearance unit. The next day was fully taken up with work at Wangkai and in the evening the clearance unit passed leaving me a message that they would go forward to the first block and wait for me. At various times I had found it necessary to negotiate lots of moving *sudd* and small blocks but this was the first time I had found myself on the wrong side of a lot of blocks and so I was pleased to be attached to a clearance unit. It was easier to clear blocks from the downstream side as the bits tended to float away after being torn out. When working from the topside one tended to work through the block, but nearly always left a block behind, albeit less dense.

The clearance unit consisted of the stern-wheeler *Stack,* the tug *Warden,* a passenger barge No. 11 and a 100-ton barge No. 254 loaded with wood fuel. The more effective members were the stern-wheeler and the tug, the two barges and *Melika* helped by occupying space in the block and by contributing labour for the manual work of tearing and pushing the *sudd*.

The following notes from my diary give the best idea of this type of work. I joined the clearance unit at Block 1 at about 08.00 hours. During the morning we were held up by a broken cable becoming wound round the propeller of *Warden* and for the right stern-wheel of *Stack* to be tightened up. The block was estimated to extend for 150 yards and we came out at 14.10 hours. We proceeded in line ahead, *Stack* leading and *Melika* bringing up the rear.

We found Block 2 just short of RP 28 and started work on it at 14.20 hours, closing down at 18.30 hours. The next morning we started work at 06.10 hours. *Stack* had worked all night and was clear by 06.30 hours with the result that *sudd* was looser in the morning and the rest of the clearance unit was worked through the block by 07.10 hours. Tow was then broken up for wooding. *Stack* and *Warden* both relied mainly on wood fuel when working in these parts and a supply was being carried on barge 254. For the next section we proceeded with *Stack* plus barge 254, *Warden* plus barge 11, and *Melika* by itself.

The clear water extended for about 1 kilometre when we found Block 3 which was not a big one. We entered it at 07.40 hours and were through by 08.40 hours passing RP 27 at 08.50 hours. We took Block 4, which was only 10 yards thick, in our stride and passed RP 26 at 09.27 hours. We passed RP 25 at 10.25 hours and stopped from 12.00 hours to 14.30 hours to change the rudder of *Stack*.

My diary indicates that we entered Block 5 at 14.35 hours and were out at 17.45 hours. The rain was heavy. We had lots of trouble with the feed-pump on *Warden*. The block, though only 200 yards long, seemed very tedious. We passed RP 22 at 19.50 hours and kept going all night, *Stack* plus barge 254 ahead, *Melika* in the middle and, at a distance, *Warden* plus No. 11 astern. The river had much floating *sudd* near Bentiu but no actual blocks. We then reverted to *Warden,* No. 11, and *Melika* formation.

The next morning we passed RP 17 at 05.05 hours. The river was fairly clear so we broke up tow and *Melika* proceeded alone, following *Stack* which was out of sight. We passed RP 16 at 06.33 hours, arrived at RP 15 at 07.00 hours, and found *Stack* busy on Block 6. This was about 50 yards long and was traversed by 07.20 hours, but, having got clear, *Stack* and its barge, now alongside, got completely wedged across the channel so that the *sudd* was quickly re-constituted for us. Half the time spent on this river on these jobs was devoted to correcting these frequent lapses! We got clear at 08.30 hours. We waited for *Warden* and No. 11, now close behind, to go ahead so as to assist *Stack* in its next lapse. *Warden* got into difficulty trying to get through, ran aground, and developed feed-pump trouble from dirty water. Meanwhile *Stack* disappeared ahead, and *Warden* got through at 09.20 hours. *Melika* passed Block 6 for the second time at 09.22 hours and set off after *Stack* leaving *Warden* to get No. 11 clear of Block 6 and follow. We passed Yodni at 09.35 hours. There was lots of broken-up *sudd* in the river. We passed RP 14 at 09.55 hours and overtook *Stack* in Block 7 at 10.05 hours. Block 7 was about 200 yards long and we were out at 12.10 hours. We passed RP 13 at 12.36 hours and RP 12 at 13.15 hours and saw lots of giraffe. We went ahead of *Stack* at 14.00 hours, and arrived at Lake No Mouth at 23.00 hours. The *sudd* trouble had extended over 140 kilometres from RP 28, and had taken three full days and one night to get moving. All this, however, was child's play when compared with blocks on the Bahr-el-Jebel, made up of large *sudd* islands many feet thick, It shows the importance of traffic being kept moving on these waterways to prevent consolidation.

Chapter Twelve

FROM MESHRA-EL-REQ TO JUBA

In January 1944 I needed to visit Wau area in connection with some Jur River problems and to look at a scheme for the emergence of the Zande people which called for a visit to Yambio. It was the close season for the Jur River and so the approach to Wau had to be by road from Meshra-el-Req. I decided to travel from Wau to Yambio by road, skirting the Nile-Congo Divide instead of by road from Juba. No extra time or mileage was involved and much of interest would be seen. I decided to take a 3-ton lorry for support with a fitter-driver and a Ford station-bus for ourselves. Here I made a mistake; I took my Atbara driver Mohd Kuku, largely for the sake of his education, and I failed to realise his lack of experience on narrow tracks and rickety bridges. This led to some hair-raising episodes. The fitter-driver came through with flying colours as he had been concerned with transport of cotton in the Nuba Mountains when we were called upon to do this at short notice. My experience on the way to Nagichot, when we lost a radiator, led me to decide to be as independent as possible and so we carried a full assortment of spare parts as well as four drums of petrol and three of water. The fitter-driver became the most popular character in Equatoria during our stay of two to three weeks. His services were in demand at practically every night stop.

I sent the transport on ahead and found it unloaded and ready when I arrived at Meshra-el-Req. I was due to meet the District Commissioner, Tonj-Dee, and travel with him to Wau. Dee arrived about 16.00 hours and immediately urged a change of plans as the following day there would be a meeting of Dinka Chiefs, and a number of District Commissioners congregated at Gogrial, and we were requested to attend. I changed my plans after amending my programme with the Forestry Department via a telephone call to District Commissioner Wau, Clark.

We slept on our launch and the following morning left Meshra at

WHEELS AND PADDLES IN THE SUDAN

10.10 hours. The District Commissioner travelled with us. The road, on a causeway, was not good and the bridges needed a lot of attention. My driver, Mohd Kuku, found a 3-metre ribbon a poor substitute for Atbara tarmac and I quickly became aware that we were heading for trouble. After 15 miles we parted from the Tonj road, bearing away to the right along what amounted to little more than a track, amidst the District Commissioner's apologies for its poor condition. Despite this we made fair time and approached the Jur and Gogrial at about 14.00 hours. However, the descent to, and the crossing of, a river 200 yards wide, if only 6 inches deep, was too much for Mohd. He sat down in the sand before getting his feet wet. With the assistance of some bathers we got out of our first trouble! We next failed in a side stream and a first section of prisoners quickly arrived and practically carried the car out of that section. There still remained the main stream to be negotiated. The car travelled 10 yards and then stopped. We paddled across and completed the journey in a Province box-car, to send down a second batch of prisoners with ropes. One hour later the car and the lorry arrived quite safely.

Our purpose in coming was, as I have said, to attend the Dinka Chiefs' meeting. There were about 40 Dinka Chiefs and sub-Chiefs present, and three District Commissioners, Hunter and Dee from Tonj, Mitchell-Innes from Aweil and Bimbashi Fyfe from Wau, with a company of Equats on a training march. The Chiefs and sub-Chiefs were accommodated in rows of temporary grass huts. They met for the deliberations in a large grass building of which they occupied one half and the public the other. Their meetings were concerned with the clarification of custom and arriving at rulings of general application. The deliberations on that day concerned payments for death arising after an interval from a wound.

Gogrial was a pleasant spot although its development had been arrested by its ceasing to be a sub-district Headquarters. The road from the river was for part of the way lined with golden mohurs and there were fine fruit and vegetable gardens with a good supply of water from wells. Gogrial abounds in doleib palms and the women round about do some very fine weaving in doleib palm *zaaf* which is almost as fine as Panama. The prison 'goo-goo', or grain store, was the finest I had ever seen. In size it was about 25 feet by 15 feet, raised 4 feet from the ground, with a small locked entrance on one side. Unfortunately it had to be scrapped in the early part of 1945 on account of white ant damage.

The Dinkas had lots of grain and *merissa,* and so their great, shining, bodies looked in fine shape. This plenty, however, carried with it almost daily fights somewhere in the area and so both the dispensary and the prison were full. The lad in charge of the former had quite a reputation for his skilled work.

The next morning we were packed up and away from Gogrial by 06.40 hours. One of the first hazards we met was the bridge over Khor Kwang. We found it unusable and so had to use the water-splash. A fine roan antelope was standing 40 yards away from the road near Gogrial, but otherwise we saw little game. At the crossroads, which we reached on time at 08.15 hours, we found Neilson, Assistant Conservator of Forests from Nyin Akok waiting to divert us to that spot for breakfast. We ferried across and were met by Marshall of the Forestry Department, an old friend. After breakfast we inspected the sawmills, seasoning sheds, gardens and plantations at Nyin Akok. I was keen to see a production policy started whereby stocks of seasoned timber, to agreed sizes, might become regularly available. Sudan Railways had large requirements and Sudan timber could play a sizeable part if only a sound production policy could be achieved. My views were very welcome at Nyin Akok. In the gardens we found a new product which we sampled — the cashew nut.

We next re-crossed the Jur and set out for Pau Mill on the Getti, 14 miles away, which was working mainly on converting vuba to sleepers for Sudan Railways and my visit was in this connection as trouble abounded. The job completed we drove on in the afternoon to Wau, 35 miles away, where Clark, the District Commissioner kindly put us up.

A very pleasant duty on a visit to Wau was to call on Bishop Ohler at the Roman Catholic Mission Headquarters. We had known him for some time and had fallen for his charm. The District Commissioner could not speak too highly of the work they were carrying out at Wau.

Next we set out to see the sites of two sawmills which had been working mainly on timber for Sudan Railways. We travelled over the Tembura road and our first destination was Nigolima on the Busseri River. It was no longer working as the machinery had been moved to Pau Mill, from where transport of timber was easier. A visit to a place of past activity is usually rather depressing, but in this case a fine nursery of mahogany and teak seedlings provided an antidote to that feeling. We had lunch at a pleasant Rest House overlooking the river and set out for Akanda, another abandoned sawmill site. The direct route was not available as the river crossing was out of order, and so we drove along the bank of the Busseri until we came opposite to Akanda; we then left the cars and paddled across ankle-deep. A large fire, perhaps 100 yards long and 40 yards across and 25 feet high, was burning at the mill site. It was all the accumulation of slash and sawdust arising from a number of years working. One drying shed had also been involved. The cause of the conflagration was apparently carelessness on the part of a charcoal burner. At night the heap was quite a spectacle.

Again there was a very pleasant Agriculture and Forests Rest House on the bluff. In the afternoon we walked to a specimen mahogany. The tree had a fine spread and the trunk measured 24 feet 10 inches above the buttresses, about 8 feet from the ground. Large as this tree was, it was said that there was one at Loka nearly twice as large. The forest trail, in addition to some fine trees, also bore the tracks of much game, including lion, leopard, and roan antelope. I was interested to learn that no goats were allowed on any Forestry Station.

We camped for the night under mosquito nets out in the open in front of the Rest House. It was not dark because of the glowing mass of the bonfire down below. The next morning our boy brought the early cup of tea amid great excitement. Our camp beds were standing on a sandy surface and on it were the clear foot-prints of lion around our beds! I have since been told that a mosquito net is a definite protection in such circumstances, though Hilary Brown had a frightening experience when sleeping in a wire mesh mosquito house at Juba with her bull terrier 'Bosun'. A leopard picked up the scent and seeking a tasty meal charged through the mesh. The next couple of seconds were very hectic but the leopard left without his supper and 'Bosun' survived as also did Hilary. Perhaps the crux of the matter is what is inside the mosquito net!

On the way back to Wau we stopped to meet Bagara, a native Chief of several groups. He was a fat, amusing and somewhat disreputable character, who agreed that with the present abundance of grain and *merissa* the times were not too bad.

Crocodiles were plentiful in the waters around Wau and it had come up in conversation that a new sport was developing, of seeking them from a boat with a bright light and a running noose. It was said that they were being caught regularly for their meat as well as their skins and that the meat was on sale in the meat market. I looked in on the market to see if any crocodile was on display but it was too late to prove the point. I was told that the meat was light in colour and rather like chicken in taste — but I have my doubts!

Later the District Commissioners took me to see improvements to the Quay of which he was justly proud, and then we visited the old blacksmith. On my last visit I had promised to send him some scrap metal from Atbara. He was an excellent blacksmith who did a considerable trade in hoes and spears. The old steel sleepers, in particular, had met with his approval and very superior lines were being forged. It was interesting that all the off-cuts were collected into *saffias* (4-gallon petrol tins) to be sold to the Gur who re-melted the steel in balls of clay to make wrought iron.

We looked in on the dairy, run by Dinka prisoners, and proceeded by a new road, being built by a large gang of prisoners from Rumbek, to the new aerodrome. On the way back we visited the shops of the large Greek merchants and were amazed at the diversity of articles still available. The answer, of course, was that Wau had always carried considerable stocks, but it was quite a treat to see such things as Sunlight Soap, Vim, Chivers Jellies and Coat's Sewing Cotton available and at reasonable prices.

In the morning we set off for Sources Yubo at 09.00 hours. We completed crossing the Busseri by 10.00 hours. The track was poor with little game around apart from one fine wart-hog. There were a few squirrels. We crossed flat, undulating country with iron-stone outcrops. Ant-hills, about 18 inches high, shaped like toad-stools, were a feature of the landscape. In general it was light forest country with a few mahogany and bu trees and a considerable quantity of vuba. Some gardenia trees were in flower. The roadside was in places lined with smallholdings. The *nass*, largely Zande and mainly Roman Catholic, mistook our wagon for that of Bishop Ohler and consequently genuflected as we passed, which was very embarrassing. They carried bows and arrows instead of a spear.

We found Mabu Rest House at 15.35 hours. After tea we strolled through low hillocks to its source of water, an extensive pool. The next morning we were on the road at 08.30 hours and arrived at Tembura about 11.30 hours. There were two Greek merchants at

Tembura with whom I wanted to discuss the collection of wild rubber, a commodity which was required for the war effort. One of the merchants was away at Sources Yubo but the other was very helpful. I was shown a sample and it seemed of good quality. The native was paid a Government fixed price of 2 piastres per rotl and the merchant got 2½ piastres per rotl on sale to the Government at Sources Yubo where the Medical Inspector acted as Government buyer. I wanted to know how the native coagulated the latex and the merchant said he wound the latex straight from the tree on to a small twig. He stated that he had handled 40 tons in the previous season but from the information I had it seemed that his figure was exaggerated.

Near Tembura were the falls on the River Sue, a very beautiful spot and one of the few examples of cascading water in the Sudan. It was a great spot for fish traps.

Away from the great outdoors we watched the large Chief's Court in action and were shown round the station by a young accountant who spoke quite good English. He had been at Busseri School near Wau for three years; and hoped to go to Juba for further training. There was a big prison and outside it a large drum made from a section of a tree and shaped like a vaulting horse. Various calls were sounded by beating on two sides with rubber-

Zande fishing party at Tembura

headed sticks. We also inspected the dispensary which seemed busy with tropical ulcers and syphilis.

We moved off at 12.40 hours. The road continued to be lined with smallholdings, plentifully studded with mango trees and pineapples. Many of the inhabitants had yum-yum hunting dogs. The *nass* also had a passion for paper, any size or kind. They were inveterate smokers.

Some 8 miles from Tembura we found the Sudanese Medical Inspector, Doctor Sayed Abdel Raziq from Sources Yubo, an old acquaintance, broken down with petrol pump trouble. We left the lorry and fitter with him. The doctor was out on inspection of fly-boy camps. The banks of the Yubo to Tembura were patrolled by groups of boys hunting the tsetse flies. The flies were sent to Sources Yubo and if particularly interesting specimens were sent on to Khartoum. The boys were paid by results.

Doctor Sayed told us there was a good rest house at Sources Yubo and regretted he would not be there himself to show us around. However, soon after we had finished lunch, he drove up and with a smile said that as his car had been repaired so quickly, he had decided to change his plans and return to Sources Yubo and show us around — and could the fitter put his other car in order, too, please?

Doctor Sayed's presence in Sources Yubo certainly resulted in our being shown this spot very efficiently. I had heard a lot about the struggle to banish sleeping sickness from the Sudan which had been waged from this spot.

These notes cannot attempt to describe the fight waged in the years from 1918. A Syrian, Doctor Baz, started treatment from scratch, moved 639 patients 25 miles to a water source in the forest that he had never seen and built a settlement. It grew to over 2,000 patients with 8,000 relatives. It required cultivation of 1,000 acres for their support. By 1929 the number of new cases had been reduced to 19. The epic is told in Lieutenant Colonel G. K. Maurice's paper on 'Sleeping Sickness'.

We drove up to a magnificent brick-built, furnished Rest House which had been the doctor's mess. We settled in and then set out with Doctor Sayed. We visited one of the Sources of the Yubo which had been converted into a grotto from which the water flowed by pipes to prevent contamination and to supply a ram. We then crossed a fine vegetable garden and on into miles of gallery forest, preceded by two fly-boys and two police. There was some splendid timber, including some fine olives.

Sources Yubo stands at over 2,500 feet, right on the French Equatorial Africa–Sudan boundary and an ornamental brick pillar, just outside the Rest House, marks the site of one of the beacons of the Boundary Commission.

The next morning Doctor Sayed called for us at 07.00 hours to start off round the hospital settlement set up to deal with sleeping sickness. The number of patients under treatment was about 40. I wonder what the present position under Sudanese administration is. We saw some of the totem-like effigies of the doctors who had served there when the settlement was at its height; they presided over the main intersections of the roads of the settlement.

We were then shown the administrative buildings, Chief's Court, dairy and another very prolific source of the Yubo. There was also a basket factory.

I had a long talk with two Greek merchants about local produce as I regarded it as an important part of my job as General Manager to ensure that everything possible was done to provide freight at distant transport points. Rubber which had amounted to some 40 tons in 1942 had dropped to 26 tons in 1943 and I wanted to know why. Three reasons were suggested: (1) Increase in price paid in French East Africa had diverted some; (2) There had been lower rainfall in 1943; (3) Rubber collection in 1942 was a new idea and the Zande quickly tired of anything.

It was also pointed out that in French EquitorialAfrica it was compulsory for each adult male to produce 15 kilos per month of wild rubber all the year round. The District Commissioner visited the area every month and collected the rubber with his own trucks. When I asked about the rate of collection around Sources Yubo I was told that a skilled collector, working at a good time of year and wanting money could collect 4 rotls per day. The figure for an average man was nearer 2 rotls per day. We also discussed the position with regard to honey, beeswax and chillies. As a memento of our visit to Sources Yubo one of the Greek merchants gave us a pair of beautiful grey Persian kittens which we named 'Saucy' and 'Yubo' and took back to Atbara with us. We often wondered from where the stock came to this outpost at the south-west corner of the Sudan.

We bade farewell to Doctor Sayed and then crossed over into

French Equitorial Africa for a short run before setting out for Yambio; we found that the other slope of the divide was very similar to the Sudan side. The road eastwards closely hugged the boundary. There were no homesteads on the right hand (French Equitorial Africa) side and no roads led up to the boundary from French Equitorial Africa. After 6 miles we stopped to see over the Leper Settlement at Bariabunde. Leprosy was a relatively common complaint among the Zande, affecting over 2 percent. It was possibly connected with the deficiency of salt and meat in their diet. The Leper Settlement was a remarkable place. Its whole aspect is quite beautiful in lay-out, buildings and flower beds. The inmates were 100 percent lepers, administration, dispenser, schoolmaster, everyone. I was particularly impressed by the caring for the old by the young. A visit to Bariabunde was quite an inspiration.

For 34 miles the road ran along the boundary. It was a good road and the country and the views were pleasant. Like all roads in Zande-land it was lined with mango trees. A post with a skirt of palm leaves attached denoted the residence of authority, and the higher the post the more important the resident. Parties of men armed with spears, bows and arrows and carrying rolls of netting were frequently passed on the road. We saw the result of one hunt in a large wart-hog killed. Rats were also a favourite food and most boys carried some of the small conical wicker traps in which they are caught.

At mile 106 we turned off to Li Rangu, another large medical settlement, but as Doctor Hunt was away we pushed on to Yambio, leaving Li Rangu for another visit.

Yambio was another lovely site and largely the handiwork of its District Commissioner Major 'Tiger' Wyld. We found the Wylds' living on an estate of 200 acres and we were graciously received and installed in a guest house which was to be our base for three nights. All the houses and offices on the station were whitewashed and thatched, designed and built by Major Wyld. I was to learn from him how all of them were saved from the ravages of white ants; all his buildings were encircled by a brick-lined trench, 3 feet deep and 2 feet across. A white ant will not go down in order to get across, and provided you did not start with white ants on your 'island' you were not troubled by them.

The estate produced revenue for Government and provided all the grain, cassava and ground-nuts required by the station, also coffee, citrus, pineapple and many other fruits. Included in the park was a nine-hole grass golf course.

The reason for my visiting Yambio was to obtain background information on a scheme being submitted to His Excellency by the Director Agriculture and Forests for a large-scale experiment of accelerated emergence of a backward people, in 30 years, to a state of educated prosperity. The aim was that they should participate in the benefits of civilisation whilst attaining to virtual self-sufficiency.

The proposed area for the experiment was in Zande-land with a centre at Nzara, near Yambio. Briefly, the experiment visualised obtaining 95 percent literacy within 30 years. It would also erect an invisible fence round Zande-land to eliminate commercial contact, and set up under a Board, with Government capital, primary industries, such as cotton piece goods, gunnies, soap and robusta coffee, designed to meet Zande needs. It would further produce an exportable surplus to the north, from which would arise sterling funds for strictly limited imports. Secondary industries were also to be set up, such as jaggery sugar, brick kilns, sawmills, iron foundry, and charcoal.

It was proposed that the lines of communication should be Yambio, Tonj, Adok. The first section was fairly easy but the second was a considerable problem. Much of my two days at Yambio was spent discussing the technical education of artisans, power supply for the industrial site, water supply, lines of communication, and the advantages of road versus light railway. The scheme had received the blessing in principle of the Financial Secretary and the Civil Secretary, but I saw two difficulties. One was that although it might prove to be a practical solution for a 'walled' community, it did not fit easily into the pattern of interdependency and therefore how did one meantime answer questions raised by or on behalf of other tribes in the Sudan? The second problem concerned the fact that about three-fifths of the Zande lived out of the Sudan and literally had to work for their living in the Congo and French Equitorial Africa. Would a Zande Elysium in the Sudan cause a wholesale migration of peoples and international complications.

I visited an interesting smallholding experiment 12 miles outside Yambio. Twenty families had been settled on 15-acre plots with an obligation to grow 2 acres of cotton each year. The land was bush and so much of the 15 acres was cleared each year and sown to food crops and cotton which was regarded as a cash crop. They were encouraged to make a decent homestead by the interest taken in the details by Government officials. Adults and children were examined by the Medical Inspector several times a year in order to keep down the many intestinal parasites which caused debility amongst the Zande. This was the second year of the scheme and I attended the first cotton market of the season. Cotton was bought for the ginning factory at Meridi; the price was: first grade 35 piastres per kantar, second grade 28 piastres per kantar, third grade 18 piastres per kantar. I was told that yields as high as 10 kantars per acre were obtained last year but the prospects for this year were not so good. About 60 kantars were bought, the greater part being first grade. There were two other similar enterprises near Yambio.

We visited a stretch of gallery forest near Yambio, then called in at the Church Missionary Society Station. The fine brick church, which was in those days called 'The Cathedral of the South', accommodated congregations of over 1,500 at festivals. It was built by Canon Gore with the aid of a sixpenny handbook. Canon Riley, an Australian, was in charge and showed us its many activities. Canon Riley features in the classic story of Bishop Gwynne who, when conducting a Consecration Service here, finding himself at a grave disadvantage, exclaimed to Canon Riley, who was assisting: 'Carry on, Arthur, I've bees in my pants', he then beat a hasty retreat to the vestry in order to rid himself of the pests. There is another version of the story which substitutes 'ants' for 'bees' but in either case the experience was uncomfortable.

There was a printing press functioning in five languages, an extensive brick-yard producing bricks and tiles, with a very ingenious kiln, and woodworking shops. Workers were engaged in citrus production and animal husbandry. There were 1,000 tangerine trees and the juice was bottled.

A stream head had been dammed and supplied the whole station with water and I was pleased to see a tung oil plantation. I regarded tung oil as a possible product capable of carrying a reasonable freight rate for carriage by Sudan Railway and therefore well worth my interest. I had sent seeds of tung to the Agricultural Department for trial as far back as 1934. In that year the research chemist of our paint suppliers had told me of the problems involved in obtaining good-quality Chinese wood oil (tung oil) for which there was no synthetic substitute. He had thought the Southern Sudan might provide a possible area of growth, and so I had asked him to obtain some seeds which he did. I had retained a few for myself but I had had no success with mine. I was also interested to see that strip cultivation was being carried out at the Mission Station.

Also at Yambio I met the five Paramount Chiefs of the Zande. They were all of the royal family of Gbudue. Chief Sangba was the largest chiefship. I spoke to his people and was shown his crops which filled nearly half of a settlement. In turn I met the four other chiefs. I sat in for a while on their Chief's Court and thereby became an Honorary Chief and was presented with my insignia of office — a very fearsome 'chopper' with a 3-inch spike balancing the blade, and a fine, squarish, straw hat which I still wear on a hot day in summer.

The days were fully occupied, and, on the veranda, after dinner, we were transported to the Steppes, for Meka Wyld would croon away about her native land to Tiger's accompaniment on the guitar and the Assistant District Commissioner — Vanderspar's — work on a squeeze-box. Tears flowed copiously and it was quite an experience. Unfortunately a few years later temperament took complete control and Meka left Tiger to finish his service at Yambio alone, but we paid a second visit to Yambio before that happened. Throughout the two days our fitter was very busy putting Major Wyld's lorries into working order, and earned high praise thereby.

Our next port of call was Meridi, 85 miles on, and then Amadi, 75 miles further on. The road crossed numerous streams; the ramps leading to the bridges and the beds of all streams cleared of vegetable growth on account of tsetse fly. Schools, each with a surrounding garden, were quite numerous. There were also many graves at the roadside. We passed a *ful sudani* (monkey nuts) plantation, the first I had noticed in the south, and roadside sellers of fruit, grain, spears and basket work. A man could weave four or five baskets a day from elephant grass. The roads were lined almost continuously with bark-cloth and mango trees. The country was quite luxurious. At Madebe dispensary we picked up the doctor from Meridi and gave him a lift back to his base. We were to require his help the next time we travelled this road as when staying the night in Meridi Rest House my wife badly cut her hand when opening a tin.

We passed a party of three men carrying a chief's ivory to the *merkaz* for stamping. In general people were becoming more 'dressed'. We passed a messenger with a letter in a cleft stick and a police post which requested that we should stop and inspect. After 20

Chief's ivory.

miles we crossed the River Iba and found quite a centre, with a Chief's Court, dispensary, school, an Agriculture and Forests nursery and a demonstration plot.

At Meridi we called on the Lavericks, a couple of elderly Church Missionary Society missionaries who had come out of retirement to staff their old station to prevent it being unfilled. They kindly gave us lunch and showed us over the station.

Meridi had gone into decline following the departure of its last District Commissioner, Clark. He had built a golf course of grass and, although now burnt off, the greens still remained green. My guide around Meridi had previously served with Sudan Railways but had transferred to the Public Works Department which he was at pains to tell me he found more congenial.

The next morning, with only 84 miles to travel, we made a leisurely start at about 10.00 hours. It was a featureless run. The bridge over the River Naam at mile 15 had been dismantled, and we had to cross by a diversion, which worried my driver and he finished up with the car spread-eagled across the track. Fortunately the fitter-driver of the lorry, which was behind us, was equal to the occasion and restored the position.

We soon ran into a heavy thunderstorm, and as it was quite

impossible to travel, we stopped for an early lunch. When we started again there was quite a lot of traffic on foot along the road. We noticed a baby slung in a very nicely constructed basket-work carrier on the mother's back. There were several blacksmith's shops at the roadside and I wondered what was the source of their raw material. The large quantity of spear grass growing near the roadside indicated that the countryside suffered heavily from bush fires, and certainly all the large trees were dead. At a new bridge, however, there was a coffee plantation, and shortly afterwards two cotton demonstration plots, so there must have been more *nass* about than was apparent at first sight. A thing that struck us was the tidiness of the road camps and the fact that the thatched roofs of schools had ventilators built into them. Both these points stood, in my mind, to the credit of the Public Works Department.

Seven miles before we reached the Mundri Bridge we joined the Wau–Juba direct road and travelled on it to the bridge, leaving it on the far side, as the direct road swung away to the right. The River Yei at the bridge was quite sizeable, and called for 3 by 50 foot spans. From the bridge we travelled straight on for 7 miles to Amadi, but did not stop there as our destination was Lui, 7 miles along the Amadi–Juba road.

Lui was a Church Missionary Society station. The story of the Frazers at Lui is quite beyond the scope of these notes. It was a magnificent pioneering work; its story can be read in the little book 'The Doctor came to Lui'. Try to obtain a copy.

When we first visited Lui there were over 20 outstations but Doctor Frazer was dead and Mrs Frazer was carrying on with the help of Doctor and Mrs Casson and Miss Collard at the hospital. There was less activity than usual as the schools were on holiday but the hospital was very busy. We had intended spending the night at Amadi but were invited to stay by Mrs Frazer as the following morning was the monthly communion for the native Christians held in Moru by a Moru Pastor, and she thought we might like to be present as it was attended by all the dispensers and teachers from the outstations. There were 75 assembled and some of them had travelled as much as 45 miles.

We attended the service and afterwards all the visitors spent the day in solving the difficulties that had arisen on their stations in the past three weeks and drawing stores before setting out on their return journey on Monday morning.

We spent the day on the station and visited a leper settlement with 90 patients from five different tribes. Our fitter's services were again in demand to repair Doctor Casson's lorry which had disintegrated as a result of having to fetch a casualty from 30 miles out over bad roads during the night.

We enjoyed the evening chatting with Mrs Frazer. She told us of the early days at Lui and it was very clear that the work at Lui was still very dear to her. The next time we called at Lui she was out of the country on sick leave and we never saw her again. She was a wonderful woman with a very strong personality.

In the morning we set out for Terakeka where we hoped to find *Sobat* waiting for us. We had to leave the lorry behind as the fitter had not managed to complete the resuscitation of Doctor Casson's lorry by the time of our departure. It was a run of 110 miles; the road, however, was not in good condition and required a lot of work to be done on it. About half-way, at Jebel Tindilo and a road junction, we met a friend, the District Commissioner, Mitchell-Innes, returning from Juba to his station, Aweil. He had taken a wrong turning and found himself at Terakeka, 100 miles out of his way. However, he was not at all depressed, quite the contrary. He brought the news that the Doctor 'Louis' Brown and Hilary had been married at Juba a couple of days before, amid great rejoicing, and he knew we would be very interested because both of them had served in Atbara for some years. He also told us he had seen *Sobat* waiting for us at Terakeka. We chatted for a while, as both Mitchell-Innes and I were interested in the clearance of the Bahr-el-Arab, and then we set out in our several directions.

We passed through pleasantly wooded country with some air-sized mahogany (small leaf) and vuba trees. A feature was the many beehives in the trees. The journey in all took us about 5½ hours running time.

Terakeka, with its great stacks of chillies, had a sweet aroma. We picked up some bullock's heart custard apples from the Rest House garden and boarded *Sobat* for the night. It was not long before our lorry arrived to tell us that another miracle had been achieved.

In the morning I decided to send *Sobat* to Juba and proceed by car to Juba across the old Lado Enclave, by the dry weather road, which was open most years from December to the end of April. It ran to the east of Jebel Lado and was a journey of 53 miles; it took me about two hours. The road had half-a-dozen, up to 300 yards, stretches of cotton soil in *toich* country. We had to cross one river and two *khors* on Irish bridges. We did not see much game, just a fine wart-hog and traces of elephant. Breakfast at Juba Hotel was very welcome.

Chapter Thirteen

INTO THE SOBAT

The entrance to the River Sobat was 60 yards wide. At low river it could be located by its smell, as there was usually a fishing camp there, using set lines to catch *aigl,* and the site was ornamented with their large heads drying off. Five miles upstream, on the north bank was the American Mission Station at Doleib Hill, standing on a slight rise, and so named on account of the abundance of palms. It had comfortable houses and excellent fruit and vegetable gardens watered by windmill pumps. The approach of the Mission was mainly educational with a school for about 100 Shilluks, who took English in the senior classes; it aimed to provide 'Southern staff' for Government posts in clerical, hospital, veterinary and agricultural work in Upper Nile Province.

The American missionaries were forthcoming folk, and I found them stimulating and they were always well equipped. It was once said that American missionaries were sent out from the USA with two books, a Bible and a Monty-Ward catalogue, the latter containing clothing, household goods, stores of every sort, right down to such items as windmill pumps, electric lighting sets, bathroom suites and outboard motors. On this occasion, an item from the catalogue was ordered for us, which I paid for in Sudan currency. Officialdom then called upon me to explain my actions to the Financial Secretary. I claimed that no local currency had been exported, merely that some dollars had been repatriated, and my defence was accepted.

Not so many years ago six young male elephants made their way to the River Sobat, by night, causing consternation as elephants had not been seen there for many years. The natives lit a ring of grass fires to contain them and sent to the mission for help. A member turned out armed with camera and rifle. In the next four hours the *nass* attacked them fiercely with spears but without seriously wounding them. Enraged at the treatment the elephants tried to cross the River Sobat submerged. The other bank was steep and

1,000 *nass* were waiting for them. They attacked, going for their eyes, and trying to cut off the tips of their trunks. Despite enormous efforts the steep banks prevented the elephants from landing and so they returned to the Doleib Hill bank. Here they were prevented from climbing out, and so made a third crossing. A still more strenuous fight ensued, but at length the elephants called it off and made a second return to the Doleib Hill, spreading out. Two eventually landed, and they got away, to be killed the next day 15 miles inland. A third, blinded and with half his trunk missing, was shot whilst climbing out to put it out of its misery. As his body floated away, there was a rush to get a line on to it and secure it to a tree.

In time two more managed to get ashore, but could do no more. They, too were shot, as the only humane thing to do. The sixth made a fifth crossing. Very weak, it just managed to climb out and was quickly killed.

There was great rejoicing. By custom the skins and ivory belonged to the King of the Shilluks. The apportionment of the meat to villages took three days by which time the carcases had doubled their size. In the Government enquiry which followed, no one mentioned that three had been shot, and so the difficult question of justification of mercy killing without possession of a licence never had to be decided.

There used to be a very acquisitive crocodile in these parts. For a long time it wreaked havoc among herds brought down to water. Many efforts had been made to get him, but he lived on. An American padre from Khartoum, Reverend Siwash, was staying at Doleib Hill for some shooting; he had a great reputation as a hunter and was prevailed upon by the *nass* to go after this nuisance. He took with him a camp stool, and settled down to keep a discreet watch over the watering place, but for some while nothing happened. Then the noise of a breaking twig made him glance round. There, behind him, no more than 15 yards away, was the old villain. He had apparently observed the proceedings, landed upstream and stalked his opponent. An accurate shot, followed by a second for safety's sake, quickly despatched him, but had not Siwash's hearing been acute, the outcome might well have been dramatically different.

Khor Filus flowed in 5 miles upstream, bringing a lot of water from the south. Unlike most tributaries, it flowed between well-defined banks, and did not spill over into *maiyas*. During 1942 a floating bridge was built across the River Sobat at this point, to carry all the motor transport that was driven up the Great North Road from South Africa. In normal times a hand-operated pontoon ferry met all local traffic requirements.

In August 1944 we did a reconnaissance up Khor Filus, which formerly was quite a waterway. For the first day's progress the width between banks seemed seldom less than 50 yards, depth of water at entry was 10 feet, and at Mulgak, where we stopped that first night, it was 4½ feet. It was in the rains, and although a sunny evening, the ground ashore was like butter. We knew that the Great North Road from South Africa ran fairly close to the waterway at this point, so we took off our shoes, and paddled off to find it. We only had to go 100 yards and there was the Cape-to-Cairo trunk route, all 4 yards width of cleared cotton soil, without formation, camber or ditches. We walked a few yards along it in wonder.

The next day we set off at 07.50 hours and conditions rapidly worsened. Two hours later, just before we reached Kan, the depth of water was down to 3 feet, and the waterway ahead completely grassed over. We had to stop and consider our return journey. Should we come out stern first or attempt to turn *Sobat*, which was 70 feet in length; there was little clear water and manhandling over the reed was implicit. We decided to turn it about, knowing that it would be a long and tedious job. Four Dinkas helped and after three hours an interpreter went in quest of more Dinka. He returned with 25, and despite problems in co-ordinating their efforts, we completed the turn-about in an hour, midst great enthusiasm from all. A local Chief then arrived and said that in another month there would be considerably more water in the Khor Filus, and because it ran between well-defined banks, the rise and fall was a speedy affair.

We moored for the night at Wunanyak and the next morning we made some calibration trials, as the reconnaisance had been carried out on a time basis. The view of the country from this point to Abwong largely depended on the time of year. During the first days of a rising river, the land on either side of the high bank was a dry arid waste, but by August or September the river was bank high, and the flat expanses transformed by lush green grass. The cattle, sheep or goats, however, would have moved from winter pastures to fresh grass near their villages inland.

WHEELS AND PADDLES IN THE SUDAN

At mile 71 Abwong was reached; it was formerly a District Headquarters and by my time boasted the first Government Intermediate School for Nilotics. Dinka, Nuer and Shilluk boys up into their twenties took their four-year intermediate course, with all teaching in English. I gave a talk to the top two forms about the Sudan Railways and Steamers Department. One of the classrooms was also the local prison, and on occasion even a murderer was put out to grass with a guard during school hours. There was also a dispensary and two merchant's shops.

Just upstream of Abwong on the south bank was the mouth of Khor Wang-Gnaish. It was said that in 1904, on the peak of the flood, *Margaret* steamed up Khor Filus to Nyerol and came out by Khor Wang-Gnaish. The distance between the two waterways was 60 miles.

The banks on either side were green *toich* with occasional small villages with *luaks*, which were outsize *tukls* in which cattle were housed at night during the rains. The river was now 120 yards wide and carried much floating grass which came mainly from the Gilla via the Pibor. On the banks myriads of weaver birds were busy over their nests and small patches of maize could be seen in the *toich*.

From Abwong the Nuer were the predominant tribe, tall and generally naked, though well decorated with wood ash and red ochre. Their permanent villages were mainly away from the river. Those that one passed were small, rectangular compressed groups of huts enclosed by a tall platted grass fence designed for privacy rather than defence and they owned large herds of excellent cattle.

The Nuer used a novel fishing spear, strung like a bow. From a canoe, the bank or whilst wading, they thrust it forcefully into the open water or amongst the rushes, until a strike is made. The fish makes off hooked by the harpoon-tip, whilst the fisherman has to get the butt of his 'rod' into his hands to play his catch on the fixed line until it can be landed. Near Jokau we saw a 100-pound *aigl* that had been caught this way.

The River Sobat was quickly fluctuating and after the first rise there was generally a fall so that the first trips in the season frequently gave rise to strandings which required a wait until one could float off on the next rise. Similarly the fall at the end of the season was very rapid and an Egyptian Irrigation Department steamer was stranded in 1942 and had to be left near Nyanding for seven months.

Nuer bow fishing spear.

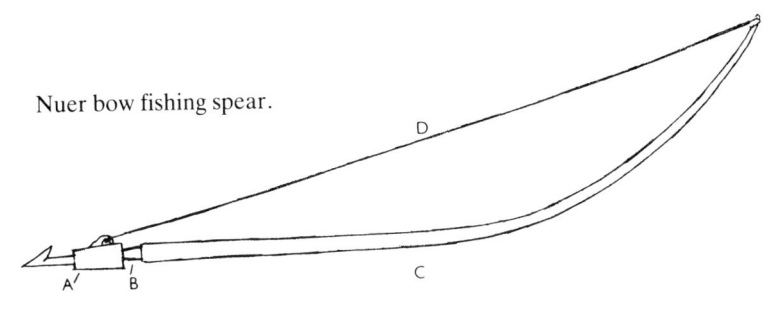

A   Detachable iron harpoon tip, attached to line D
B   Tapered horn point, freely releasing A
C   The 'rod', sometimes two-piece, and up to 12–14 feet
D   Plaited line of wild asparagus root fibre

From Abwong the scenery was less austere, with lower banks, the *toich* a little greener and occasional trees. At Khor Nyanding, 134 miles from Sobat Mouth, we found an Egyptian Irrigation Department launch in trouble, having cast off its barge and apparently high and dry. A lot of Nuer were pushing, and its engine was racing when we came within hailing distance. We stopped and threw her a line and joined in the struggle to get her off, but she was too firmly aground. There was nothing for it, but to wait for an expected rise of river. It was cold comfort save that the grounding was opposite a village. Khor Nyanding was a fine sheet of water, fed from the south, but after 12 miles it was completely grassed-over although water was still 8 or 9 feet deep.

The Nuer had a definite code for indicating distance. If a man pointed with his tongue, that is stuck his tongue out, it indicated that it was a matter of little exertion, perhaps a mile or so. If he pointed with his arm it meant exertion, perhaps two to three hours or even up to ten hours. If on the other hand, he pointed with his spear, considerable exertion was required; the mark was over the horizon and perhaps two to three days away.

The country became more varied as Nasir was approached. There were scattered trees and villages. The river divided round an island and there were some good patches of maize on the bank. At mile 179 we reached Nasir, the Headquarters of the Eastern Nuer District with two District Commissioners. Connection with Gambeila during low river season was maintained by the police

WHEELS AND PADDLES IN THE SUDAN

with the aid of a dozen dug-out canoes, which were probably the finest specimens in the Sudan. The *suk* was not large; the merchants had a hard time as it was difficult to get their imports in and their exports out with only three sailings per year. Nasir was the largest station of the American Mission in the south. It was opened in 1913 and there were usually about six workers.

We arrived on a Sunday morning. We tied up in front of the Mission houses, each surrounded by a prolific fruit and vegetable garden with its windmill. After breakfast of waffles and maple syrup we attended Church service in a large Dutch barn, with an orchestra of drums and a xylophone. Over 100 *nass* sang hymns energetically. One Nuer made his entrance in his 'Sunday best' consisting of a pair of red and black ringed football stockings, a gent's straw hat and, apart from a broad smile, nothing else!

After service we met the staff. The padre and his wife, the Adairs, were a rather serious elderly couple. Ray Huffman was an energetic middle-aged nurse, who had already translated one Gospel into Nuer, to her credit and Miss Soule, of whom, more anon. We had breakfasted with Doctor Doherty and his family, refugees from Abyssinia, marking time. The staff were fully employed on medicine, education and evangelism.

The nurse, Ray Huffman, was very interested in evangelism, particularly among Nuer women. She used to combine it with her village clinics and, when she returned to Nasir, would continue her Bible translation work.

The last member was a sweet old lady, Miss Soule, who ran a school and orphanage for girls alongside the Mission. When she retired as Matron of a large hospital in the USA, she decided to undertake missionary work and came to Nasir. She was known to us as the Steamer Engineers' Mother. Whenever a steamer was in sight, or tied up at Nasir, there was an extra place laid at her table and no-one ever sailed from Nasir without their larder being well-stocked by Miss Soule. She was very sick in 1944 and, although eventually moved to Egypt, authority refused to transport her back to America as she was too ill. After a while she improved and came back to Nasir. She settled down with her girls and was very cheerful; when her time came she wanted to be at Nasir, and it looked as if she would not last long. We saw her in 1945 and though very frail she cracked a joke about a former visit, but she passed away before the end of the year. Her last Christmas card had a photo of four

WHEELS AND PADDLES IN THE SUDAN

Nuer luak (cattle shelter).

Nuer lasses.

Fowal village.

Nuer lasses paddling in the river; although not definitely so stated, I took it that they were some of her 'girls'.

Upstream of Nasir there were fine patches of maize, scooped out of the *toich*, and groups of *tukls* with their *luaks* scattered about. It is customary in these parts to add to each a sort of petticoat of thick grass, tucked in under the eaves to distribute the run-off, often referred to as the Nilotic fringe. Many of the huts had an ornately thatched porch. There were herds of cattle about, and flocks of sheep and goats. The banks on either side were very flat and there were a few trees on the horizon.

We met a merchant bringing down a consignment of hides from Jokau. He had three large Nuer canoes, spaced about 4 feet apart, and poles laid across them. On this platform parcels of hides were stacked to a height of 5 feet. Each canoe had a paddler fore and aft but they were low in the water and the merchants got the wind-up at the sight of *Melika*. We stopped in mid-stream and called on him to paddle past us which he did, with relief, as it would have taken very little to swamp him.

After a while there were stretches of grassland with low trees, bushes and ant-hills on one bank and *toich* on the other. Trees were scattered except for lining one or two waterways in the distance. The river took winding sweeps as it progressed from bend to bend. There was only one sizeable settlement, on the north bank, between Nasir and Pibor Mouth, but every here and there was an individual *tukl*.

The River Pibor joined the River Baro to form the River Sobat 26 miles upstream of Nasir, flowing in from the south. Much of its water probably came from the Bar-el-Jebel north of Juba. Crocodiles cruised across its mouth. Sixteen miles further on we reached Adura Mouth.

The Adura was the southern channel, separating Adura Island, about 40 miles long, from the south bank. Therefore at the downstream end of Adura Island was a choice of two routes; the usual one was the Baro via Jokau and the other, more obstructed and seldom used, was the Adura Channel.

Following the Baro one found oneself in a swift-flowing red-brown stream which, in the flood, was bank-high and overflowing. *Toich* extended for miles on either hand, the island being without trees on its northern side whereas there were a few trees on the other bank. After 7 miles Dumbirau Island was reached and boats

WHEELS AND PADDLES IN THE SUDAN

used the left-hand channel. At low river this area was well populated but not so in the flood, although we noticed a canoe and a mosquito net erected in grass 6 feet high. The river was now clear of floating grass. We saw water-buck, a pair of saddle-bill storks, and weaver bird colonies. The river varied in width from 60 to 120 yards and was very winding and fast flowing. We had our first view of the mountains of Abyssinia.

At Khor Machar which took off to the north and which during the flood drank heavily from the main river, returning the water on the falling river, we passed the Egyptian Irrigation Department launch and barge which had just completed a discharge measurement. Nearby some Nuer were fishing from canoes with bow-spears. Some 12 miles further on, after a stretch of very fast flowing water, lay Jokau where there was a Sudan Railway shed to afford protection for goods. After Jokau both banks were Abyssinian territory. Jokau was the first Italian post on the river during the occupation of Abyssinia and a certain liveliness was exhibited here during the war.

Some 8 miles above Jokau was the end of Adura Island at what was called Adura Head where the Adura took off in a channel 150 yards wide. In the old days, when the Gambeila service was in full swing, *Annuak* and *Nuer* used to handle ten or even more barges. Coming downstream they would, at this point, cast off all barges in excess of six to float down the Adura Channel, one by one, each with two sailors aboard to keep them moving. Then the steamer with six barges would drop down to Jokau for the night and pass through the swift water down to Adura Mouth to await arrival of the barges and re-marshal the tow.

The alternative route, by the Adura Channel, was more interesting and picturesque, but involved some trouble and delay. The maps showed a waterway wider than the Baro but it was ten years since barges had been floated down and the waterway was much obstructed. The first 12 miles was a fine open waterway starting 120 yards wide and never less than 60. Adura Island, on the left, was *toich* whilst the other bank was low-lying land with trees and many scattered groups of *tukls* and *luaks* each with maize plots. The Nuer were quite friendly. After 12 miles the main channel took off sharp to the left and it was then that the fun commenced because the grass growing in the stream formed a very real obstruction. After 2 miles we tied up for the night and set off next morning at 05.30 hours. At 06.30 hours we stopped at a Nuer village for milk and the natives were intrigued with the boat. A couple of handfuls of salt and of onions were considered generous exchange for the milk.

Both banks were now sprinkled with trees and in the dead ones sat big baboons. On the left bank were white-eared cob and on the right a pair of buffalo. The stream winding through the grass was about 30 yards wide. At 08.30 hours we chose the wrong channel and ran aground on to hard sand in 3 feet of water. The result was 5½ hours work. Then, 2 hours later 100 yards of *sudd* took 3 hours to clear. It was quite a busy day for Ramadan, the month of fasting. The crew nevertheless considered their performance was below standard and requested permission to complete the Adura section before tying up for the night and so it was 23.45 hours before peace reigned on board.

From Adura Head onwards the scenery along the Baro changed to some of the most pleasant on the waterways of the Sudan. Trees became more plentiful and at some places the vegetation along the water-edge formed a solid green wall much favoured by *warana* lizards, 3 feet in length. Lengths of *toich* still occurred but there were always trees in sight and strip plantations of maize.

Again, whilst one could go almost anywhere at high flood the journey was much more adventurous at the beginning. Travellers had to pick their way with care and much sounding and were certain to get stuck several times. The Baro could rise as much as 2 metres in the night and fall nearly as rapidly.

We were now in Annuak-land, and the Annuak were interesting people, polite and very cheerful. Their royal house resided at Pachala on the Akobo River and the tribe lived on both sides of the Abyssinian frontier. It was not a fighting race and had suffered much at the hands of the belligerent Nuer. Their villages were different from any other type of riverain village. Their siting was essentially strategic and defensive — on the outer bank of a bend, and therefore with permanent water available at all states of the river, surrounded on three sides by a ditch and stockade built on top of the spoil from the ditch. Generally there were two gateways, one upstream and one downstream, about 15 yards from the water's edge, which could be effectively blocked with boughs of thorn.

The Annuak hut is built on a 9 inch plinth of mud, with two rings of posts to give a low 3-foot wide verandah. Thatching is generally a flat coating with a low pitch. The walling is of woven grass; the inside is mud plastered as is the outside on either side of the opening for a distance of 4 feet, which is adorned with wavy lines and lots of small pieces of shell.

There were a number of *kapok* and other shade trees growing between the huts and in the stockade, as well as bananas, paw-paw and castor oil. The outstanding feature was the cleanliness of the village. The ground was swept and polished by hand; one felt almost ashamed to walk across it.

Their cooking hearths were ingenious; they would first excavate a hemisphere, then cut out three or four-quarter spheres so that a pot would rest on the points of intersection, leaving space to feed the fuel. It was always left scrupulously clean after use. The bed was a mat about 3/4 inch thick, woven of bamboo strips about 1½ inches wide on a narrow framework, giving the same finish on both sides. The pillow was a miniature gymnasium horse about 8 inches high, cut from natural growth.

Their canoes were the finest on the river, carved in one piece, solid, long and well shaped. Large spoon-shaped paddles were used, which gave a firm grip on the turbulent river, and also came in handy for baling out.

Most Annuak were over 5 feet 9 inches tall. They generally wore khaki shorts while the 'elders' also had a cloth to throw round their shoulders. The women wore short black or dark brown skirts with bead ornamentation. They were very cheerful and had no fear of the evil-eye (or camera). They were polite, bringing my wife the Chief's chair and a small boy came over to her of his own accord and allowed himself to be picked up and played on her lap with a fly-swish. They were very clean in their person and free from smell in the mass. Their 'wants' were fish-hooks, paraffin for lamps, razor blades and new and old male attire; their 'likes' were salt, onions and dates.

Wigada Alumu, Chief of Fowal, stood well over 6 feet. His bead necklace was interesting; it consisted of white oval and green cylindrical beads in groups of seven to nine beads. It was stated that these particular green beads were of the same sort of value locally as gold — one bead was said to be worth about eight cattle. With over 40 of them in his necklace he was clearly a man of standing. He told us about his eight wives and four sons and it turned out that the little lad who had sat on my wife's lap was one of them. So when the following year, we brought him a framed enlargement of the lad he was very pleased. He invited my wife to meet his latest wife. He first

E.W.W. and small boy.

swept the scrupulously clean plinth at the entrance to her *tukl* with his hand to demonstrate that there were no partially buried poisoned thorns protecting the threshold, he then invited my wife to enter.She found a girl in her late teens, good looking but very shy, clad in a beautifully embroidered apron and a fine collection of necklaces. On her right arm she wore a 1 inch diameter heavy gold wristlet and one of ivory on her left. Immediately below the centre of her lower lip a hole was pierced to house 8 inches of thin reed or similar substance. After a while she relaxed and my wife persuaded her to come outside for a photograph, to which she charmingly agreed, after first covering her beaded apron with a length of cloth.

One visit to Fowal involved my wife in a very lengthy first-aid session and we became very interested in the occupants. They lived in a very pleasant spot, their way of life was simple but it retained a number of highly commendable qualities and we felt we were always very welcome.

The main activity of the Annuak was growing two crops. The first was always, and the second generally maize, though some of the second might be *dura*. The early crop was a rain crop and was harvested in August. It was sown along the river bank so that some of it could be watered by hand should the rains fail. The 1943 early crop was a tragedy and the *nass* lost heart. On the falling river a second crop was sown. In 1944 and 1945 the picture was different, because the rains had been good. There was maize all the way and we were pelted with corn cobs out of sheer *joie-de-vivre*. There were also small plantations of *tombac* (native tobacco).

Travelling upstream the mountains of the Abyssinian Plateau became clearer and then several foothills took shape. To the north the Nyagwom Hills were viewed from many angles and the outline was like a large recumbent statue of the great Duke of Wellington.

At the beginning of the flood, the mass of crocodiles had to be seen to be believed. One could count up to 1,000 in no time. They make their nests well up on the sand banks and beaches, towards the high water mark and the nests contain many eggs, but whether this is the result of single or communal effort I know not. I shot one of 16 foot on this section.

Near Pachuri on the south bank was a wood which sheltered an enormous number of baboons. A little further upstream in 1943 we ran aground several times in the shallows and as a result got sand into our circulating pump; we tied up just upstream of an Annuak

Crocodile nest and eggs.

village and the Chief was a little worried about his cultivation. The rope was, however, made fast high up and so no plants looked like being injured. We were given poultry and in return gave three handfuls of salt, their greatest desire, and some old razor blades.

There was not much game to be seen while the river was open, though turtles were numerous. Fish traps abounded all along the Baro. Bird life was plentiful and there were some wonderful colonies on the islands. Species represented included three kinds of egret, two herons, two cormorants, one moorhen and several kinds of ducks. Pelicans were very numerous and roosted in the trees along the river's edge.

We wound our way along between islands and we decided to tie up for the night at Itang, a long straggling series of Annuak settlements. The Chief himself helped a sailor to carry our anchor inland and settle it in the ground. It was a quiet, peaceful night.

It was, however, for an unfortunate occurrence on another trip that we most remember Itang. We were sleeping on the upper deck when a storm broke. In doing up the bedding I must have included my wife's false teeth in her roll, which the *reis* picked up. As he reached the bottom of the companion way there was the sound of something hitting the deck followed by a splash! My wife exclaimed: 'My God, my teeth!' She was quite correct — they had fallen into the swiftly flowing Baro! The *reis* sounded and we found 5 feet of water and a hard bottom. Salvage would be attempted in the morning. We arose at 05.40 hours to witness operations. The *reis* had a pole driven into the bottom, well forward, to which a sailor was attached by rope. Holding onto the side of the launch the *reis* worked his way along, feeling with his feet on the bottom, and within five minutes he thought he felt them. The sailor dived down and a minute later, came up grinning with the denture in his hand. The rescue was fortunate for the prospect of no spare available, and the nearest dentist a fortnight's journey away, was unpleasing.

Near Pakou, on the north bank, there was a short heavily wooded section with colobus monkeys, and then on the next long stretch, also on the north bank, the map showed 'low hill'. It was 100 feet high and one of the few definite landmarks after Jokau.

The river, which had been anything up to 300 yards wide for many miles, narrowed as we approached Gambeila, and the current became more rapid. There was a wide sweep to the south, with a dangerous rock near the north bank, known as the Nasir rock, as in

1930 *Nasir*, leaving Gambeila on the last sailing, ran aground on it and sank. It was salvaged in 1931, an operation that was one of the epics of the Steamers Section. The advance salvage party included *Sobat*, a small cone-propelled launch, a steel *felucca* and a wooden *felucca*, under the command of Chappell from Khartoum North Dockyard.

From Sobat Mouth to the wreck was around 290 miles. Nearly half of that was through shallows of 1 foot depth at most, which meant at least one *felucca* being manhandled by her crew. *Sobat* had to be abandoned after 130 miles for lack of water. The heavily over-laden launch gave persistent mechanical trouble due to design fault, so it too needed manhandling over long distances. Miles of channel for navigation through sandbanks had to be scooped out by hand, and the greatest trouble of all came from a shellfish, rather like an oyster, called *mchar*. It formed ridges, up to 6 feet in height, presenting edges like broken glass; their shells, too, were covered with tubular spikes up to 1 inch long. It was a most unpleasant hazard and the crew were more chary of them than of the crocodiles. It took 18 days to reach the wreck, but their morale remained high, despite little shelter from sun or mosquitoes, fresh food being unobtainable, and the enormous physical slog. In his salvage report Chappell wrote: 'The spirit shown by *Reis* Darrag and Leading Seaman Abdel Karim Idris enabled us to carry on, and the spirit shown by the men was very creditable'. The journey by the main salvage party, which followed with the materials to effect a temporary repair, the repair operation, the floating off of *Nasir* from the rock on which it was impaled, and the journey home on one boiler made inspiring reading. I happened to be in Khartoum North Dockyard when *Nasir* arrived to a great welcome. It ended on a sad note; *Nasir* had to be scrapped, but at least its hulk was not left simply to rust away in far-off Abyssinia.

From this point onwards one had the impression of being above the surrounding countryside. This was indeed the case, because through the years the river had deposited its silt on bed and banks. The little Jebel Gambeila showed clearly between the trees as the river pointed towards the gap in the foothills leading up to the plateau. After 322 miles from Sobat Mouth, we came to Gambeila on the north bank, at the limit of navigation of the Baro.

Whenever I think of Gambeila I always remember its District Commissioner, Jack Maurice, a larger-than-life character, but the

WHEELS AND PADDLES IN THE SUDAN

history before and during World War II should first be considered.

Gambeila Trading Station, to give it its full name, was a concession from Emperor Menelik to Queen Victoria. The enclave of 1 square mile was administered by a District Commissioner and 30 police as part of the Upper Nile Province until the Republic of the Sudan handed it back to Abyssinia. Its principal articles of commerce were coffee for export and salt for import. Pre-Abyssinian war export of coffee was 4,000 tons in a good year. By 1942 it had dwindled to 2,000 tons. Gambeila's main link with the outside world was its wireless station although a second vital connection had also recently been added. This was a landing strip of 1,050 yards. It was humped and normally over-grown with grass left as a protection to the soil, but could be cut by 110 men in half a day, a length of warning that was always available. Its merchants were very friendly; on my first visit I was presented with a fine goat's milk cheese from Gore, repeated at subsequent visits, but when their generosity grew to a 200-pound bag of best coffee it had to go to the Catering Section and Sudan Railways for a time served some very fine coffee.

Gambeila had mixed experiences in the years from 1935. The position of the Enclave was one of some difficulty. Major Maurice was instructed to extend generous hospitality to any who were willing to accept, and so most of the officers at Gambeila on any night were to be found at the District Commissioner's house. The majority, particularly the cavalry, were charming, but the police officers were most objectionable. The degree of espionage that existed would scarcely be credited. The Admiral from Massawa, after being entertained, wrote a letter of thanks from Saiyo, 30 miles away; instead of being sent down by runner in the usual way, the letter was sent to Rome for censoring.

When the Duke D'Aosta visited Gambeila he handed all his telegrams to Major Maurice for wireless transmission, stating that otherwise they would all be sent first to Rome and requested that under no circumstances should they be returned should any official attempt to retrieve them be made — and the effort was made!

When Italy entered the war the position of the staff at Gambeila was uncertain. The Duke was prepared to let the District Commissioner and his staff be treated as consular staff but the Foreign Office could not agree to this convenient irregularity. Eventually the Duke granted safe passage down the Baro at two hours' notice.

WHEELS AND PADDLES IN THE SUDAN

Much had to be done; cyphers, codes and secret files had to be burned, but, on time, the District Commissioner, his *merkaz* staff, police and wives set out in 12 canoes. There was trouble with two Fascist officers on the frontier at Jokau, but the District Commissioner was to play the Duke d'Aosta card and thereby obtain passage.

There was something very likeable in the Duke's character. He had a sense of humour. When he was passing through Malakal on his way south as a prisoner of war he remarked to the Governor: 'By-the-bye tell your District Commissioner that when he returns to Gambeila he will find his official files where he left them — behind the bucket of the office latrine!'

After the evacuation the inhabitants of the Enclave had a poor time. The record of the Italians was unpleasant. When they departed they left the roads, aerodrome and District Commissioner's garden littered with mines. In return for the hospitality received over five years from the District Commissioner those in his garden were of a special type — made of beer bottles! As usual, however, most of them were 'duds'.

The return of Abyssinian power to Gambeila Province brought little change. The Governor General in 1945 was a son of Ras Casa, a young man who had been educated in England for seven years. I talked with him one evening; he was very dissatisfied with the state of affairs. The position in outlying areas like Gambeila was hopeless. All the old troubles were back again and he talked of returning to England and leaving Abyssinia for good. I was asked by a Chief why, when we had defeated the Italians, we did not deal with the Amhara. I replied that while the former were enemies the latter were, as Abyssinians, our allies. He could not understand it — he said in his experience they were equally bad!

And what of the man? Jack Maurice was one of a large family from near Marlborough, from which establishment he would tell you he was rejected on account of failure to acquire knowledge sufficiently rapidly. After a spell in Canada he took a job in Ruthenia, which required him to take readings of a plant, of which he knew nothing, making tanning extract and also to spread the culture of an English country gentleman. He imported a pack of fox hounds and for several years had a fine time. After World War I, spent with a mounted unit in Palestine, he came to the Sudan in connection with the improvement of horse rearing in Darfur and then in 1928 to Gambeila as District Commissioner. Here, in near-isolation, he flourished.

Jack had an enormous fund of stories about life in Gambeila. One concerned the funeral of a Greek merchant; it was a long tale and told with a wealth of detail. The main point was that custom required that the corpse must be decked with a bowler hat which on this occasion was difficult to find. The mourners were all gathered about the house with the corpse reclining in a propped-up coffin for inspection but the local pundits refused to carry on with the procedure until a bowler hat was produced. It took nearly a couple of hours!

A bit of a fatalist, and feeling that times had changed so much that England now held little attraction for him, he would take you to a shady tree just outside the little cemetery, and show you the plot he had reserved for himself, alongside one of his favourite dogs. However, when we visited Gambeila in 1945, he told us he had changed his mind. Whilst on leave earlier in the year, they had buried a Greek in his plot, and without a bowler hat too! He had decided after all that he would not leave his bones in Gambeila but would retire to Tanganyika.

In 1943 our launch was the first craft to arrive at Gambeila on the rising flood. We stuck many times but just managed to creep in. Two days later, however, the river fell and we had to stay a week and await a rise. Life was hectic! The rule at Gambeila was that all visitors dined with the District Commissioner; after many drinks one sat down to dinner at 23.00 hours and after many stories one would rise from the table at 01.00 hours and with luck be away at 02.00 hours. After a week of this routine, my wife said she could not stand the pace anymore. Although the river had not reached what we considered a safe level our *reis* thought that with daylight travelling, and care, he could take *Sobat* through, and so we set off after breakfast on the eighth day and were thankful when, after a couple of hours, Gambeila was out of sight. A little beyond Nasir rock we ran hard aground on a sandbank, and it took us three hours of hard work to get her off. We had a number of further groundings, but nothing serious, as we made our way back to Pibor Mouth.

Chapter Fourteen

UP THE PIBOR

The crocodile was on guard as usual as we turned into the Pibor River. He was about 20 feet long and I always refrained from shooting him as he was the largest I knew.

Toich extended for miles on both banks, that on the east being a particularly fresh green and the river was very dirty with grass from the Gila River. In dry weather there were many Nuer cattle camps on each bank. The east bank, right up to the mouth of the Akobo River, was Abyssinian territory. There were a few trees ahead and *maiyas* were visible away on the east bank. The first tributary was Khor Macap on the west bank which we passed after half-an-hour. Then came Khor Makwai, on the east bank, after 1 hour 25 minutes, connecting with the Adura.

The river was running very full, spilling over to *maiyas* and canoes were engaged in fishing in the *toich* using double-ended punt poles. On higher ground there was cultivation and magnificent crops of red *dura* were nearly ripe. The occasional strip of dry land carried scrub and some ant-hills.

After five hours we reached the Gila River, on the east bank. Our progress was slow owing to the quantity of grass in the river, but it improved later and we passed Wanding, where there was normally a merchant, after a further 1 hour 40 minutes. Towards Akobo the river became more confined between banks. At 58 miles from Pibor Mouth there were two village schools of the American Mission, one at Burawil on the west bank and the other at Dibock in Abyssinia. They gave a two-year elementary course in English, arithmetic and Nuer in phonetic characters.

Half a mile before Akobo was the American Mission station, the home of the Maclures. It was designed and built by them. Based on the *tukl*, it looked rather like a catamaran ashore. It was a sound job though I sometimes wondered how long it would stand against the ravages of white ants. The Mission carried out fine work with a practical approach. A big drive to improve the condition of the

Annuak was under consideration which if developed would make Akobo the centre of a very interesting experiment. Annuak-land was thought to offer scope for real achievement.

At mile 66 we reached Akobo, a District Headquarters with a District Commissioner and his Assistant. Wireless was of vital importance to Akobo which was accessible by river only from mid-June to mid-December and by road from mid-January to mid-May. It was situated on cotton soil and in the rains possessed some of the finest mud in the Sudan. Two tribes were administered from Akobo, the Annuak and the Merle, each extending over both sides of the Abyssinian frontier.

On my first visit we arrived, in rain, at nightfall and tied up at the *meshra*. In the morning it was still raining as I set out for the *merkaz*. My arrival coincided with that of the District Commissioner, 'Kid' Lewis. We went inside and reviewed the position. In a few minutes the clerk arrived, a fine tall Nuer lad. He stood on the threshold for a moment, removed his *luah*, a yard of calico, knotted over the left shoulder — wrung it out and hung it over the back of a chair to dry; he sat down and got on with his touch-typing. I learned something of the difficulties of living and working in an outpost like Akobo and then the District Commissioner came back to lunch with us on *Sobat*.

On another memorable occasion, on *Melika* we made an effort to reach Pibor Post which had been without river connection for a number of years on account of the vegetation in the river. From Akobo the journey proceeded through pretty country. For the first 20 miles the river flowed mainly between well-defined banks of cotton soil which gave a cloudy appearance to the water. The river turned through a considerable bend and the Akobo wireless masts assumed many unexpected positions. The first village of any size was Dimmo, situated on a knoll on the east bank. The American Mission had once considered the site and the Chief had been prepared to sell it and clear away all buildings for two bulls!

In 1943 there had been a very high river and marks on the bank indicated that the peak had been about half a metre higher than when we made the journey. The river was free from floating grass and an indication of its high level was a canoe being used to stand in while picking *dura*.

With the rains and the flood the trees looked very fresh in their young leaf. One, if not both, banks were covered with trees touching the water. The prevailing tree was the pale yellow-green *thip*, with its tassels of white flower. Mingled among them were *akat* with their edible berries and a tall well-shaped tree called *thau* which elephants delighted to eat.

The reach between Akobo and Agwei Mouth was at certain times of the year a favourite fishing spot with sometimes as many as 15 canoes proceeding abreast fishing with bow spears. At mile 86 Agwei Mouth was reached. The Agwei was much the same size as the Pibor at the confluence but its banks were higher. In 1943 we went up it for some two hours. It was mid-June and the river was then much lower and consequently narrower. We were much hampered by wooden weirs erected in connection with low river fishing enterprises. Eventually we called it a day on account of the width of the river. In fact, we had underestimated by 5 feet and we had to excavate 5 feet from one of the banks in order to manhandle the 70 feet of *Sobat* round. It took us about 1½ hours. The Agwei gave a cloudy effect to the water passing Akobo. The Pibor above the junction was somewhat obstructed with grass but after about 1 mile a clear stream unfolded itself. From this point onwards the river was quite unexpectedly wide and deep, and the scenery was beautiful, although flat. There were no hills until some miles beyond Pibor Post.

The inhabitants of this area were the Merle, a primitive people of a low type. They did not bury their dead but merely dragged them clear of the village. When a Chief died they made an exception for him and left him in his hut with the door mudded-up and in due course the whole structure collapsed on him. Nor were they faddy over their food. They ate lion, hyaena, snake, frog and any kind of insect, as well as more generally approved items. Their canoes were as roughly constructed as their huts and the Merle were not good boatmen.

The men were about 5 feet 9 inches tall and naked except for a cape. One of their favourite hairstyles was formed of matted hair nearly one foot high, like the bottom half of a pea flower. Their women were not good-looking and did little to improve their appearance. The lower part of the body was clad in a leather skirt and their ears were a mass of 2-inch iron rings of blue beads and some wooden pegs making a bunch the size of an orange. Their babies were carried on their backs in skins rather similar to rucksacks.

WHEELS AND PADDLES IN THE SUDAN

The scenery along the river from Agwei Mouth onward was, however, much better looking! Trouble was experienced at the points at which *khors* joined the main stream due to grass covering the surface but elsewhere it was a fine stream, much of it 200 yards wide between banks with 100 yards of clear water. Trees lined the water's edge.

During the flood little game was seen. We saw 22 giraffe on the open ground and several couple of reedbuck at the water's edge and a few waterbuck. Bird life was well represented; the biggest and fattest of spur-winged geese abounded, as also did Nile geese and whistling teal. Guinea fowl and fish eagles were numerous.

Until the last 15 miles from Pibor Post there were few villages or even habitations and with the many winds in the river it was not easy to spot one's position on the map. We stopped at a merchant's hut at Mauta-karo, 11 miles from Pibor Post. From here we took a sick Merle woman into Pibor Post. The Merle believed in good and bad spirits. As we passed some fine trees at Lochli on the way to Pibor the Merle man who accompanied us prayed to the trees on one side of the river and then to those on the other. We tried to make a fast run over the last part of the journey in order to get the women into the dispensary before dark, but we were unfortunate and got stuck in grass at Wingkok which, we were told, had been the limit of navigation for several years. We reached Pibor Post, 172 miles from the mouth, after dark. Our arrival was quite unexpected as there was no wireless. We stopped at the merchants' huts and police soon came across from the lines. There was some doubt whether we could approach the *meshra* as an earth bridge had been thrown across at low river and was in the way. The woman was taken ashore.

Pibor Post was one of the farthest outposts and one of the most inaccessible. It was open by river, in theory, in September and October only and by road from September to May. It had a landing ground but it was very wet during the rains and was virtually under water during our visit. Outside the Post was a signpost giving the direction, destination and distance along each track for Cape Town, Khartoum, Cairo, Paris and London. On the post was an iron plate as a memorial to Captain Hutton, RMA, District Commissioner, Akobo, 1912–1915, killed in the Nuba Mountains 1917.

After taking soundings we decided that the launch could safely cross the bridge. We were warned by the police to keep clear of two trees just by the *meshra* in which there were beehives. We passed the site of the bridge and the beehives without incident and then on past the Rest House which had a pleasant view upstream.

After 20 minutes we came to the junction of Khor Kengen from the left and the River Lotilla from the right. This point was presumably the start of the Pibor River. The Kengen was a clear stream, of greater volume at that moment than the Lotilla, which came from the cotton soil and was cloudy. We took the Lotilla which, though pretty, turned out to be very winding. There was plenty of water but with bad luck we touched a sunken log and lost a blade of our port propeller. We passed very considerable flocks of crested cranes, in places standing on the tops of the trees, silhouetted against the sky-line.

We continued upstream for 1¾ hours but the stream began to lose width and the bends proved tiresome to a launch the length of *Melika* so we turned at a convenient spot with Jebel Lother visible away to the west. There was plenty of water but *Melika* was not suitable with twin propellers and high superstructure for exploratory work. It must have been years since any craft had visited these waters. It is recorded that the Seignora, Miss Tinne, in 1862 reached Gondokoro, near Juba, and returned via the River Sobat, which meant that she must have crossed the swamps to the Veveno, a tributary of the Lotilla, and come down the Pibor. A map I had showed a spot in the area with the caption: 'The place of the Long Chimney', which almost certainly referred to Miss Tinne's journey. I had hoped to get close to that spot but my craft was not suitable. With regret we turned for home.

Chapter Fifteen

A JOURNEY UP THE BLUE NILE

The Blue Nile, which rose in Lake Tana in Abyssinia, was the main factor in the Nile flood each year. It was said that the eyes of Egypt were fixed on Roseires or more correctly on the Roseires gauge, for the gauge reading, by specific agreement, had to be telegraphed to Cairo daily. Prior to the building of the Makwar Dam, services to Roseires were run, during the flood, from Mogren. Later, when the railway was built, they ran from Medani. When the dam was part-built, decisions had to be taken as to which craft would stay permanently above the dam as the last chance of crossing was on the flood of 1924. For a while after that date, services were run from Kassab-el-Doleib, which was rather close to the dam, and so, with the opening of the Gedaref line in 1929, a small river terminal was made at Suki. The dam not only impeded the movement of craft up and down the river, but also of the fauna; the crocodiles, however, soon learned to trek round the ends, leaving a trail.

The flood commenced in June and peaked about the end of August. The river had a very reduced flow when the peak was passed and was only navigable to Roseires from July to mid-December under normal conditions. The reservoir effect was, however, felt as far as Zamurka and navigation within the reservoir was extended by three to four months until the end of March, and between Suki and Singa until mid-April. The repair period for the fleet was April to June. The fleet consisted of: *Fateh*, a large wood-burning stern-wheeler; *Abuklea*, a medium diesel; *Sultan Hussein*, a wood-burning side paddle; *Puma*, a large wood-burning tug, and *Wilful*, a small wood-burning tug.

Native boats were not numerous, and all available serviceable boats had been taken over to assist in meeting the very heavy demands for space. In 1943 we had to handle about five times the quantity moved in pre-war years.

By far the most important feature of the Reach was the sunt

forests dotted along each bank. From them the Three Towns got their firewood and charcoal and Sudan Railways got 40,000 very good sleepers every year. Local opinion was that the sunt forests dated from a very high flood in 1906 which spread seed from a few parent trees into all the *maiyas*. The banks of the Blue Nile were either low with a *maiya* or shallow lake behind them, or high and steep, particularly on the outside of a bend. Sleepers were first cut, as half-round type, from Azaza Forest for Gebel Auliya Dam construction in 1933. Little, if anything, was done to develop timber production prior to 1932. Experimental work was, however, now being carried out and one could see plantations of mahogany, neem, sisoo, oil palm, bamboo and teak.

I decided to make a trip up the Reach for several reasons. I felt that Headquarters ought to be more aware of the splendid work being done on the Suki–Roseires Reach with limited resources. I also knew it would give an opportunity for any complaints to be voiced. Finally, future requirements, after the war, had to be assessed, particularly railway extension in the light of mechanised agriculture, possible dam construction and fleet renewal.

It was July 1944 when I made the trip, and Suki, like so many other riverside stations at that time of year, had plenty of mud. I reached it by motor trolley as the track through the cutting did not allow my saloon to approach the riverside. Before embarking I looked at the grain-cleaning plant, the sawmill cutting firewood to short lengths and the charcoal briquetting plant. The last two were very busy.

We embarked on *Fateh* and sailed at 15.00 hours. The Reach was very pretty; a wealth of green vegetation on each bank. The river was seldom less than 400 yards wide and frequently much wider. In flood its average speed was about 4 miles per hour, increasing considerably where constricted. It was, of course, of rich brown colour with its high silt content.

On leaving Suki the river took a big 'S' curve to the right and the first village of importance was Ramash on the west bank. This was a large Taisha settlement with a fruit garden. As the river swung to the left we passed the first two sunt forests, Dabkhara on the west bank and Dangada opposite. On the east bank there was a long curving bluff with the village of Abu Gara halfway along and then came Wad Gasouli Sawmill, busy cutting sleepers for Sudan Railways. Right opposite was the Forestry Station of Mina, which had been cut out and replanted. Round the corner on the west bank we came to Singa, 16 miles from Suki.

Singa was once the capital of the Fung Province and its *merkaz* was situated in the old Mudirieh, a fort-like building, with aradeiba trees in front. Its glory had departed, possibly with its last Governor, who was 'played out' by the Province band as he walked for the last time from the Mudirieh down the avenue to the river steps to board *Sultan Hussein*, one of the last side-paddle steamers in service on the Nile.

Another relic of more prosperous days was an extensive garden along the river bank, now somewhat unkempt. However, it was a delightful spot, with cool deep shade, and contained much fruit. The golden mohurs were a mass of scarlet bloom. From its situation it required two sets of pumps, one for normal irrigation and the other to pump it out should it be flooded during the peak. We were told that boats on occasion floated into the garden and, therefore, it was very necessary as more than four days' immersion was likely to prove fatal to citrus trees.

Singa had suffered much from erosion and was horribly scarred. Early town plans, dated about 1905, showed a site for a railway station and development had commenced in that there was a small modern soap factory.

Immediately upstream of Singa, on the east bank, was the village of Hillet-el-Mek, standing on a bluff which curved away to the right. It was an unpleasant sight standing in an eroded wilderness, created by man and his goat. When the vegetation was stripped from the soil, the rain ran off quickly and cut numerous small gullies to the level of the river. Their nakedness stands for all time and the size of the gullies will continue to increase until the science of soil conservation is applied.

We next passed an island notable for its trees. All other islands on this Reach were flooded at peak and without trees. On the west bank was Azaza Forestry Station. This area was the first to be cut and was later replanted. A little further on was Hariri Sawmill, busy cutting sleepers from Hariri Forest. Ahead lay a wide, open sheet of water.

Patches of sunt were numerous in this part and on the east bank we soon reached Gezeia, a forestry station with a colossal *gemeiza* tree at the *meshra*. The forest had been cut out and replanted. It had extensive nurseries and we picked up a large quantity of neem shettles, done up in bundles in canvas, for distribution to forestry stations, along the Reach. The river now curved away in a long sweep to the left with a high bank commencing at Bahasu and finishing at Barobras. On the west bank was Lembroa Forest. Opposite the end of a long island was the extensive village of Sabonabi. From now onwards one noted *goo-goos,* which were little *tukls* raised about 4 feet from the ground for the storage of grain.

We passed relics of Turkish days — small abandoned fruit gardens consisting of some half a dozen date palms and lemon trees, and in Karkoj, which we were approaching, were traces of that era. Its inhabitants regarded the town as being much more important than Singa.

Karkoj, standing on a sandy bluff, boasted a local court, a dispensary and elementary schools. It exported *dura, simsim,* gum, soap and *garad,* as well as small quantities of many other commodities.

The building, however, of the Suki–Gedaref railway line hit Karkoj rather hard as the town used to be the gathering point for all products from the Abu Hashim area on the Dinder. Subsequently much of this produce went to Dinder station. Nevertheless, it still had a soap industry said to be more than 200 years old, using *simsim* oil, making a product widely used in the Sudan.

Upstream of Karkoj was a long low island and we took the western channel which was only possible during the flood. On the west bank lay the village of Serou and, on the east, Dentai forestry station, now a replanted forest. After 6 miles we reached Abu Hagar which was almost at the limit of the reservoir and had a good area for transhipment. During the flood it was necessary to lift all the forest products from upstream of the reservoir area and the shortage of craft compelled us to dump the greater part at Abu Hagar for on-transport during the reservoir period. Abu Hagar possessed a dispensary and a boys' school but was another ghastly example of erosion.

From here the river turned to the left in a great sweep of high brown cliffs. We walked the 2½ miles to Lawni whilst the steamer battled its way against the swift current. A steep bank swept round to Zamurka village on the east bank and Lawni village on the west, just 6 miles from Abu Hagar.

We then entered the longest straight of the journey, which was 10 miles. We passed Zamurka Forest, on the east bank, followed by Capsoon, a Felata village and an off-shoot from Suki, and Wad Bugheiga Forest. On the west bank was Baraukwa Forest and village. At this point, approaching Abu Tiga, the current was very fast. Abu Tiga itself used to be an important gum centre but the trade has since declined.

The next section, of 22 miles, stretched to Bunzuka. On the west bank lay Baraukwa and, on a high red bluff, Abu Naama and its forest. Coming out of an 'S' bend we entered a straight 4-mile reach at the end of which was a Taisha village, Tangaru, on the east bank, and Lokandi and its forest on the west bank. At the head of the next reach lay Gaabat on the east bank, opposite the end of the Lokandi Forest, which finished at a bend with a clump of doleib palms which looked strangely out of place. We next came to Hugeirat on the east bank and on the west bank, Hidibat Sawmill, which was busy cutting sleepers for Sudan Railways. Seven thousand were awaiting transport.

We took on firewood at Hidibat and I had a look round. The foreman complained of belt-trouble with the rack bench; the belt broke three or four times a day as it had for the past 15 months. I was not surprised as the mill had been set up with the driving pulley 4 inches out of line. As the mill was working for the railway, I lined up the pulley for him, had the concrete cut away from the shaft foundations and saw it working before leaving.

Continuing on our journey, on the east bank, on a flat curving bluff, lay Sabonabi and on the west bank a *khor* led to Wad El Nail, 3½ miles inland. It was a trading centre and on the telegraph. Bunzuga, a forestry station on the east bank, had been replanted and had a small trial plot of oil palms.

We passed the tug *Wilful* with a barge. It was a real circus with even a camel on board as a passenger on the barge.

At the last forestry call we picked up Waterson of the Agriculture and Forests and I was able to have an interesting talk with him about their policy in this Reach. Waterson's special responsibility was regeneration of the cut-out areas, which was a very important function. I asked him if he could find any lime-free soil, situated on hillsides, and, if so, to try tung oil in this area. He knew of a spot and I promised to get some seed and cultural instructions for him.

The next section was 25 miles, from Bunzuga to Saoliel. The first stop was at Galgani, an extensive village on a ridge about ½ mile back from the river, with a brick-built *suk*. From Galgani we glimpsed the only two jebels you see on the whole journey, Jebels Okalma and Kardos, which could be reached by a road from Mehala. Omdurman was a big village on the east bank and then we passed, on a straight reach, the Felata village of Abdul Khaleg on the west bank and Um Basid on the east bank as were Abu Zor, the Felata villages of Dowd and Tertora, and Saoliel with its extensive forestry reserve of neem.

The next section stretched 10 miles to Bados. On the west bank was Harun Forest. Bados lay 2 miles inland, behind a *maiya*, in an extensive area of cultivation. Along these reaches bird life flourished, but at this time of year little animal life was visible.

The last section extended 22 miles from Bados to Roseires. On the west bank we passed Abu Kok, a Felata village before the river took an 'S' bend between red cliffs and a Berta village called Beida, on a bluff on the east bank. All along the banks was a thin belt of maize cultivation and generally higher ground, perhaps 60 feet above river level, at a distance of a quarter to half a mile. On the west bank lay Serew, a large Felata village, and Disa, with a large *khor* and a forestry Rest House well known to those wishing to indulge in lion hunting. Also on the west bank lay Abu Ramad where a sacred war-drum was supposed to be buried. At one time navigation used to be impeded here by a rocky channel between an island and the west bank, but this nuisance was greatly reduced by blasting in 1937. Throughout the whole journey we could see habitations, which could hardly be said of any other river journey in the Sudan.

Roseires next came in sight. The first thing visible was the District Commissioner's house, on a hillock looking down the river. Next one noticed the pylons carrying the telegraph line across the river, and the *meshra,* shady and bright with the scarlet of Golden Mohurs. Total steaming time to Roseires was 40 hours if one was lucky, though a fast-rising flood can add considerably to that figure.

Roseires lay on the east bank at the foot of the Damazin Rapids. The buildings were perched on small hillocks, about 60 feet above river level. The gullies between, as well as the hill tops, carried little vegetation, and with heavy rainfall erosion had been considerable. The administrative buildings were connected by fine avenues of neem trees. Roseires also had a *merkaz*, hospital and boys' school.

Roseries *suk* dealt in locally produced gold. Gold washing was taken seriously in *khors* upstream of Roseires, particularly in the Beni-Shangul country. It was found mainly as dust but occasionally sizeable nuggets turn up. I was shown one the size of a pigeons egg. I asked a Greek merchant how big was the largest nugget he had seen and he pointed to an office paper-punch.

Roseires was an extensive centre for trade generally. Salt was imported for sending forward into Abyssinia. Gum, coffee, hides and bursh matting formed the main exports. There was land line communication to Khartoum via Sennar and, as already mentioned, the Sudan reported the Roseires gauge reading to Cairo every day. Roseires also maintained wireless communication with Kurmuk.

I visited the hospital to see an interesting case. A young lad had been attacked three times by a crocodile and got away each time by putting his fingers into its eyes. He was badly mauled on arms, legs and buttocks but was progressing fairly well.

Before 1938 it was felt in certain directions that it was only lack of enterprise which caused Sudan Railways to declare that Roseires was the limit of navigation. It was said that there were rich areas upstream only awaiting river transport for development and in that year Sudan Railways decided to explore the Abu Shendi and Damazin gorges. A small motorboat with cone propulsion was taken up by lorry and Messrs Chappell and Holman of the Steamers Section set out. It was April and the river was low. Abu Shendi Gorge, 3 miles in length, was first traversed on foot; it proved impossible to get even a small boat through the rocks. The launch was put into the water at Abu Zagholi. It took three days of hard work to get to the head of the Damazin Gorge and the launch had to be portaged over a number of obstructions. The Damazin Gorge itself, 7 miles long, was traversed in a day and took nine hours work. The entry proved very difficult, it took two hours to get through the fast-running shallow water and a whirlpool. The middle section, of deeper water, was less thrilling but the last 2 miles were the most difficult, and 1½ miles of them took four hours of hauling, dodging rocks and general back-breaking toil. The verdict of the explorers was emphatic — Roseires was the limit of navigation! The question of navigation beyond Roseires became academic only, when, 25 years later the Roseires Dam was built across the Damazin Gorge.

Chapter Sixteen

SENNAR TO MALAKAL BY ROAD

The purpose of this journey by road in February 1946 was to make a general reconnaissance of the country with a view to development. I, of course, was more particularly interested in the transport angle coupled with water supply, population and commodities. It was an expedition *en famille,* occupying two station wagons and a 3-ton lorry, but catering and camping arrangements were for the first time, as far as we were concerned, in the hands of our Catering Section. The *Wakil* (man in charge) was excellent and the cook, Mahmoud, had sailed with us twice on the Blue Nile. We took five servants in all as staff went down with malaria quickly in the south.

The motor transport was not new. It gave our Transport Superintendent many troubles before he had it overhauled to his liking. The drivers were all old hands and two of them had gone through Equatoria with us in 1944. The head driver had driven for 19 years in Sudan Railways. Our fitter-driver kept our cars in good order and was general mechanic to the expedition. We carried sufficient petrol for each section with us, generally 280 gallons in seven 40-gallon drums. There were also three 20-gallon containers of water for use in emergency or at bad wells. It was quite a sizeable load before anything else was ever added.

SENNAR TO SINGA

The first afternoon's run was just 40 miles to Singa. It was reserved for after lunch and the pack-in was easy because the camping and catering equipment had gone by rail to Suki for loading on to *Fateh* which was to be our floating home for the night at Singa. We left the saloon at 14.45 hours and drove down towards the dam and, crossing the railway line, made our way through Sennar *suk* to the open flat country bordering the reservoir.

At this time of year the reservoir was brimful. The water at the

WHEELS AND PADDLES IN THE SUDAN

edge was very shallow and covered with birds. Very soon we were running through dry grass about 3½ inch high. The water of the reservoir viewed at this flat angle was a beautiful blue colour. Every now and then we passed small villages and the Roseires telegraph wire lay away to the right.

At mile 10 (all distances are given as miles from Sennar) we came to the extensive Fellata settlement of Maijumo. The road was flat, mainly cotton soil and the going for the most part quite good. A few lorries were passed but the traffic was not heavy. At one or two spots there were pleasant groups of trees in the water at the edge of the reservoir. A number of hides gave indication that duck shooting was enjoyed in these areas.

The country was on the whole flat and open with scattered trees away to the right and occasional areas of small trees and bushes. Smallish villages were passed and the telegraph wire was visible most of the time. After an hour's running we waited eight minutes for the lorry to catch up. Egyptian Irrigation Department benchmarks, belonging to the precise levelling to Roseires, occurred from time to time. It became clear that the main cultivation was further inland.

Singa, at mile 40, was, as already mentioned, no longer at its best. Viewed from this approach, it was even worse. We drove through the town and down to the landing-stage, arriving at 16.15 hours.

Fateh lay at her moorings. We called on District Commissioner Disney and then settling ourselves on board, spent a comfortable night. Next day we laid out all camping equipment on the deck of the barge for inspection. As space was limited we loaded essentials first. All personal baggage was put into the back of our station wagon — back seats had been removed from both of them at Sennar and left in the saloon — and this with boxes of drinks, sodas, cans of 'Flit' and paraffin and two pressure lamps, three passengers and a driver made a fair load.

The next station wagon was loaded with camp beds, mosquito nets and mattresses for four two camp wash-stands and baths, three trek tables, ten folding chairs, hurricane lamps, four servants and a driver, and it was felt that it would hold the road well. The lorry was called upon to find room for the catering equipment, supplies of food, our bedding and all the servants' belongings. I watched a sack of white flour — most precious of stores — placed right on top and thought it was safe there but I know better now!

SINGA TO WAD-EL-NAIL

We set off at 09.00 hours. Our route lay straight up from the waterfront to the end of the built-up area and on to a flat expanse of cotton soil. It was probable that the railway station would be in this area, about a mile from the river. The first section of about 14 miles was to Dar Agil, passing Hariri Forest on the left and one or two villages. The banks of the Blue Nile formed a succession of small sunt forests, each of which required for its existence a shallow *maiya* which was filled during the flood season and then drained away.

Over much of the Sudan between the thirteenth and tenth parallels the predominant tree was the *heglig* and the area through which we passed was no exception. From its fruit, or more correctly from the kernel of the stone of the fruit, could be obtained *lalob* oil. Imperial Chemical Industries was interested in this oil. Locally the oil had many uses. In the north the fruit was fed to goats who spat out the stones which could be gathered and processed. The husks provided fuel and the kernels yielded valuable oil and good cake. Although not the practice in the Sudan, spirit could be made from the flesh of the fruit. A local soap-maker in Singa experimented with 300 kantars of kernels which cost him 25 percent more than for *simsim* and reckoned it was thoroughly economic. The Sudan only required a simple, preferably hand-driven, decorticating machine and then a virtually new and valuable industry could exist.

As we approached the village of Dar Agil on the right, mile 54, the trigonometrical point of Jebel Gereirisa lay ahead. Dar Agil was situated on the edge of the slight depression, an old river bed of Khor Um Ishsh, and there was consequently a good supply of water from numerous wells. The village had a busy *suk* of 25 shops and was a centre of the *simsim,* gum and *dura* trades. It had a promising sub-grade school and was a court sub-centre. It was altogether a flourishing spot. A new well had just reached water and lining with bricks was commencing. We were escorted to the site and saw a neat job in progress.

We crossed the shallow depression and set off in the next section towards Abu Hagar. Much of the country was covered with *kittir* bush which meant that the soil was good for *dura*. The approach to Abu Hagar, mile 64, showed terrible gully erosion. We arrived at 10.30 hours to find the gum market just closed. The *suk* contained about 40 shops and did a fairly big business in *simsim*, gum, and *dura*. Transport on the Blue Nile was possible for rather longer from this point as Abu Hagar was at the end of the reservoir area. The village contained a main court, dispensary and boys' elementary school.

After a stop of ten minutes we set off for Abu Na'ama. The going was rather up and down and the route for a railway would have to be sought further inland but would probably not be difficult to find. On the left lay Lawni Forest Rest House. The road dropped down into Khor-el-Gara with its dense sunt and then climbed out, soon to reach the village of El Keneiza which lay opposite Zamurka Forest with its fine stand of neem trees. Away to the right lay Jebel Abel with Wad Buheiger Forest away on the far bank of the river. We passed a number of Fellata villages. One village, called Amara Abd-el-Ghaffar was a very decayed spot. The village shop had recently collapsed and there was no *suk*. It was like coming into fresh-air when we left.

A few miles further on, at mile 78, we crossed the telegraph wire and came up to the village of Abu Na'ama. It was situated on a bluff which would provide the starting point of the scheme to pipe water into the interior in order to increase agricultural production should this method be decided upon. The whole of the vast area in these latitudes lying between the Blue and White Niles was of cotton soil, admirably suited to produce *dura, simsim* and gum. It had three main drawbacks — lack of water supply, scanty population and poor transport facilities. Abu Na'ama had a *suk* of about 15 shops and dealt in the usual commodities of these parts.

The last section of the day's run was the 18 miles to Wad-en-Nail. It was generally too uneven for a trace for a railway — that, we were assured, could be found quite easily inland — and really consisted of a quite good motor road designed for the administrative purpose of joining up centres of population. The first village was Tangaru, a Ta'aisha settlement; and then passing through thick trees for a distance and leaving the telegraph we came to the village of Ga'abat with a *suk* of 15 shops. After more ups and downs, we went down past the village of Shamiya Yousif and to a glorious enclosure of sunt trees which was too small to interest the Forestry Section for its sleeper production programme. The road led on out of the depression to the village of Shamiya Umar standing away to the right. A couple of miles further on, a turn led down to the left to Hidibat

Sawmill. *Habil* trees figured widely in the landscape from now on. The soil was for the most part alluvial, and after Ruweina, where a new forest reserve was about to be proclaimed, we crossed Khor el Malwiya.

Soon we saw the first full-grown dom palms and from here southwards dom had its place in the local economy. There was a flourishing industry in *zaaf,* the dried ends of the palm fronds, and the tree was placed on the protected list.

At mile 96½ and 12.20 hours we drove into Wad-en-Nail and were welcomed by the Nazir of the Rufaa-el-Hoi, Sheik Ahmed Yousif Abu Roaf, who was to be our host. We found ourselves in very comfortable quarters. Over refreshment we congratulated our host on the Robe of Honour recently conferred on him by His Excellency the Governor General. The occasion was marked by barbaric ceremony. As His Excellency drove into Wad-en-Nail, five bulls lined up at the roadside were slaughtered with appropriate acclamation and the entry was made in a blood-bath. Eastern magnificence! He did not receive a Robe of Honour in his home town every day of the week!

Wad-en-Nail stood on an open site. It was on the Roseires–Singa telegraph line and had a *suk* with 16 shops. Its trade was increasing, and it had become a centre of administration, and was quite prosperous. One well gave a copious supply of water.

After lunch, I set out on a short diversion of ten miles, about south-west by west to Jebel Tozi. I wanted to look at the type of country inland through which a suitable trace for a railway might be located.

The going was not good over cotton soil, though quite flat. After about a mile there was some improvement. For most of the way there were trees or clearings for cultivation among the trees. Much of it was through *talh*, the red-barked acacia which yielded inferior gum and had white straight thorns which were used for office pins in the Fung. I was puzzled at the constant size of large areas of *talh*. A possible explanation may have been that in 1930 locusts ate off all the grass and so there were only a few, small fires the next year and the young trees got a good start.

I was interested in the agricultural possibilities of this area. The planned agricultural settlements were to have three strips and rotations: Years 1–6, agriculture; years 7–12, young acacias, with cattle and sheep allowed in among them; years 13–18, bigger acacias with camels and goats allowed in, and providing timber for housing needs.

I passed through some grass which was excellently suited for *hareig* (burning off). The best type was called *anis* and possessed the desirable quality of lying over. The feathery grass was not so good. *Hareig* was done by protecting grass from burning by means of fire-lines for three years and then burning it off in the fourth year when the young grass was just beginning to come through. If too wet and too late, the burn-off would not be effective. If too early, germination would not be complete. It followed that the crop sown would be late and if *dura* was sown it would still be in the milky state when the birds arrived and liable to suffer heavily. The year after the burning of the grass was called *kamadob*.

The new scheme was to grow *simsim* in the fourth year, after burning, as it was a late crop and to plant an early *dura* crop in the *kamadob* which would then be hard before the birds arrived.

The new scheme of *hareig* visualised grids of permanent fire-lines, 80 yards wide, made with two cuts of a hay cutter, one up and one down, and 80 yards apart. The area in between was for subsequent burning-off.

Ground which was burnt accidentally was called *mahal*. It had a poor growth of grass and weeds in the first year after the burning but could carry a fair crop of *dura*. Nomads deliberately fired areas to produce good grass in the second season after the fire, their purpose being to obtain good grazing and freedom from ticks. The first season's growth of grass for pasture on *mahal* would be poor.

The last mile or so to Jebel Tozi was across open plain. The *jebel* had twin saw-tooth peaks and a small detached peak. They rose about 100 feet from a plain as flat as a pancake. There was a small *hafir* (reservoir) at the base and the site had every sign of having been occupied over many hundreds of years. Climbing the *jebel* produced a splendid view over grass and open forest which appeared to be mainly gum. *Jebels* protruded from the plain in most directions.

I discussed with a local chief the terrain between Jebel Tozi and each of the other peaks. I could obtain no information of deep *khors* or other obstacles and it seemed probable that a flat direct trace from Singa via Dar Agil to Wad-en-Nail could be found.

The night spent at Wad-en-Nail was pleasant. The only disturbance was the lorries using the road northwards by night. Doubtless the night air suited their venerable engines — and darkness cloaked illicit movement of rationed goods!

WAD-EN-NAIL TO ROSEIRES

Next day we were packed up and away soon after 08.00 hours. The day's run followed the river closely and was unsuitable for rail location. It was, in fact, unsuitable for a road and one on an improved alignment further inland was under construction.

Our first leg was of 9 miles to Galgani. The road started on alluvial soil which stands up well to heavy diesel transport. We passed through the remains of *dukhn* (bullrush millet) cultivation; in these parts they sowed *dukhn* to extract the last bit of energy from lighter soil after it would no longer carry *dura*. The road dropped down 20 feet into Khor Malwiya and quickly climbed out again, and then joined the telegraph line. Every now and then we passed an Egyptian Irrigation Department bench-mark. The soil changed to cotton soil and new trees began to make their appearance.

It is helpful to know the names of various trees. My companion regarded it as one of the first duties of a District Commissioner and instanced an example. He had instructed a new Assistant District Commissioner to start learning names. Within a week the translator brought in a tiny piece of paper carrying a number of seals, saying it meant just nothing at all. Disney saw it was a list of trees and concerned the boundaries of a piece of land. The sheiks had walked the bounds from trees to tree and recorded them in Darfur names which meant nothing at all to the translator.

One of the trees was new to me the *leiyun* which grew rather like a chestnut and carried a cluster of small round fruits at the end of the bough. We dropped down into two more depressions and in the second found another of those delightful patches of sunt which made ideal camping spots.

Galgani was at mile 105. It was a large and entirely Fellata settlement with a Sultan. It had a superior *suk* of 20 brick-built shops. Several *assaras* (oil seed grinders) were at work, and *ful sudani* was an additional commodity in this area. Galgani was laid out with wide streets to minimise fire risk and was one of the few villages with trees planted and cared for by private enterprise. At the south end of the village the trace for the new road to Sereyu took off. The survey was rather a stout effort on the part of a Gordon College boy on vacation in the summer of 1945. He got on to camels with camp gear and instruments and ran a very creditable line through. At this time of the year able-bodied males at home in Galani were few on account the financial attraction of picking cotton in the Gezira.

As we left Galgani two more trees made their first appearance both of them very beautiful with flower. They were the *khash-khash azraq* with its lilac-like flower and the common *khash-khash* with flowers of light and dark mauve.

One of the first views after Galgani was of Jebels Okalma and Kardos, almost in line, with Galgani Forest reserve in the foreground. We passed some more *dukhn* cultivation. The road led through a small thicket of *hashab* gum and we stopped to look at the process of gum-growing. The *hashab* is tapped by making a cut in the bark fairly low down with an axe, prising up the bark and giving a long upward tear. In the course of time large blobs of white gum exude from the scar, as big as a golf ball and bigger. Small trees were tapped from four to ten years old. The crop was worth about a million pounds a year to the Sudan. The product was used for Rowntree's gums, high-class printing and stiffening straw hats. The best gum was grown between the twelfth and thirteenth parallels. The legend of the forest with jewels on the trees was probably a picture of the sun shining through a gum forest.

Our road threaded its way up and down with some of the declivities as much as 40 feet deep. New trees included the *selag* which looked rather like a birch. *Tebeldis* were by this time fairly common, great obese growths which were rather sinister. The pith round the seeds was said to be rich in cream of tartar. In Kordofan they were hollowed out and used as water tanks, but here no such use was made of them and they were troublesome to cut up.

Soon we came to the village of Ahmar Mogi on the left and the first *terter* trees with their pinky bark, rather like a plane, and *babonus* (ebony) with its lightish green leaves. There was a fine view of Abu Hagar Forest across the river just before we dropped down into the newly dug *maiya* of Abdel Khallag. On the edge of the *maiya* was a plantation of *adas* (lentils) and a quantity of maize. The *maiya* bed provided some excellent grazing for cattle, and carried some sunt which shaded the road. The village of Abdel Khallag was a Fellata settlement.

The road then breasted a rise and we passed a number of people carrying freshly cut *zaaf*. From here onwards the dom palms were very much clipped. *Zaaf* was laid out in the sun to dry. In the early rains the woods were a mass of bulbs which the natives regarded as edible, giving them the name *basal el kelb* (dog's onion). The bulbs generally grow in groups of three and when dug up they usually consisted of one old and *afin*, (stinking) one fit to eat and one too small. They would almost always replant the small one to let it grow on for another day.

At mile 117 came the boundary between the Rufaa el Hoi and the Fung Kingdom; it was marked by a curiously bent rail. A bit further on we came to the village of Merabi on the left. And so we drove on through very pretty country, up and down and past a group of *kapoks*. These cotton trees were once very popular in the Fung until it was decided that they harboured stainer bug which was a menace to Gezira cotton. The destruction of the *kapok* trees was demanded. The reply of the Governor, Dupuis, on hearing this, lives on: 'We like our kapok trees better than our entomologists. They'll stay!'

The road surface as we journeyed towards Roseires improved. The district owned two disc harrows and the quality of the surface largely depended on doing the work when the ground was at the right consistency. Obviously it was impossible with animal haulage to do the whole amount of work in that period. As the Roseires 'ploughman' drank less heavily than the Singa one, here the roads are better. We passed through some stretches of *talh* and remnants of *simsim* cultivation and, in open woods, a lot of *khash-khash* in flower.

Again we dropped down into a depression, to Abu Kuk Forest, and the shade was pleasant among the sunt and dom palms. Some of the *tebeldis* appeared to be pollarded. In Kordofan this custom was followed to make them grow straighter and provide a better tank — but the reason for such action here was not clear.

At Sereyu we saw the end of the new trace from Galgani. Near the road was a particularly fine *goo-goo,* about two-thirds full of maize heads. Maize was always stored on the cob until required. Sereyu had a *suk* of 15 shops and was a marketing centre for a grade of *simsim* which had a high oil yield and was keenly sought after.

Shortly after the village there was another by-pass which avoided Disa, a spot beloved of lion-hunters. We were the first convoy to use it. The route was pretty but still too up and down for a railway.

Nevertheless there were indications that much flatter country existed a bit further in. *Leiyun* trees became very numerous. A mass of *khash-khash* was a beautiful sight and we passed the first gardenia tree, still in flower and with a lovely scent. After a while and skirting Disa Forest we joined the old road. Bird life was well represented; numerous grey hornbills with their distinctive flight, gloriously multi-coloured Abyssinian rollers and blue-black tree creepers. It was significant that we did not pass a single lorry during the day's run; night was more suited to their activities.

We were now nearing Roseires, and before dropping down from the higher ground to which we had worked our way, we had our first view of Jebel Gerri which lay to the east of Roseires. It was a bamboo reserve, being the source nearest to Khartoum and was cut on a three-year rotation. We then dropped down and wended our way through eroded hillocks to reach the river bank opposite Roseires. Here were a number of corrugated iron warehouses where the trade goods, largely salt and cotton piece goods, were held for trade with Abyssinia. The heavy stuff like salt was brought up by steamer during the flood for on-carry by lorry during the winter in exchange, mainly for coffee, at Kurmuk. Here too was a small Sudan Customs Post. Trade with Abyssinia was funnelled through Geissan or Kurmuk. The Sudan Government preferred the latter and encouraged it at the expense of the former.

Turning left, a further 200 yards brought us to the Rest House at mile 155½ and 12.25 hours. We settled in and conversation at lunch turned on whether the present staff of Government were quite as peculiar as those of 15–20 years ago.

After lunch and a short shut-eye we were ready for the afternoon's excursion. It was almost in the nature of a religious observance for visitors to Roseires to be taken, weather permitting, to the Damazin Gorge and whatever the state of the river the scene was always beautiful. Roseires was the limit of navigation of, at least, the Sudan portion of the Blue Nile. For seven miles upstream there extended an area of cataract, known as the Damazin Gorge. Although in 1937 a small motor launch was manhandled through the Gorge with considerable difficulty at dead low river, the Gorge represented a complete obstruction. We were ferried over to the other side and at 15.30 hours met our host, District Commissioner Lindsay. Our transport was the *merkaz* lorry as it was not considered worthwhile to ferry one of our cars across. We made ourselves comfortable for the half-hour drive over rough roads. Having threaded its way through the town the road twisted away to the south. There were some promising market gardens along a branch of the river, whilst a 6-inch pump scheme had just been started on one of the islands. *Tebeldis* trees were everywhere. After a while the road forked away to the right and, after crossing the aerodrome, which was bombed several times during the war, made its way down to the river edge in the middle of the Gorge. The scene was lovely, in many ways prettier than when the river was in flood and nearly all the rocks were covered with heavily silt-laden water. This time the water was clear, there were long sandy beaches, and the rocks, polished by the water and turned purple by the sun, towered out of the water which flowed fairly quickly. Fishing at this time of year was excellent. It was altogether a pleasant outing.

ROSEIRES TO WISKO

Looking down the Blue Nile at dawn with the first rays of sun touching the little promontory of Abu Ramad was a sight not easily to be forgotten.

During breakfast Mek Hassan called he was an intresting character. He was a direct descendant in the main line of Sultans of Sennar from Amara Dunkas who founded the Dynasty about 1540. As 'Nazir of the Fung Gism', he had an independent budget of about £20,000 and contributed about £10,000 back to Government. He still had the original *nahass* ceremonial drum, with Amara Dunkas' name on it, and beat it on occasion, such as VJ Day. He was a character of some importance!

We were under way soon after 08.00 hours, down the avenue and past the piles of salt. Salt was the most popular trade article to Abyssinia at that time, wresting pride of place from cotton piece goods owing to salt having been cornered by the Imperial Black Market. We passed the Customs Post and climbed out through the eroded gullies to the plateau which was well covered with *talh*. There were small ups and downs but the going was quite good. We were in an area of which the local Forestry Officer had remarked in connection with the indigenous trees 'The Sterculia-Combretium association is commercially uninteresting but connotes conditions suitable for *neem* growing'. Along the river bank and on the islands at the end of the gorge the locals raised tobacco both the short kind, *tombac*, and the taller variety, *gumsha*, and they were great *bursh*-makers.

At mile 166½, before dropping down into a khor bed, we got a good view of Jebel Maba ahead with its long flat top. The *khor* bed was about a mile across and during the war formed the advanced base of one of our defence units. At the village of Kharaba, mile 168, we turned right, the road going on to Geissan. The *tukls* from now on had wattled sides, generally of split bamboo.

Jebel Gargarda was now in sight ahead, a rounded hill with tree-clad slopes. At the village on the south side was a go-ahead community growing a good type *dura* and considered worthy of encouragement. The Ingessana Hills area got rain in April so their *hafirs* had to carry them over from December to March and they usually did so. The soil as we approached the *jebel* was chocolate-coloured and considered very good for growing grain. The predominating tree was now the *habil* which, after burning, was now putting out fresh light green leaves. On our right we passed Jebel Bamsak and shortly afterwards debouched on to the edge of a plain with a magnificent view of boulder strewn hills rising from a wide expanse of golden grass. The main massif of the Ingessana Hills lay to the left of centre. Jebel Bamsak was sharp right.

The grass was all *anis*, the type best suited for burning-off, and similar conditions were said to exist southward for at least 20 miles to Khor Uffat. It was a possible area for agricultural development and particularly mechanised agriculture. I asked from whence labour could be obtained because it was obviously of little profit just to move people from cultivating on one spot to make them cultivate another when additional transport facilities would be required at the new spot.

There was a steady flow of slaves from Abyssinia who were freed on arrival in the Sudan and settled in villages along the Blue Nile between the mouth of Khor Uffat and Abu Sheneina. These settlements were steadily increasing, both from new arrivals and breeding. They were industrious and adaptable and given water on the plain would be keen to undertake cultivation there. There was at present good cultivation along the banks of Khor Uffat but the elephants were causing enormous damage. The elephants had vacated the Dinder National Park because the poachers made it too hot for them. Recently the police lost one camel, killed whilst capturing five poachers and some Italian Anti-Personnel bombs. It was hoped that the brands on the poachers' camels would lead to the discovery of the true owners. The poachers had thrown a bomb at the Assistant District Commissioner and killed a Police Officer in the previous year. It was desirable to have more elephants and less poachers in the National Park.

There was quite a lot in the choice of late-maturing *duras* for these heavy cotton soil plains. As we drove across we saw some lovely heads not yet ready for cutting. For the very heavy soil they used a slow-maturing type, planted late, named *butalig*. It had a feathery, open head some 18 inches long and was not ripe when we passed and probably would not be matured till March. The less heavy soil was sown to *tilling* which was not quite so late. Most of the grass was *anis* with an occasional patch of the feathery *lanzura* which stood up and did not give as clean a burn-off.

By this time we were approaching Jebel Bagis, a typical rounded hill, boulder-strewn and covered with dom palms and *gemeiza*. Round the base was a large grove of *tebeldis*. The road wound between Jebel Bagis on the right and Jebel Kilgo on the left, there being perhaps 200 yards between them. In the gap was a little Rest House, a point of strategic importance during the war. At the foot of both *jebels* were a number of *hafirs*. We looked round and under a tree I picked up several red seeds about three-eighths of an inch long with a black spot. They were known as *Habb-el-Arus* or Brides' Beads, and had been used since the dawn of time for weighing gold.

After a quarter of an hour's stop we set out hugging the side of Jebel Kilgu and stopped to inspect in detail one of the *hafirs*. With hills composed largely of piled boulders the run-off was reasonably free of sediment and it was possible to make more tidy contraptions. Coming to the end of the *jebel* we struck out across the plain for the nearest corner of the Ingessana Hills proper, near Bubuk. Our road led through *soufar* trees. We were looking forward to seeing the Ingessana, who were receptive to new ideas.

As we made for the end of the massif, Jebel Buk, our immediate objective came in sight. We crossed some small *khors* and reached Bubuk Fork. The road went straight on to Wisko, where, we proposed to spend the night, but we made a deviation to the right to Jebel Buk, along the road which led west, right across to the White Nile at Renk. According to the aneroid we had risen 570 feet since leaving Kharaba. We now skirted the base of the Ingessanas keeping them on our left hand. The going was rough over chocolate

WHEELS AND PADDLES IN THE SUDAN

soil. As we were running about 100 yards from the base of the hills *khors* were fairly frequent but not wide. We overtook a party of 30 Ingessana women and boys, carrying loads in gourds suspended by netting from a pole carried across the shoulder. Loads went flying and it took 15 minutes to restore confidence. The Ingessana handshake is the squeeze of a finger between the first finger and thumb.

It was interesting to see that the hillsides were terraced, a relic of soil conservation of many years ago. Small *hafirs* abounded on all sides but all were dry. The frankincense tree, *luban* or *terak-terak*, came into prominence here. It was curiously shaped, tending to a flat top with bunches of pinky-purple buds at the ends of the branches. Its wood burnt with a pleasant aromatic smell, but its gum, like so many Sudan products, just missed being attractive to traders in frankincense. It had a leaf like the ash. A small Rest House at Gebenit was passed on our left and some two miles further on we left the main massif and struck out for Jebel Buk, 7 miles away.

The chocolate-coloured soil was soon left behind and we passed on to the cotton soil and through trees in grass. There were some good stands of *dura* along the roadside and a small plot of rain-grown cotton. Whilst the Ingessana grew late maturing *duras* in the plain, round their houses in the hills they planted some *feterita* type *dura*. This could not mature on account of the rain and so they cut off the heads and dried them in their houses. It was a sort of catch crop to keep them going until the main crop arrived. When we struck the base of Jebel Buk we circled round leaving the *jebel* on the right hand. The main village was soon reached, with some two or three shops, but we carried on to a smaller village on the west side from which a track ascended the *jebel* where we arrived at 12.10 hours. Altitude by aneroid was 540 feet above Kahraba.

Guides were soon forthcoming and we set off up the *jebel*. The climb was nothing more than a hot scramble, but a path had to be cleared of leaves and grass. A sharp rise of perhaps 50 feet brought us to a small village. The *tukls* and *goo-goos* were made of thin mud walls. An elementary cotton gin was standing outside one of the houses and stones for grinding corn were let into the ground in batteries of three. Another 50 feet and we came to a larger village on a saddle between the two peaks, with a small *hafir* which, according to the locals, still had sufficient water in it to drown a camel. So far we had been along well-used tracks. From this point our guides had to clear a way. There was some discussion as to the best route, for the hill was not often climbed. At length the line was decided upon and off we went. I had taken the precaution to put on rubber-soled shoes and it proved worth while. With a scramble and a bit of mutual help, in which the guides were most solicitous for my welfare, we soon reached the top, short of wind and rather moist. A fine view awaited us and oranges provided welcome refreshment. By aneroid the summit was 345 feet above the base. An enormous expanse of grass and open trees lay before us stretching away to the west to Jebel Gule and to the various outlying hills of the Ingessanas to the south and east. We gathered that a line of approach from the north-east, going on to the south, through the gap between Jebel Ahmar and Jebel Balmut might be a possible location for a railway. The downward journey was certainly easier than the climb and lunch very welcome on our arrival at the foot.

The shade of the *tebeldi* was so attractive that no one was really in a hurry to resume the journey. However, we left at 14.18 hours to retrace our steps to Bubuk Fork. Where we expected to find the other station wagon and lorry in camp as they had not accompanied us to Jebel Buk. The land immediately round the base of Jebel Buk was very worked out. Springing up on it was a thorny bush called *la'ut* which seemed to delight in exhausted land and kept out the animals allowing better trees to get a start. We did the 18-odd miles back to Bubuk Fork in a little over an hour.

We were now making for Wisko. The original station in the Ingessana Hills was called Soda. A change of station was required and the new site needed a name. Whisky was half-humorously proposed; it stuck and has passed into geography as Wisko. The first village we passed was full of pigs, which were common in the Ingessana Hills. After 3 miles we entered a large amphitheatre in the hills and then after about the same distance we came to the village of Merik with a Rest House. The village up to a short while ago had a sub-grade school but it had been seen off by a devil!

We continued over some uneven ground, preparatory to the next obstacle which called for skilled driving. Some 3 miles from Wisko was a steeply ascending pass known as the *mintig*. It was in two pieces, with a soft surface at the bottom, and allowed no run to be taken. If one was aware of its existence it was nothing very terrible but to come on it unawares generally put a driver into difficulties. It was known to all our drivers and we safely surmounted it. The remaining run to Wisko, mile 208, was quickly covered and we drew up at the Rest House at 16.10 hours. The aneroid indicated a height of about 2,500 feet.

Wisko was delightfully cool and after a wash and tea we went down to the *suk*. There were about 12 shops. Gum, grain and cotton seemed to be the main export commodities with nicely made wooden bowls about 12 to 15 inches in diameter and 1 inch thick. There was a court house and a busy dispensary. Water supply was quite good.

Our quarters were excellent and we spent a restful evening among the Ingessana. They totalled about 25,000 men, women and children and have a relatively high density of population per square mile of territory by Sudan standards. Their unit was another confederation of seven hills — Togo, Tabi, Tagha, Torda, Kurban, Gebanit and Jegu — ruled over by seven *Meks* who carried the title of Aur.

They had managed to maintain their existence more or less inviolate, largely owing to their hill positions. They had never been enslaved. Their colouring was shining black. The men had bobbed

Wisko suk

hair which was frequently anointed with white fat. They wore bead necklaces and kilts of homespun, kept up by a leather belt. On their left arm or shoulder was usually a reticule made of monkey or serval-cat skin and over their right shoulder typically a *colbeita* or throwing knife. Their womenfolk wore skirts of homespun and in party rig two triangles of chain mail, apex upwards, covering each breast, slung from a necklace. They carried their loads in baskets slung from a pole.

WISKO TO KURMUK

Next day we were under way by 08.30 hours and speeding along the road to Kurmuk. We were still in the amphitheatre of the hills and after about 4 miles dropped down into a biggish *khor*, Khor Doleib, which threaded its way through a large dom palm thicket. In the bed were a number of wells with people drawing water and preparing *dura* for *merissa*-making. For the latter the women made a hemispherical hole in damp sand, spread the *dura* thinly over the greater part of the surface, covered with a layer of leaves and a final layer of wet sand. The local name for the spot was Toga.

The soil varied between black cotton and chocolate-coloured alluvial in alternating patches as we gradually made our way out of the hills. Jebel Burka, a tree-clad hill, lay right ahead and before long we were debouching out on to the cotton soil plain and leaving the Ingessana Hills behind us.

The road led on towards Jebel Danderu with other hills on the horizon through a welter of low burnt trees. The surface was not bad and we made good time. We crossed Khor Miska which actually flowed to the west and not as shown on the map. At mile 226 we reached the base of Jebel Danderu running for a while with it on our right, then passing through the hills we skirted the other side of the remainder coming to the Rest House at the far end.

New hills were constantly coming into view and the road developed rather into 'witching waves'. Much of the grass had been burnt and whole lengths of the country formed a sort of blasted heath. We were back again on chocolate-coloured soil. Jebel Kukuli with its 'Cap of Liberty' profile was in sight in the distance ahead and then Jebel Beni Shako 5 miles away with its great smooth dome.

The road was crossed by some small but deep *khors* and was now

WHEELS AND PADDLES IN THE SUDAN

Ingessana girls

Ingessana man with 'colbeita'

almost entirely on cotton soil. Before dropping down a small hill to approach Jebel Beni Shako we had a fine panoramic view with isolated hills showing on the horizon. Jebel Beni Shako — one wonders at the origin of the name — terminated in a smooth dome of igneous rock. It was inhabited by Hamegs who were coal-black and a lower type than the Ingessana. Their main village was on a saddle rather more than half way up and a stiff climb. Their pigs could not get down and had to have their water carried up to them. From the road it formed a striking picture.

We continued, up and down and through bamboos in some of the *khor* beds. The view of the mountains of Abyssinia was at times impressive despite the haze. The peaks of Beni Shangul were striking in the distance.

We never actually touched Jebel Kukuli leaving it away on the right and after crossing Khor Gulbus, a very pleasant camping spot, we made our way to Jebel Tornasi — sacred hill of the Hamegs. Its height was given on the map as 4,100 feet. It was tree clad. Visiting was discouraged locally and it was considered as endowed with all sorts of ju-ju. There was, of course, a luminous snake which was always the first deterrent. The branch of the tribe who presided over these rituals was reduced with only a few left. Rumour said that there were supplies of running water up in the *jebel*. Their village was extraordinarily well camouflaged and blended into the hill-side remarkably well.

Immediately to the south of Jebel Tornasi lay Jebel Fasulia, with candelabra trees and the village of Keili at its foot, at mile 250. Keili was the capital of a small Fung Kingdom, the Fung only now existing as a ruling caste. Keili had an unapproved dispensary set up by the Sudanese acting Province Medical Inspector because he felt that something was required. It was an excellent example of action and, moreover, was staffed by a local. At the cross-roads of Keili was also a 'corner-house', a further token of progress. Brick kilns were hard at work producing bricks for four more wells which the *Mek* was paying for with his own money.

Gold mining or washing was carried out round Keili and nuggets were sometimes found by cracking open large pebbles in gold-bearing streams. Any nuggets found round Keili were the perquisite of the *Mek* and, in return, he provided shrouds for all his people when they died.

Whilst at Keili we heard that there was rather a disturbing

outbreak of some illness in one of the neighbouring hills with a number of fatalities. The Medical Assistant from Kurmuk had gone up to endeavour to find out the cause.

We stopped at Keili for about half-an-hour and then, work and civilities completed, we got on our way. Crossing many little *khors* we came next into the Berta country which extended along the Blue Nile and all the way along the frontier from the Blue Nile to the Yabus. There were also Berta on the other side of the frontier. All those in Abyssinia were slaves and those in the area which was now the Sudan had been raided for centuries. Enslaved Berta dressed as poor Arabs. Their women wore black, white, red and yellow beads in their hair and red bead elbow bangles. They carried their loads in two fern baskets on a bamboo pole. Gourds of water were normally carried on the shoulder.

Before long Jebel Kurmuk was in sight, but the road continued to be rough and up and down through trees. At mile 259½ the road forked back to Geissan but we ran on across a terrible blasted heath and a mile and a half further on the road crossed, almost without it being noticed, the watershed between the Blue Nile and the White Nile. After another 200 yards we came to Khor Ahmar, a considerable stream in the rains, flowing away to the west and to be met again later on. At the *khor* there was a Rest House and fine views away to the east of the Abyssinian Mountains and the Beni Shangul peaks. This part was almost without *tebeldis* but the other trees were doing their best by putting forth fresh shoots after the fierce burning. Bamboos were quite common and blue starlings flitted about everywhere.

Jebel Kurmuk now lay 9 miles away. Before long we touched the north corner and skirted the east side. We were only a few hundred yards from the Abyssinian frontier. Almost the first building was the little Customs Post and then came the *suk* of 30 brick-built shops, the hospital and other Government buildings in a wired enclosure. We took our choice of two Rest Houses and were glad to get into camp.

The afternoon was rather warm but at 16.30 hours we set off to see the sights. The hospital was in the course of being re-thatched. It was a co-operative effort by 50 to 60 chaps from a Berta village who had undertaken the job for a certain sum. Whilst we were there Doctor Sayed, the acting Province Medical Officer, drove up. He had come non-stop from Sennar — 272½ miles — on hearing of the outbreak at Keili.

We also saw the police post, the Wireless Station, office for visiting District Commissioner and a *tebeldi* tree. The photo of this tree is probably the most widely published after the Californian Redwood! At the base of the trunk was a doorway and inside a storeroom. It was used as an advert for Guinness — and suggested that whereas the *tebeldi* in Kordofan was used to store water, the officials at Kurmuk had found a better use for theirs!

We enquired in the *suk* about the rate at which coffee was being brought in and the prospects for trade. Export from Abyssinia was always difficult for the exporter, with many obstacles, both official and local. Nevertheless there was a steady flow of coffee which nearly met all the needs of the Blue Nile Province.

I wanted particularly to find out about gold sales. In a small way there was quite a bit of gold handled here. The largest Greek merchant told me that he bought from 4 to 6 ounces per day and probably 15 to 20 ounces were bought in the *suk* daily. On 7 February 1946 the prices were as follows:

Buying: per oz of 30 grammes £18.200

Selling at Omdurman: per oz of 32 grammes £E19.650

Why should gold fetch a price so greatly in excess of the Johannesburg price? This merchant said that he had never handled a nugget larger than a currant. I was surprised at this after what I had myself seen at Roseires during former visits. The shops were well stocked and my wife purchased several small things which she had not seen for some time.

We continued our walk round by the Customs Post and the sub-grade School for boys, and returned to the Rest House for tea. Very shortly Doctor Sayed turned up to see his patient. He diagnosed the complaint as dysentery and fortunately had with him sufficient sulphoguanidine. Pam was well dosed and it was hoped that rest for a day or two would make her fit to travel. Kurmuk had a bad reputation for disturbed nights with a wind tearing round the *jebel* all night. It was at its worst in cooler weather, after the grass and been burned-off. We went to bed prepared for the worst. I in fact had an excellent night in the open. That of the family was not so peaceful.

A DIVERSION TO WADEGA

Next day I set off with Disney at 07.00 hours for Wadega. It was a beautiful morning with the Abyssinian Mountains covered in mist. We took the road to the south-west over flat cotton soil. Jebel Faragamindo lay ahead and was suggested as a possible site for growing tung oil trees. Just before turning right to Wadega after 6 miles the road dropped down into Khor Malagine, an obstacle 200 yards across and 50 feet deep, the bottom of the bed being 40 yards across.

The road to Wadega led first of all practically due west towards Jebel Mafwa. It ran on chocolate-coloured soil over easy up and down grades through trees in grass. The colour of the soil changed in places almost to the red of Devon.

The *jebel* was in the heart of the Hill Barun country. These natives lived mainly on four hills, Kurmuk, Jerok, Maiak and Mafwa. They were very independent and retired into their hills at the least provocation. When Government first wished to discuss matters with them the Barun retreated up into their hills. McLarèn, the District Commissioner at the time, played his bagpipes and marched round and round the foot of the hill, skirling for all he was worth. After a while the Barun came down — they could stand it no longer!

After another 6 miles and a few ups and downs we reached Jebel Mafwa, passing a number of gardenia trees — their wood provided the white handles for Arab knives, known as *Abu-um-gawi*. We turned left to skirt the base of the *jebel* which sheltered a fine grove of *tebeldis*. The hillside was covered by smaller *tebeldis;* and must have been very pretty in the rains when all the trees had light green leaves with large creamy-white flowers. We stopped for 25 minutes at a fine *hafir* (reservoir) on the west side of the *jebel*. It was a new effort and said to hold 7,000 cubic metres. It had been constructed at a cost of only £15 so was very good value. It was, however, dry at that moment.

The Barun of Jebels Mafwa and Maiak were still real hill-dwellers with large caves. These caves were originally used against the Abyssinian invaders. There were certain broad differentiations between hill and plain dwellers in these parts. No hill-dweller, but all plain dwellers, carried bows and arrows. The leather what-not — a skin used for pants — was mainly worn by hill-dwellers as a seat protection on hot rocks and was called a *furwa*. It was normally worn hanging loose at the back. Their womenfolk wore ropes of green beads round their necks and a small apron.

Having finished our investigation of the *hafir* we set out for Wadega, 9 miles distant, at 08.35 hours. Our road lay across a much burned flat cotton soil plain which had only very few remaining trees.

To the right, Jebels Maiak and Eiro. As we progressed we came into open woods with lots of the birch-like *selags*. The soil changed to chocolate and gravelly and about half-way a shady *khor* called us to breakfast. We got under way again just before 10.00 hours, the road on chocolate soil slightly falling through open scrub. There were no folk walking along the road and only an occasional gazelle to be seen. Two miles before reaching Wadega we passed Jebel Fombulij covered with frankincense trees, and threading our way through open woods, came to a dry swamp. We dropped down some 20 feet to cross an old friend, Khor Ahmar, 40 yards wide in its bed. This *khor* bed provided permanent water by wells for Wadega which we reached at 10.07 hours. Height by aneroid 2,160 feet.

Wadega was a busy little spot. It had one brick shop and half-a-dozen others and was a collecting centre for surplus grain for export. There were several *assaras*. The southern migration of the Rufaa-el-Hoi extended to the country to west and south of Wadega and their affairs were in the hands of El Nur Riheima who was based at Wadega. These migrating Arabs were a problem as they were not by nature respecters of other peoples' rights though very insistent on what they regarded as their own. They needed a strong hand and in El Nur Riheima it seemed to me they had a real master.

The tribe in this area was the Jum-Jum. They lived round Jebels Tungya and Terter and at Wadega. Their wits had been sharpened by constant contact with Arabs. The males were pink-haired, by application of fat and coloured earth. Their women wore a thick skein of string round their waist and had shaven heads. They carried enormous baskets on their heads.

We set off for Jebel Wadega to get a birds-eye view of the countryside. It was 2 miles away with a fine grove of *tebeldis* at base. As usual some discussion took place as to the best route of ascent. The granite hill was of smooth bare rock, boulders and lots of grass. The instruments we carried to the top, compass, binoculars, aneroid and camera and maps, much impressed the *nass*. I had carried all the instruments up but our guides insisted on relieving me of them for the descent as they felt sure that in my case it was likely to be accelerated involuntarily. They certainly took such care of me that we got down quickly and safely.

Back at Wadega, El Nur Riheima told us that he had applied for a licence to shoot elephant. We asked him for what purpose and he said to get some fat for his folk. We raised our eyebrows for the Arabs wallowed in fat produced from their herds. I pointed out that a licence fee would cost £15 and that was rather a high price for fat. We felt that what he was really after was the ivory. In due course he was to get his licence.

An hour passed pleasantly, and we rose to depart. Discreet enquiry was made as to whether I would accept a 4-gallon tin of *semn* (native butter). The answer was in the negative. The merchant then presented me with two finely woven leather bound *bursh* mats, nice examples of local handicraft, made by the women, probably an euphemism for slaves, of his household. We said our farewells and set off for Kurmuk, arriving as the police guard was striking 14.00 hours.

My last remaining job here was to visit the garden which was the special pride of the Police Inspector. We had a date with him for 16.30 hours and noted the number of house-owners at Kurmuk who were trying to grow *ingil* hedges, started from wild plants growing on the *jebels*. It was a practically leafless plant, poisonous to goats, which with clipping grew so dense as to become impenetrable. We arrived at the garden on time and found it was an acre in area and newly constructed since the war, when the old one had died of neglect. It had been planted up with citrus and mangoes. It was already producing bananas and paw-paw. There was a good selection of vegetables but the Sol complained of the difficulty in obtaining seeds. Watering was by *shadoof* from a big shallow well. We complimented the *Sol* on his efforts which did him great credit.

Doctor Sayed came round after tea to see his patient. She was progressing excellently and demanded a poached egg for supper. Professional caution caused him rather to frown at our suggestion of setting out the next morning — and in deference to him the actual decision was left to the morning but my wife was quite sure that recovery would be rapid. We turned in wondering what sort of a night lay ahead of us. The bad reputation of Kurmuk had been deeply impressed upon us before we arrived. All was peace.

WHEELS AND PADDLES IN THE SUDAN

KURMUK TO YABUS BRIDGE

My wife's prognosis had been correct. Pam was almost herself and we decided to travel. The journey was not a long one and we had anyhow proposed to have the following day as a holiday and felt that all would enjoy it more at the Yabus with its running water. Camp was quickly packed up and we planned to have breakfast half-way, at a convenient Rest House at Ora.

We set off at 07.05 hours along the same road as the previous day, not turning off at the Wadega turn. The going was undulating over chocolate soil. A mile beyond the Wadega turn, a road took off left to Jebel Jerok, the south slopes of which had a curious rock formation which gave a silhouette of 'the elephants and children, pa, ma and two little ones' climbing the hill in single file. The countryside was open trees and cultivation. A bataleur eagle surveyed our passing. Almost simultaneously we saw ground squirrels and a pair of ground hornbills. By native reckoning those were good omens.

The going changed to cotton soil, but continued quite good going through small trees. There were fine views of the Abyssinian Mountains away to the left with Jebel Gangan very much in evidence. After 12 miles we came to three Berta villages of settled freed slaves. These were called Deim Mansur, Amara (=Settlement) Gedima and Amara Gedida. All Berta were so abject that it was generally difficult to get them to speak up and obtain their freedom though there were signs that this was beginning to change.

About 15 miles from Kurmuk the road forked giving choice of route to Ora. We took the right and 4 miles further on came to Khor Abu Seifein, a fair-sized stream in the rains. The story goes that in the early days an Egyptian mamur, riding a mule, with a large sword hung at each side of the saddle, came to this *khor* during the rains. He refused to cross the ankle-deep water and waited till the *khor* ran dry. He is still remembered.

We were now about 5 miles from Ora. The District Office was originally at Keili but was moved to Kurmuk simply because the army had camped there. It ought to have been sited at Ora which was much more pleasant, had no howling wind — but caught any breeze which blew along its north to south valley — and had running water. The chance was missed in 1930 and again after the Italian occupation.

The way into Ora, at mile 295, lay between Jebel Horo on the left and Jebel Ora on the right. The approach was through trees to a large cleanly swept square. In the middle was a fine Rest House standing on a plinth, approached up a ramp. The roof was made of bamboos, accurately spaced and tidily finished. The walls were of bamboo walling plastered with mud inside and out. Ora was renowned for its Omda's hospitality and his fine products of lemonade, tea and coffee.

In the square outside was a fine *teraya* tree, rather like a witch elm, a court-house and a dispensary. We spent an hour in Ora, and left at 09.30 hours. The road led past various gardens and — mark this! — through a real water splash. There followed a short sharp climb out of the valley to the west and then the road continued in an undulating fashion through a belt of frankincense trees.

Away due east of Ora stood Jebel Faragamindo, already mentioned as a possible spot for tung oil trees. It formerly was used as a high pasturage for cattle but had ceased to be popular since it became the alleged home of a huge luminous snake!

Jebel Chali soon became visible ahead and 5 miles after leaving Ora we turned right to Chali. Our purpose was to visit a station of the Sudan Interior Mission. A mile down the road was the village of Montesoro, a settlement of freed slaves who once belonged to Sitt Amna, the Queen of the Slave Trade and wife of the chief of Beni Shangul. She was tried at Kosti in 1928 and received seven years. Then, after another mile and a half, the road crossed Khor Bunda where we entered the Upper Nile Province and led on through wooded country. After a while we were joined by a direct road from Kurmuk and soon reached Chali 'Town' which consisted of little more than one merchant's shop. One of the missionaries — Reverend Forsburg — was down at the shop and he accompanied us back to the Mission, about a mile away on higher ground. There we met the rest of the personnel. The station was rather depressing. One of the houses was having a new roof fitted and almost nothing had been done about planting trees or making a garden. The hospitality, however, was impressive, especially the ice cream. The Fosburgs' two small boys were both down with dysentery and although they had a supply of sulphoguanadine they were not aware of the correct dose; we could at least give them information from our experience.

We were soon back at the main road and turned south for the Yabus. Almost immediately we came to Jebel Montesoro on the left and two miles further on, situated on rocks to the left was the site of Sitt Amna's castle, also called Montesoro. The *suk* at Montesoro was under the large *aradeiba* tree to the right of the road.

There were a number of *khors* crossing the road owing to the proximity of the *jebels*. At the village of Wad Gumaa, an alternative route to the Yabus Bridge took off to the left but we carried on across a blasted heath to pass between two small *jebels*. Away to the left was Bel Magdoli, 'the hill with the twisted head', and quite an apt description too, which was still inhabited by a few freed Berta and had a small amount of permanent water. A little further on was Bel Arabu.

From just before Chali we had been in Uduk country. It was one of the most backward parts. An Uduk *tukl* generally had reversed curves to the thatch of the roof. Their womenfolk had shaved heads and wore plain aprons.

It was about 12 miles to Yabus Bridge. We crossed several small *khors* and the country was open woods with 'hydrangea trees'. The soil was continually changing, cotton, red and sandy. The Abyssinian Mountains unfolded in a magnificent panorama away to the left with Jebel Bange ahead.

At the roadside were many small holes about 4 feet wide and up to 6 feet deep. We had now entered the goldfields. The *nass* dig up the gravel and carry it in wooden bowls for washing in the *khor* a mile away. In that the holes were very numerous we presumed that the effort presumably was worthwhile. The Uduk preferred to wash for gold rather than grow grain and it had been found necessary to stimulate cultivation by illegally ordering that there should be no gold-washing during the cultivation season. To the right of the road was the extensive village of Abungoro — the Jo'burg of this corner of Africa — and reproducing most of the features of its prototype. In a few minutes the road dropped down some 25 feet into Khor Buldidni, which was a considerable stream in the rains. As we climbed out of the *khor* we passed a striking clump of six *lohinga* trees. From this point the road fell gently towards the Yabus and at mile 324 we reached a high bank overlooking the river 50 feet below. We went down a concrete runway, over the Irish Bridge among the rocks and splashing water and up a similar slope the other side into camp at 13.30 hours. Height by aneroid was 2,270 feet.

WHEELS AND PADDLES IN THE SUDAN

YABUS BRIDGE

The accommodation at Yabus was almost palatial as His Excellency had stopped here for two days recently. The site on the south bank overlooking the river was delightful, which at this time of year was clear. The banks were clad with trees nearly up to gallery forest standard. The bed was of polished purple rock. The bridge itself was 15 feet long, and at this time of year the water rushed underneath with 2 feet of daylight. The bridge was about 1 foot thick and in flood I should think there was about 3 feet of water over the roadway. Heavy concrete continued over the breadth of the bed and also under the wheel tracks for the greater part of the slopes. The bridge was built by Engineer Troops in 1932 and had had no repairs since. It stood as built — a splendid piece of work.

The road from the Yabus Bridge to Daga Post, for which the bridge was constructed, featured in a White Paper in the House of Commons dealing with slave trading. One episode was known as the Shimi raid and another affray was the subject of a poem entitled *The Pillage of Pill* by our late Financial Secretary (Sir Francis Rugman). The road had been quickly constructed by Engineer Troops and the impression was given that armoured cars patrolled the frontier day and night on account of slave-raiding. In fact, the road went out of action in the rains and it was only in the early rains that slave-raiding activities took place. However, the road was built and everyone seemed satisfied. The road was now completely out of use, largely because the District Commissioner concerned regarded motor cars as dangerous innovations.

The terminus of the road, Daga Post, was an interesting spot. Disney recounted a visit. He arrived at a stockade with a sentry housed in a crow's nest above which floated the Union Jack. As he approached he heard: 'Guard turn out!' It was Sergeant-Major Kalam Sakit giving the order in perfect English. Disney entered, and after a wash, sat down to breakfast with his host. A perfectly cooked kipper was brought in by a mess waiter wearing not a stitch of clothing.

We found the prospect of two days at the Yabus pleasing. Donald of Upper Nile Province, who was our pilot from this point, walked into camp bringing his fishing rod during the afternoon, but before he could start fishing the family decided to bathe in the swift-flowing shallow pools. We went to sleep that night to the sound of splashing water.

Early the following morning we visited some colobus monkeys in gallery forest among the islands upstream. The monkeys gave a magnificent display and we had some pretty views of the main stream during our walk. After breakfast Pam watched Donald fish and wanted to do likewise. We fixed her up with a bamboo pole and some line and Donald supplied the hook. Sport was quite good. Donald's best was a barbel of 4 pounds and Pam's somewhat smaller. Fishing and bathing filled the day very pleasantly, and in the evening we discussed the programme for the following day. The run to Boing was only 34 miles, taking less than two hours. As Yabus was more pleasant than Boing it was decided that we should defer our departure until after lunch. A very satisfactory decision on which to go to bed!

After another restful night I decided to try for photos of the monkeys but Pam opted for fishing, Donald had promised her 15 piastres for the first fish plus 15 piastres for the third and every additional fish. She landed two barbel of about 1½ pounds.

The morning passed very pleasantly and all too swifty.

YABUS BRIDGE TO BOING

We packed up and left punctually at 14.00 hours. The three vehicles negotiated the crossing without incident, not sticking on the incline as one lorry had done earlier in the day! The first 5 miles retraced our tracks back over Khor Buldidni and then we turned left at Abungoro. Passing a bataleur eagle was a good omen. There were graves at the roadside in Abungoro. The road crossed small deep *khors* making their way down to the Yabus. The countryside consisted of small trees in grass on cotton soil, fine views of hills away to the south. The *nass* along the road seemed taller than any passed recently and were ochred and dripping with sweat and oil. We passed the village on the right of Belbubulo (which word has in the local dialect some connection with a good belch!)

The going was good and flat, passing a dry swamp to the left and several small villages. The green valley of the Yabus lay away to the left before Boing. The country was pretty with open woods and *khash-khash* trees in flower. Some of the *tukls* had stepped thatch and entrance was by a round hole with the threshold about 18 inches from the ground. After a few more miles we came to Jebel Slingi, about the last hill to be passed, covered with frankincense trees, and a good view of Jebel Benomore south of the Yabus. We passed a party of Uduk women carrying big hemispherical crates on their heads. I have to confess that our approach led to chaos and the destruction of contents. Their menfolk frequently had a feather or two sticking out of their much plastered hair.

There were various villages along the roadside, each with a good complement of pigs. The countryside continued pleasant and park-like with *tebeldis* and various good-sized trees away to the left. Dom palms became numerous and cotton soil predominated.

Three miles from our destination we came to another Sudan Interior Mission Station, Doro. We drove on to Boing Rest House, mile 348 arriving at 15.55 hours.

There were two Rest Houses of wattle and mud walls and thatched roofs in an extensive compound surrounded by a 6-foot wattle fence whose main purpose was to keep out goats and pigs, but its efficiency depended on all the gates being shut at night.

We quickly settled in and then visited the Mission in Donald's company. The staff consisted of Reverend and Mrs Morrow (and daughter aged two) who had been on the station several years, and Reverend and Mrs Major who had recently arrived. They were all Americans. They were working among the Maban, and had a small school for boys. It was interesting to watch the little girl's reactions on meeting white children of her own sex for the first time. A bougainvillea was flowering nicely outside the house but otherwise the station was as depressing as Chali. Discomfort was a pronounced feature of their life and yet a *tukl* under the shade of a tree, with its surroundings swept, a *bursh* on the floor and a raw-hide strung *angareeb* or stool to sit on, has a degree of comfort and well-being. Perhaps personal discomfort was regarded as a desirable state.

Whilst we were having tea the Reverend Forsburg arrived. He had started from Chali at 05.30 hours on a donkey but I fancy that they had both walked the greater part of the way. My respect for him was much increased as the journey was about 35 miles and he had done it in 12 hours of daylight. From him we learned that his two children were practically recovered from dysentery. We returned to the Rest House just before dark.

Boing was one of the few administrative centres of the Barun country. The Maban and one or two other tribes were the non-hill Barun. Boing had one brick-built shop, owned by Mohamed

Abdulla of Melut, a very enterprising merchant. It had a police post with six mounted and four foot police. Recently a dispensary had been approved with a Shilluk Medical Assistant and a Barun working under him. It had possessed a local court, without a warrant, for the last three years, which involved the District Commissioner in seeing all cases afterwards. The bench was rather heavy with punishments. Boing was well administered from December to April but during the rest of the year it had to get along on its own as it was inaccessible during the rains.

The Maban favoured communal cultivation. A man who wanted to cultivate on a big scale brewed a great quantity of *merissa* and announced that a *nafir* (communal party) would be held. There was usually a good response and if the *merissa* was sufficient the job would get done.

The night was disturbed. Some of the gates in our compound fence had not been closed and at 01.00 hours I had to get up and clear out pigs and dogs which were rootling among the kitchen gear and making the dickens of a din, which disturbed the servants not at all. The roaring of a lion set all the dogs off and it sounded as if there were a hundred of them. It was half an hour before peace reigned again.

BOING TO AWAD-EL-BAQAR

From Boing the journey was very flat but the surface being largely cotton soil, was not good. Donald and I got away at 07.00 hours in his lorry leaving the family to follow more leisurely but by 08.15 we had so shaken the lorry that a front spring pin nut had been lost and the pin was half out. Our programme was to get to Awad-el-Baqar as soon as possible and then go on a diversion into Dar-es-Saqiya, but it looked as if the going would defeat the lorry. The wear and tear on cars over these roads was very heavy and 50 miles was enough to convince me that the rest of the journey would be made in a station wagon and not on a grain-collecting lorry. The District Commissioner had lost his own box car which was awaiting a spare part and had to travel in a borrowed lorry.

Throughout this run of 52 miles to Awad-el-Baqar the countryside was more or less covered with trees. *Hegliegs* were probably the most common. Most of those near the road had been half cut through to facilitate making road blocks quickly in 1940–41 had there been any retreat to the Nile. There were numerous stretches of *talh* and usually a *tebeldi* in sight. Dom palms were not so numerous as on the previous stretch and there were many *selags*. *Khash-khash azraq* was common and there were a few *aradeibas* and gardenias and we saw one euphorbia. The frankincense tree was no longer to be seen.

Villages were few. The first was Bella at mile 353. Then came Yousif Batil at mile 361. Soon after this we overtook a pair of ground hornbills in flight, one on each side of the road. By folk-lore the omens for the day were trebly good: two of them, and in flight and one on each side of the road!

Bird life was well represented. There were many colourful Abyssinian rollers, and blue starlings. Smaller hornbills frequently glided across the road whilst *hoo-poos* got up into the trees. We passed coveys of guinea fowl and vultures were busy on the corpse of a diminutive goat.

Yousif Natcha was located at mile 373 and soon afterwards we passed the only four-legged game seen in the day's run — a pair of red-fronted gazelles. Shortly before reaching Kidwa Wells we passed Jonguls Post.

North of our route there was some surplus grain and strenuous exertions were being made to get it out and sent down to the White Nile at Melut for forwarding on to the consuming areas. At each of the larger villages stood heaps of grain that had been brought in in small quantities. Lorries were working at right angles to our route and from Awad-el-Baquar two diesel lorries and trailers were taking loads of 150 sacks to Melut.

At Kidwa there was a brick-built merchant's shop and two bull-driven oilseed grinders turning out *simsim* oil used mainly for anointing the bodies of the locals. We walked across to the wells which were situated about 400 yards away. They consisted of a number of holes varying in diameter from 5 feet to 10 feet with water about 8 feet from the surface. The water looked most repulsive, like curry sauce but the wells had not yet been cleaned out and brought into use. The grass in the neighbourhood had recently been burned-off as the site was for dry season occupation. All the Barun were further south in the swamps on cultivation but were expected back shortly. Nearly all the houses in surrounding settlements were unoccupied, a state of affairs proclaimed either by a bunch of thorn or piled logs in the doorway. The road was bad and the mattress on the lorry's front seat — and no springs — was most uncomfortable. We had another hour's run to do, through grass and trees, much of the former burnt. There was one patch of *talh* in flower. I was not sorry when we reached Awad-el-Baqar, mile 400, at 10.45 hours. We decided to leave the diversion over to the next day.

Awad-el-Baqar had two Rest Houses, less elaborate than at Boing, in a compound enclosed by a wattle fence. Just outside the front gate was a large *gemeiza* tree much beloved by the pig population of the village on account of the ripe figs which kept falling from it. Our drivers camped under it but they had to dispute possession with the pigs frequently. The picture of these Mohammedans saying their prayers in a mass of rootling pigs verged on the grotesque!

Awad-el-Baqar was a centre of the Maban. The men here were of good physique and good cultivators. They kept lots of pigs and were great tobacco growers. They also fished quite a lot and were keen hunters and it was quite common to see two or three nice looking greyhound-type dogs on leash as they moved about.

In the afternoon we went round the village of Awad-el-Baqar. It was a straggling collection of houses along a line of water holes. The water supply arrangements were very primitive and the animals seemed to be able to clamber down into most of the holes and help themselves. In one of them five sheep seemed to be fairly well bogged down; eventually, by throwing in small clods of earth, we persuaded all except one to extricate themselves by their own exertions, but the last one was firmly stuck in the mud. Donald clambered down and when encouragement failed finally lifted it out bodily by its fleece.

The pounding of *dura* into a coarse flour was interesting. The women used a mud-lined hole in the ground for the mortar and not a wooden *fonduk*. The holes were surrounded by a carefully prepared mud-floor and the grain swept into the hole as required with a brush made of a bundle of grass tied round. The pestle, a piece of wood, about 4 inch diameter and 7 feet long. It was used with extreme accuracy, coming down at the centre of the bottom of the hole every time and never striking the side. Preparations for making enormous quantities of *merissa* were in hand. Three women were pounding grain non-stop and we discovered the brew-house in a *tukl* where five women were kneading the coarse flour after moistening, and accumulating great piles of balls of dough, one of the intermediate stages in the manufacture. The prospects of the final result filled all with merriment. Having watched the energy devoted to these two processes it was not difficult to understand why a fat woman is rare in these parts.

The village contained only one shop, housed in a glorified *tukl*. Coarse calico, *wizn ashera* as it was known, was the only cloth in which the people were interested. Beads were a good selling line. I was surprised at the prices paid. One would think they yielded a nice profit to the seller.

AWAD-EL-BAQAR TO MELUT

We left Awad-el-Baqar at 07.00 hours in one of the station wagons as the previous day's riding on a lorry had been too hard on my seat. This meant that our staff who had so far had the comfort of travelling in a station wagon had to be content with less comfort.

Our route lay 11 miles along the main road to Paloich and then a diversion along a new road northwards into Dar-es-Saqiya, made for grain-extraction purposes. The section along the main road was of excellent surface although cotton soil. It had been opened early and had a scraper over it in January. There were wide expanses of grass on either side, very suitable for *hareig* cultivation. At mile 402 we passed the last Barun village on the main road. Trees became less numerous, just a few large *hegleigs* and some *soufar*.

Animals were more common than usual. The highlight was two giraffe and an ant-bear which scuffled across the road. Bustard, francolin and several large coveys of guinea fowl gave interest to the journey.

At mile 410 we turned right towards Dar-es-Saqiya. The purpose of the road was to allow grain to be brought out, and it followed that the location was to a large extent fixed by the points at which the grain was situated, and the merchant concerned had had a lot to do with the siting. This road also led across a wide grass and cotton soil plain except for a narrow ridge of alluvial soil, 50 yards wide and 2 feet high, at mile 4, which was covered with dom and trailed away to left and right like a great snake. At mile 7 and a mile away to the right lay the village of Sheik Keiga Una hidden in dom palms and trees round an old *bafir*. Two miles further on and away to the left was the village to which these folk would shortly return and which possessed shallow wells which would be used as soon as the *hafir* was dry.

Up to this point we had seen little or no cultivation, though the grass looked excellently suited for *hareig*. From now on there was usually some in sight. It was either self-sown from the previous year's cultivation or excellent stands of this years *dura*. There were some good grain heaps at last year's cultivation.

The going so far had not been at all bad, for a temporary road over cotton soil. Some of the grass had been burned and there were a few trees. At mile 16 we came to the village of Dudu, situated on two *debbas* (knolls), 300 yards apart, Between the knolls ran a shallow *khor* bed which served two *hafirs* with thatched covers. I had never seen a thatched *hafir* before and it would have been interesting to know how much loss due to evaporation was reduced thereby. An ordinary *hafir* typically lost a centimetre per day from this cause.

We went into a huddle with the head Sheik of the villages to obtain local opinion of local geography, which did not always confirm what our maps indicated. The Sheik gave the course of a local *khor* as through Sadan and Bansarra to Jantoka, quite different from the map. Asked if a better route in the rains than the present main road existed, he stated that in the old days, when folk travelled on donkeys, during the rains no one would have thought of trying the present road but passed through Dudu and made for Paloich. He further said that one could *ride* on a donkey from Dudu to Paloich at any time in the rains whereas on the road you had to unload and carry loads on head. In good weather the journey took 1½ days from Dudu to Paloich and in bad weather two days.

We then continued along the road, which was deteriorating. After 4 miles we came to the village of Ban Ulga to the left, at the moment unoccupied, and with a small thatched *hafir*. After another 4 miles the road became so bad that we decided that respect for the car compelled us to desist. It tok us 40 minutes to do the 8 miles back to Dudu. With careful driving, we sustained no damage and were back on the main road at 11.35 hours. It was clear that more work would have to be done on the road before lorries could be sent up there to collect the grain. Labour would have to be collected and it was thought that some Shilluk could be hired at Melut.

The road now stretched away to the west over a wide expanse of cotton soil covered with grass. Two miles further on and away to the

WHEELS AND PADDLES IN THE SUDAN

right was the solitary *hegleig* tree at Tim Shol; it was sufficiently outstanding to be a trigonometrical point. At mile 417 we forked right at Daw and the appearance of the ground indicated that the area was very wet in the rains. We passed a clump of dom palms and could see an occasional tree on the horizon but they gave no relief to this colossal flat expanse of dry golden grass. At mile 424 we turned left off the road to Miadol Wells, several water holes in clumps of dom palms with a single *gemeiza*. The wells were not yet in use. There was quite a bit of game about, red-fronted and teital.

Road work was in evidence as a new trace was being tried, but it did not depart far from the existing road. Work was done by a grader during the winter and every effort made to keep traffic off it. It was allowed to consolidate during the rains and was then scraped. In cotton soil, providing the traffic was kept off and the scraper applied on time, the results were good.

Five miles on we came to the large Dinka village of Agor Dit, situated on an extensive *debba* (knoll) which indicated many centuries of occupation. There were surprisingly many males in residence and we were soon surrounded. Would we go and see a lad with a bad leg. He was in a terrible way with a lion bite nearly three weeks old which one could smell from 20 yards away. His father promised to send him in on a lorry which would be passing later in the day but the tragedy of it was that lorries had been passing every day during the previous three weeks and no one had done anything about it! It was nearly spring time, and the Dinka lads had marvellous arrays of beads on. Dinka houses had neat thatching, done by the women, and clever provision of a porch, but the general effect of *tukls* on a *debba* without a blade of grass or a tree was very bare. We found the grader parked here and the crew miles away in Malakal — one of the trials of trying to carry out work with Sudanese supervision.

We next set off to the north-west. The journey was still over grassy plain with some plots of *hareig* protected by fire lines. At mile 435 there was a fine *fula* (shallow depression filled by rain) to the left. It was just covered and surrounded by thousands of ducks and geese. Donald got out to try his luck. Stalking was of little avail, so he waded out into the middle and loosed off. Clouds of birds arose and started to circle and cross the *fula*. As they came within range he more or less took his choice. Small boys splashed about to pick up the fallen. I thought he was unlucky to have only six brought to the car.

At the nearby village of Mbako we discussed with elders the possibilities of travel, during the rains, say due east from Mbako. They said such travel was possible without undue difficulty. The route they recommended was more or less direct for Dudu, the village we had visited earlier in the day in Dar-es-Saqiya. The points passed would be a village called Deraful, about 5 miles away and 'visible from Mbako in the morning light' and an old cattle camp site, Wunaboich, about half-way between Deraful and Dudu. All very interesting when taken with what we were told at Dudu. We bade the elders farewell and continued our journey.

It was another 13 miles to Paloich. We passed several Dinka villages mainly to the left and a *hafir* and crossed the new graded road several times. It looked as if we would miss Paloich, which was visible from some distance, away to the right. However, the road took several turns and we finally came in to the Paloich–Melut road a bit to the west of the village. It was mile 448 and 14.30 hours. Paloich was a small administrative centre. There was an office for a visiting District Commissioner to use and an Agriculturist was stationed there. The Government well was a failure; it was said that after tapping the water stratum it had been carried through an impermeable layer to further sands which let all the water flow away! We were met by the Sudanese Agriculturist and had a talk about fire-lining which was his main pre-occupation.

A quarter of an hour later we set off on our last leg for the day. This was the 23 miles to Melut. The road surface was lovely and it took us only 35 minutes. We passed several villages. Away to our left lay trees and a small dam across a *khor* in this area had held up water from the last rains in a promising manner. Elephants were frequently seen along this stretch, but we were not lucky.

After 20 miles we struck a *khor,* which was a branch of the Nile, and turned north. Before long Melut was in sight and a white blur which was in all probability our launch *Melika*. We drove through the Mission and on past the Police Post to the foreshore, stacked with grain, where we received a cheery hail from the rest of the party on board *Melika*. It was mile 471 and 15.20 hours and lunch was very welcome!

I promptly went down with a sore throat and so missed the last road stage which was 124 miles to Malakal. Old age and the day in the lorry left their mark. I needed two or three days rest to get going again and then journeyed by launch. Donald took the cars and making several stops for administrative purposes reached Malakal, mile 549, at 14.30 hours. He admitted that a station wagon was much better travelling than a lorry or a box-car and with that opinion I heartily agreed.

Chapter Seventeen

THROUGH THE NUBA MOUNTAINS

For most of my journeys in the south I was concerned with the operations of Sudan Railways. Our trip through the Nuba Mountains was, however, more the result of a personal invitation from the District Commissioner of the Western Jebels, Rex Harrison. It was an interesting part of the Sudan and deserves a mention.

It was March 1946. We had completed the journey Sennar–Melut and had intended to reconnoitre the proposed route Adok–Tonj–Meshra-el-Req, but weather conditions prevented this. It did not, however, prevent us carrying out the last leg of the trip. We tied up at Tonga in the evening and found the transport already unloaded. Our head driver reported that all was ready for a start in the morning.

We got away at 08.20 hours for a run of 98 miles to Talodi for lunch. The Nuba Mountains were clearly visible in the distance. We crossed Khor Lolle on a causeway — the *khor* ran parallel to the White Nile, about 2 miles back from it for 50 miles. We passed groups of *tukls*, studded about on a grassy plain. An unusual feature was that almost every group contained a tree in addition to patches of cultivation. The road was rough in places but we made fair time. There was not much game in sight.

A little further on we came to a village, Es Soufar, with some big trees and cultivation. We passed on into scrub with all the signs of considerable devastation by elephants but none was visible. At mile 23 we crossed a *khor* which was the Province boundary.

Population was as scarce as animal life as we closed in on the Nuba Mountains, straight ahead. The road was much improved allowing a speed of 25 miles per hour over black alluvial soil which gave way to ironstone. We passed a group of *nass*, one armed with a fine *baggara* (broad-pointed) spear, with their *afsh* (belongings) slung from poles. The soil changed quickly back to alluvial, through trees that were quite unfamiliar to me.

At mile 43 we approached the first *jebel* and a camp of woodcutters. Both types of euphorbia, some growing very tall in the shelter of other trees, were prominent. We saw Jebel-el-Amira ahead over a burnt-out section. We stopped at the old Rest House at mile 49 in rocky terrain, which was a half-way point. It had taken us 2½ hours running time.

We got under way again at 11.20 hours. We could see the foothills of Jebel Eliri ahead and drove through a mass of frankincense trees in flower. The road surface had deteriorated and changed to a yellow colour. Before long, however, we were back on the ironstone with lots of *khash-khash* and hydrangeas. At mile 56 we drew level with Jebel Eliri on our right with Dallas village at its foot and it was noticeable that the thatch on all its dwellings was stepped. Our road skirted the *jebel,* passing through a grove of large *tebeldis* and brought us to Tungari village with an old *merkaz* building and *suk.*

The road continued sandy, but good, with Jebel Musmar to our left. We crossed some small *khors* and passed several villages with attendant palms and extensive patches of bamboos. At mile 71 we drew level with a small rocky knoll to our left covered with frankincense trees in flower and a ground squirrel crossing ahead of us indicated that the omens foretold a lucky day.

The soil changed to ironstone and bamboos came back into the picture, with tall grass. We passed through several miles of sunken road. At mile 85 we got our first glimpse of Jebel Talodi and crossed the telegraph line. Soon the white rock summit of Jebel Abu-Gir lay ahead, its slopes covered with frankincense trees. We skirted it, leaving it on our right and passed a party of travellers mounted on a bull, a horse and a red donkey.

The going was pretty poor but it was only another 10 miles to Talodi. We skirted Jebel Hagarat and passed over a small bridge to open woods with Jebel Talodi just ahead. Over another causeway and bridge we made Talodi Rest House at 13.37 hours.

After a good lunch we were packed up and away at 15.15 hours. This was rather late but the next section to Kadugli was only 52 miles. Our road continued to hug Jebel Talodi, tree-clad and rocky; it was wide with a good surface, through open grassland with lots of *khash-khash* trees in flower and small *tebeldis* at the foot of the *jebel.* The trees grew larger as we approached Khor Azraq which was crossed by an Irish bridge, as was a second *khor* soon after. A number of hills lay close ahead, the Limon Hills and Jebel Tabuli to the right and Jebel Doleibaya straight ahead. All round were lots of *sabils*, like silver birches, with a well near the road.

After 13 miles we came to Doleibaya Rest House near the foot of the stony-sided *jebel* of that name and breasting a slight rise we came on some firm going. Khor Dabaker was crossed on a diversion as work on a new causeway and bridge was in hand and shortly afterwards we caught sight of a striking pinnacle rock on Jebel Limon. At 20 miles the road passed close to a low spur at the foot of which were several well-camouflaged villages. They were constructed in stone and mud, and abounded with pigs.

Soon after this, despite the favourable omens, we ran into a spot of trouble. It was our only involuntary stop on the trip; a back spring came adrift. However, the staff were unperturbed and brought tea. We might have been on the veranda of the Grand Hotel in Khartoum. A waiter came over from the lorry with our tea set out on a large plated tray, as was the custom there. In 1½ hours we were continuing our journey.

By now we were well into the *Jebels*. At mile 27 we passed Jebel Umm Dorein with a number of clustered habitations at its foot and some curious balanced stones. From this point the road led across a bowl between the hills, with a *suk*. At a fork in the road we took the right arm, leading to open park-like country. We crossed a *khor*, with a small spring in its bed, by an Irish bridge and skirted the base of Jebel Lebu on our right.

On account of the mechanical trouble we were running a bit behind schedule, into a very fine sunset. The telegraph line crossed our road and we crossed small *khors*. There were some remnants of cultivation. We passed a village on our left but by now dusk was falling. The road was on cotton soil and not in good condition. At nearly 19.00 hours we arrived at Kadugli.

We spent a good night and after breakfast I 'made my number' with the Assistant District Commissioner, a Senior Sudanese, and so it was nearly 11.30 hours before we set out on our run of 77 miles. The terrain was curious. It was a layer of 2 inches of gravel on top of cotton soil. The road allowed us to make good time.

After 20 miles in 40 minutes we came to El Geimaya Rest House and Jebel Keigat Turmmero ahead, with the curious formation of gravel on cotton soil continuing. We crossed the many channels of Khor Kueik by means of small bridges with an Irish bridge over the main channel. Alongside was the village housing the road gang.

After 31 miles we drew level with Jebel Keigat Kolo on our left which looked as if it had a white limestone summit. Guinea fowl were plentiful and soon we passed Jebel Debu with a number of balanced stones, and a view of the Dasol Hills ahead. We stopped there for 5 minutes to enjoy the view, and then spotted a wayside cafe in this most unexpected position, though no one was at that moment enjoying its facilities. Half-way, 39 miles, was reached in 1¾ hours and we stopped for lunch.

The road led on through low stony hummocks to the beginnings of the Dasol Hills.

There were graves near the roadside covered with stones. The Rest House at mile 44 had been burned down. *Khors* were frequent and the Temein Hills began to show up on our left with a more rugged sky-line. At mile 52 were a number of wells and Ghulfan Dispensary. The going was good and passing some cultivation we came to the village of Umm Garbo with large wells and many animals. Soon Dilling lay ahead and we passed the ginning factory and the brick-field to cross over an Irish bridge and on up a mahogany avenue to arrive. We drove on to the Harrison's house and were warmly welcomed.

DILLING

My knowledge of the Nubas and their way of life was scanty, and Rex had promised to do his best to correct this. We were to attend a *la'ib,* a gathering for dancing and wrestling, pastimes which were taken seriously as the representatives were maintained at the public expense. I would sit-in on the dispensing of justice which was always the quickest means of learning something of native mentality.

The Nubas were by nature among the finest soldiers in the world and excellent marksmen. His Excellency's comments on them, and he was entitled to speak because he had fought on nearly every Hill, was: 'Nubas are like bees — they sting when you least expect it'. They were very independent and disliked external authority. Until the 1930s their villages clustered round the tops of the hills; there were many caverns and it was difficult to dislodge them. It was necessary to send a patrol to one or more of the hills nearly every year. Now, with few exceptions, they had to live at the base of the hills. Nubas formed the backbone of the Sudan Defence Force and many battalions fought in North Africa in World War II, winning high praise.

In that the Nubas lived on hills their administration was based on groups of hills. In the Western Jebels there were three such groups or Confederations, Nyimang, Ajang and Hawazma.

I was visiting the Nyimang Confederation of Seven Hills, Salara at the centre, surrounded by Tendra, Kurmetti, Nitl, Fassu, Sultan and Zanki. These were surrounded by an outer ring of Hills, not all speaking Nyimang. President of the Nyimang Confederation Court was Amina Dirdimma, the *Mek* of Salara. The Court met on Fridays and went on trek.

In order to begin to appreciate how the Nuba ticks, one must know something of the parts that the ancestors, the *awaid* (the folk-lore or customs), the *kujur* (a sort of priest) and the *sibr* (a wide term covering all sorts of religious exercises) play in his mental make-up. The Nuba regards God as far away and rather beyond his realm of comprehension. Next come the ancestors and then the *kujur* who holds the spirits of the ancestors in his hands and can intercede with them. The *awaid* are the customs which are the basis of life for the Nuba. The *sibr* is presided over by the *kujur* and is a great release of mental tension for the Nuba. The Nuba is liable to brain-storms and without *sibrs* is a difficult proposition and virtually useless. The *kujurs* have a considerable knowledge of simple surgery and medicine and psycho-analysis; they understand the people, who have complete faith in them and on this basis they are frequently able to succeed where western science fails. If a soldier on leave asks the District Commissioner for an extension to attend a *sibr*, the District Commissioner always sends a wire to say it should be granted. To illustrate this point Rex quoted from his own experience. There were two promising recruits to the local detachment but their shooting was hopeless and they said they wanted a *sibr*. Their Bimbashi asked Rex what he should do and was told: 'If you will take my advice you'll give them leave. A prisoner even gets out of prison for *sibr*. He is quite useless if he wants a *sibr* and you deny him'. The Bimbashi took his advice and in due course they came back, shot the course and put every round in the bull.

The *awaid* (customs or lore) form a point to which the Nuba always returns. Any catastrophe, famine, epidemic or other general trouble is caused, in his opinion, solely because the *awaid* are not being properly observed, and calls for a return to the *awaid* and the abandonment of new ideas. From this, one can see the enormous disadvantage under which the missions worked. The *awaid* are in the hands of certain of the *kujurs* and some of the *meks*. They are not over-clear about the *awaid*, which are very complicated, and are for ever recollecting further ones. This habit can be wearisome.

The Police were a very important element. They formed a corps d'elite. There were 160 names on the list, waiting for a vacancy, ranging from a complete savage to an ex-*bash-shawish* (Sergeant-major). The District Commissioner claimed that it was the best police-force in the country and absolutely loyal, though only 27 were literate. The force contained a number of the *Mek's* sons and cousins. When there was any trouble on a Hill he would send one of these and an old sweat; the former had the prestige and contact, and the latter the police knowledge. In dealing with Nubas he claimed that the personal touch was the main key.

Nubas have little respect for Sudanese or Egyptians. Abdel Eff el Agab, Assistant District Commissioner at Kadugli, was a Sudanese and he cut no ice with them. When the District Commissioner was away on leave and he was left holding the fort the Nubas generally stayed away. Their attitude was *enta wahid Sudani* 'You are just a Sudanese, you don't know anything about it!'. Fortunately Agab Eff had the sense to laugh.

The *Mek* and the *Kujur* of a Hill had been at loggerheads for many months and they barged into Rex's office for the n'th time. They were told that if they could not settle their difference outside he would send them both to the *ajang* — the *Mek's* Court. I asked if this Court would have any difficulty sorting them out and was told none whatever. They would give the District Commissioner the answer and he would approve it and the two disputants would be put under guarantee to adhere to the finding; if either broke it he would be put in clink. It was quite common to have a *kujur* in clink, and then a request would come that they wanted the *kujur* out to perform a *sibr*, which no one else could undertake, and out he would go on ticket-of-leave and, incidentally, back he would come. Prisoners were quite unofficially allowed leave to attend a *sibr*. 'It may seem curious' said Rex, 'and it would certainly shock the Legal Secretary, but it is sound common sense and it prevents the Nuba from becoming disorganised mentally'.

The *Mek* and the *Kujur* incident was quickly followed by the appearance of three prisoners with their committal order — two men and one woman — sentenced by the *Meks'* Court to 9, 5 and 4 months respectively for adultery. The District Commissioner reviewed all sentences and his signature made them operative. The 5-monther was asked if he had committed adultery with the woman and he said 'No'. The District Commissioner then asked the woman if she had committed adultery with the 5-monther. She tittered and would not answer. The 9-monther was then asked if he had committed adultery with the woman and he admitted that he had. The District Commissioner then asked the woman again about the 5-monther, and asked whether he had committed adultery or just sat down in her house. She said that he had come to her house to commit adultery but he had run away without partaking of her pleasures. The result was 5 months sentence reduced to 3, the other two sentences to stand.

Rex said that since the men and the woman concerned had both received sentences of imprisonment, adultery had been much reduced and also the serious crimes arising therefrom. Sentence for putting a woman in the family way was always 12 months for both parties. There was a strong element making for public security in the length of the sentence. In Nuba-land you could be put in prison for looking at a married woman. When the adulteress came out of prison she would probably be given a second chance by her husband who would expect her to have learned her lesson.

It was now time to set off for the *la'ib*. The condition of the roads in this area to a great extent depended on the interest taken in them by the District Commissioner. The Nuba liked roads and did not mind working on them. We were approaching Nitl with villages all round its base — a very populated area. It was here that whilst on patrol in 1917 Capt. Hatton, whose memorial we had seen on the sign-post at Pibor Post, was killed.

We next came to Nitl and then Kurmetti and encountered many natives enroute for the *la'ib*. We drove through masses of people mobilised for the *la'ib*. Prominent was a party of young women with a bunch of fur strips hanging down from the back of their necks, indicating that they were newly married. Next came a contingent of dancers with blue beads round their waists and a tail with a blue finial at the back and a length of blue bead-work in front. On one leg they wore the equivalent of ankle-bells made from dom palm leaf with a pebble inside. Their bodies were most weirdly and wonderfully painted. There were a number of pairs of women dancers; one pair was clad in red and yellow vertical striped skirts with brass and red 1½ inch belts. Another pair sported purple and yellow *rahads*, a short skirt made of narrow leather strips, and another pair with white cow-hair fringes from the waist. All their lips were painted bright blue, and one had the distinction of a shaving mirror hung around her neck. A number carried cow-horn sticks.

The men were much painted, in red-ochre, purple and bronze, relieved by all sorts of designs. A number had a black sheepskin attached to the waist and hanging down as a very elaborate *furwa* (seat protector). Others wore all sorts of loin-cloths and bathing shorts; one had a sweater on, upside down, and many had a feather or two in their hair. They sported all sorts of neck and arm adornment and fibre bells round their ankles.

En route we overtook a number of contingents marching in from Nitl, Tendra, Kurmetti and other Hills. It reminded me of the Gathering of the Clans at the Braemar Gathering. The Nuba loves marching for marching's sake and the contingents showed a considerable degree of order. If they lacked the regularity of the dress and equipment of the Mac Duff and Balmoral Highlanders they made up for it in colour and good humour. Everyone was in the best of spirits. The Tendra contingent was led by a venerable sheikh in a mauve *kuftan* astride a donkey and they marched to the sound of a bugle. Multi-coloured sun-shades added to the gaiety of the scene. The *la'ib* was to be held on a flat spot among the Salara Hills — a large natural amphitheatre with hills all around. A big *tebeldi* gave a point of vantage of which many availed themselves, and a long *rakuba* (shelter of poles and grass matting) had been erected as a grandstand and to this we were driven. We were received by Mek Amina Durdima, President of the Nyimang Confederation, and a number of other *Meks,* who posed for photographs.

The huge arena was well filled with dancers for most of the time, moving round in groups. They were representing their Hills and were encouraged by a lot of local support from the onlookers. There was a decorative rugger scrum with a ruff hanging from their necks and a skirt — a sort of two-piece costume in grass. There were some concerted numbers in which many dancers participated. It was all very colourful but not easy to describe in detail. I was very busy with the camera.

We adjourned for lunch at 14.15 hours. The Rest House had a

The five Meks.

glorious view with the Cathedral Rock of Salara and the Church Missionary Society Station at its foot. The Rock received its name from the cavalry patrol in 1917–18, long before there was any thought of building a church in these *jebels*.

At 15.45 hours we were informed that the wrestlers were ready to commence, so we returned smartly.

The wrestling was interesting. The wrestlers were public figures, representing, and being maintained by, the Hill to which they belonged and the onlookers supported their representatives very vocally. The bouts lasted 1–2 minutes and were presided over by a referee whose ruling was instantly acceptable. I took many photos and at the conclusion I thanked the President, Mek Amina, for the splendid show that they had arranged and handed him the price of four bulls to provide a feast for the performers. Honour was satisfied. We then made for Dilling and home.

As we left for the *merkaz* the following morning I learned something about Rex's driver, Issa Saadan, a great big black. He was Nuba only by residence and came from Bedairi, near El Obeid, married to a woman from Salara he was the best known man in the

WHEELS AND PADDLES IN THE SUDAN

Nuba wrestling.

Nuba dancing.

Nuba wrestling.

Nuba dancing.

District. He was generally greeted by name before the District Commissioner. Philip Broadbent, who was in Dilling for five years, trekked very extensively and thought that he knew and was known by everyone. At his departure his successor, Arthur Hankin, asked a man at the roadside, 'Did you see the District Commissioner pass along the road?' 'No.' 'Did you see the *Merkaz* car?' 'Yes, the *Merkaz* car passed.' 'Was the District Commissioner riding in it?' 'I don't know.' 'Was there any Britisher in it?' 'There was a Britisher alongside Issa Saadan.'

We next visited the prison; there was an air of peace and security. It was 11.00 hours and Musa, the murderer, of whom I was to learn more later in the day, was asleep in a ward, the weapon with which he had committed the crime was in the arms store and his daughter in the police area for protection. 'Come and see the adulterous women' said the District Commissioner. 'They all get one year along with their paramours'. Among them was one of the *Mek's* daughters — it happened while he was away in North Africa visiting the troops — most unfortunate!

Rex told me of a shooting case involving a lad. He had taken his *atira* (sweetheart), to a party. In one of the dances the man pointed his rifle at his partner. At that moment the lad had a friend's rifle in his hands. It was unfortunately loaded and had a hair-trigger. By great bad luck it went off and the girl dropped like a stone. The lad came in straight away and gave himself up. It was not murder and he got one year's imprisonment. He was quite content to be away with the Government for a year; in fact to be in prison was the safest place for him during the year of his sentence.

Our discussion took us on to what was the basis of our control of the Nuba; it was reckoned there were 15,000 rifles in the Western Jebels and Rex related a recent conversation with Mek Amina on his return from a three month visit to Egypt and North Africa at the end of the previous year. Whilst there he saw a lot and a lot of what he saw he did not like. The *Mek* started the conversation with 'Is there any news?' Rex replied that there had been rioting in Egypt. 'Ah,' said Amina, 'I meant to have spoken to you a few weeks ago about this. I heard *tabit-tabit*(on the grape vine) that they want to throw off the British rule in Egypt. 'Is this true?' The District Commissioner pointed out that it was not quite true to say that there was any British rule in Egypt. To this Amina replied 'But I saw British troops everywhere in Egypt'. The real cause of their presence was explained to him. Amina then went on 'But is it true that the Egyptians want to return to the Sudan?' Rex said there was some truth in the statement. All present — Mek Amina and the other *Meks* — laughed uproariously at the idea. Mek Amina continued 'It seems clear to me that the British have in them the quality of being able to rule. In the Sudan the British will last as long as time'. In the event history confirmed the truth of the dictum that nothing is permanent except change. Rex continued by pointing out that this belief in the rightness of our rule tended to be embarrassing. 'Whatever decision is given they will accept — providing it has some modicum of reason in it. Their phrase at all times is Nazrak kafia — loosely translated whatever you say goes'.

In the afternoon we set out in our car to another of the Hills, Tendra. As our driver was a stranger, Rex was responsible for navigation and it quickly became clear how much he relied on Issa. Tendra Police Post was very elusive.

We dropped the family at a well to prepare tea and continued the search. Eventually we were successful. Returning to the well we found women drawing water and with them were two small boys age five years, each with a little bow 2 feet in length, and a long, very thin arrow. One had the result of his hunting with him — 1 tiny rat and six large grasshoppers! There is not a lot of game left in the Nuba Mountains, unless you include a few jackals and hyenas; it was all cleaned out. But it was not always so; I have in my papers a letter dated 27 December, 1954 from Woodall who was in charge of a motor transport unit that we had to provide to carry un-ginned cotton to the ginning factory at Dilling:

Leopards (Illegal shooting of)

For your information, Suliman Mousa shot three full-grown leopards this morning from the box-car in three successive shots with a 12-bore gun and No. 4 shot.

This must be a record. One was killed instantly. The second dragged itself into long grass where it was considered unwise to go after it, and the third recovered while the men were commencing to skin it thereby causing awe and despondency among the troops.

If he gets hold of any No. 3 shot I am afraid Suliman will be run-in for shooting elephants.

After we had finished tea I took some photographs of girls drawing water from the well, and then we set off for home via

Funda, another of the Nyimang Hills. I had been shown the policeman in the *merkaz* lock-up — Musa— a Fundawi, who could not return to his Hill. His story was rather interesting. A Corporal and Musa left Tendra Police Post to arrest a deserter. The soldier was in his house. He came out to discuss the matter and said he was not coming. Argument ensued and at last he made a bolt for it — up the hill like a goat. After him went the Corporal and Musa. As they were not gaining on him the Corporal said 'shoot' and Musa shot, and being a Nuba killed his man. That was 'blood' — *dihm*. The police came down the hill quickly, hotly pursued by Nubas. They made for Tendra Police Post as quickly as possible, but their chances of holding it were slight, and so the garrison made a dash for it on their horses. The countryside was swarming with Nubas and it looked thoroughly ugly. Again the Corporal said 'Shoot one of them off' and another Nuba was killed. The police made Dilling safely but Musa had been employed in the prison ever since — for his own safety. Under the *awaid* there was blood which must be expunged. The individual must cleanse himself and must not come near his house for two years. He could by means of *sibr* cleanse himself; there was no question of *dia* (compensation). Should he appear in his home area during this period he would promptly be killed.

On the question of *dia*, Rex said that it had been the custom that for a Nuba life *dia* of seven cows should be granted, but recently a Nuba had made an impassioned appeal against that figure. 'Why not thirty-three? Arabs, Turks, Nubas, are not all one? Is not a Nuba life worth as much as an Arab?' Result, thirty-three in future.

After dinner I asked Rex how his plans for conservation of rain water were progressing as I knew he wanted to build some small dams in the Hills, and I was told of a happening in this connection. He had climbed to a vantage point and was sitting on a rock making a sketch of the area that seemed to offer possibilities. Whilst he worked he became aware of someone approaching from behind and looked round. He saw a Nuba hesitating in his approach. The Nuba was quite unclad except for a straw boater, which he raised. Rex invited him to approach, whilst he got on with his sketching. The Nuba stopped a few yards away. After a little while Rex enquired as to what activity he was engaged upon. The Nuba acknowledged the purport of the remark with a slightly wry smile and said that his condition had been such that the necessity of *sibr* had been absolute.

Rex agreed that such circumstances could arise, and, perhaps it would be better if he gave the details, and his story unfolded. For over two years he had played the saxophone in this and that band on Broadway, mentioning names of two well-known bands of the early 1940s. Then an inescapable urge had struck him, he must *sibr*. He threw up his connection with the world of entertainment, went down to the docks and signed on as a fireman on a cargo boat sailing for Suez via the Cape. He was discharged at Suez and made his way back to the Sudan and his Hills. His *sibr* had been accomplished, he was now free as the air he breathed. One of the questions to which we had given considerable thought on the Governor General's Council was how would 28,000 troops, mainly Nubas, who had served in North Africa and had 'seen the world' react to the basic life of the Nuba Mountains on their return? I wondered whether we had need to worry quite so much!

We said goodbye to the Harrisons in the morning after a very full couple of days and many happy memories.

The 87 mile run to El Obeid lay for the most part over flat, sandy ground with a number of *khors*, many crossed by Irish bridges. We passed a few *jebels*. Compared with the earlier sections trees were scarce; just a few *tebeldis* and round euphorbias. Many miles could be described as open scrub. We passed a road gang engaged on extensive repairs, some broken-down lorries but only two villages, a wayside cafe, very little cultivation and few travellers. We were not sorry to arrive at El Obeid at 14.40 hours.

Chapter Eighteen

FAREWELL

In the spring of 1946 came signs that I might be able to get away in the near future. I was past retirement age and I wanted to give my staff the move up that was their due. As soon as the news became public all sorts of presentations were planned. I managed to suppress a scheme which the native staff put in hand to have a 'gold' collection from the whole Sudan Railways staff.

The Municipality of Atbara gave us an enormous tea-party in the open-air cinema. There were speeches galore in Arabic, and I was presented with a large double ink-stand in Omdurman silver, adorned by three date palms, which was the Province badge. The Sudanese Club as representing the staff of Sudan Railways gave an equally large tea-party at their club on the river-bank and obtained an enormous iced cake from Khartoum from which I unfortunately got food poisoning! I was put on eight large tablets of sulphoguanadine to be chewed, dry, every four hours for three days, and I survived as a very limp specimen. The Atbara Sports Club gave a farewell dance and a lovely Omdurman silver bowl, and the ladies of Atbara similarly endowed my wife.

We were very touched by the expressions of goodwill.

Our farewell party to the British staff aimed to match these efforts. We called on the technical resources of the Mechanical Department and our slightly elevated sitting-out space overlooking the Nile was converted into a water cascade down a huge pile of glass battery boxes with subdued flashing lighting in them. The flowering trees and the house were flood-lit. A large flashing sign of a locomotive climbing the 'bank' with a full blast of steam coming from the chimney was quite impressive and a dance floor with a fountain covered the middle lawn in front of the house. The tennis court was used for the dinner tables while a Sudan Railways dining-kitchen car set on our siding provided the facilities.

It was a fancy-dress affair and the 120 guests entered into the spirit of the evening. Our Governor, from Damer, arrived dressed

General Manager's house, Atbara.

as a 'Bash-Shawish' of Police, leading a camel on which his wife was riding in a sun-shelter, dressed as an Arab bride. I remember a very amusing 'Gert and Daisy' double act and there were many more. We started with a whist drive, still in those days a popular activity, and then had dinner, with speeches kept to a minimum. Dancing followed and lasted till late. It was quite a good party.

Our farewell to the Sudanese was a tea-party followed by an open-air Arabic film-show in the garden. Despite rationing, sufficient sugar was made available to ensure that everyone had a good cup of tea by Sudanese standards. The cup was filled to the brim with broken *ras* sugar before the tea was poured in — and the Arabic film was, as Abdel Sayed Eff had promised, of sufficient length and pathos to give satisfaction.

Between times I said a few goodbyes in Khartoum.

We visited Sir Sayed Abdel Merghani, SAM as we knew him, first. He was a charming, puck-like, little man and very quiet. His followers held him in the highest of regard, crediting him with almost magical powers. We had tea with him in a shady corner of his garden. About a week later we called on the other Sayed, SAR,

WHEELS AND PADDLES IN THE SUDAN

Sir Sayed Abdel Rahman el Mahdi, who had let it be known that he was expecting me. A wonderful tea-party was laid on. His gleaming white mansion stood on 2–3 acres of magnificent lawn, edged with rose-beds and with a few shade trees in the corner. SAR was very different from SAM, being a large swash-buckling, rather likeable villain, who was a very painstaking host. He was particularly gracious to the youngsters. He paraded three of his racehorses round the lawn for inspection as he said he understood that the youngsters were very interested in horses. He then invited Pamela, the youngest, to mount and ride a beautiful grey Arab. She complied, with some diffidence. I can still see SAR bouncing up and down in his arm chair, clapping his hands together and calling in Arabic 'Faster, faster!' He was not happy till he saw the turf of his beautiful lawn flying in all directions. It was an example of real eastern hospitality.

About a week later, I received a telephone call from Khartoum telling me that extra places were available for the journey home if I could arrange my own transport to Aswan on the next Tuesday. All space on the main party, on train and Nile steamer, leaving on the Wednesday was filled but it was thought that I could arrange my own transport outside these limits and thus take up, in Cairo, the places which had become available. I agreed, provided that Khartoum would open the office for visas and warn the bank that I needed money. I took our elder daughter with me to Khartoum that night, leaving my wife and the younger to cope with the packing. Arrangements for travelling to Aswan did not present any great problem. We put on a goods train to Wadi Halfa for 15.00 hours on Tuesday to which my service-car could be attached and, with 24 hours in hand, a small spare steamer would get us to Aswan in plenty of time. The night train from Aswan had spare sleeping accommodation available.

We arrived in Khartoum early Sunday morning to learn that a spectacular air-drop was scheduled for 09.00 hours. A mild sandstorm was blowing and the drop looked doubtful. However, on time, some 200 parachutes were seen. They had a rough touch-down; there were many casualties and the Commanding Officer sustained a broken arm. The gliders and troop-carrying planes made fair landings.

I managed to get all our visas and travellers' cheques. I went to the Palace to take leave of His Excellency and was requested to

WHEELS AND PADDLES IN THE SUDAN

delay my return to Atbara for a few hours to enable me to dine at the Palace for the last time. I also managed to say farewell to the Secretaries and many Heads of Departments. After a pleasant dinner I made my departure at 22.00 hours amid copious good wishes. The driver of the train, not to be outdone, made up two hours on the journey and we arrived in Atbara at the normal time. I had just 30 hours in which to put my affairs in order.

It was hectic. After lunch on the second day we pushed all the unpacked gear into our service-car, changed and drew up on the platform a quarter of an hour before departure. There was a big crowd there to say farewell. The band played at its best. My last job was to bid farewell to the bandmaster in those famous Kitchener blues.

The train drew out and we were on our way. There then followed four hours of packing and by 17.00 hours we were reasonably straight. We were on express timings and made Wadi Halfa at 07.00 hours. *Ambigol* was lying ready and we quickly transferred, picking up a pile of farewell telegrams, and set off.

The main party arrived at Aswan and we all set out for Cairo to find on arrival that no one knew anything about us or would do anything for us. To cap it all, Khartoum claimed that we were no longer their responsibility. Faced with the probability of a long stay in Cairo, my wife agreed to keep house for Bishop Gwynne, and we retired to the Bishop's house to await developments.

Every day I visited the Sudan Agency and Thomas Cook and other possible sources of help without success. After a fortnight we had a 10-minutes option on three seats on a KLM plane to Amsterdam for the next morning. I accepted, and, when seeking visas at the Dutch Embassy, enquired after our friend the Dutch Ambassador at Jeddah. I found out that he was at that moment in Amsterdam. When handing my wife her tickets I warned her that if she got into trouble in Amsterdam she should call on Mr Van der Meulen.

I saw the family off at 03.00 hours. They had a rough passage. Despite promises of connecting on-flight to London, nothing was available and everything became very difficult. My wife remembered my advice and requested the officer to get her a line to Mr Van der Meulen of the Foreign Office. The atmosphere changed completely: 'You know Mr Van der Meulen? We will see what we can do'. In 20 minutes a plane was available to fly them to London and in due course they reached my wife's home in Reading. When

I arrived at Somerton I found that my wife was still at Reading, recovering from pneumonia. I brought her home.

And so our Sudan wanderings were finished! Our children went back to school after spending rather over two terms with us; I do not think, on balance, they had lost anything. We had to do some adjusting, to climate, lack of help about the house and garden and many other things, but soon acquired plenty of local responsibilities. I used to say that I had to work harder then than when I controlled an undertaking with some 20,000 staff because, in that sphere, I had had a marvellous staff of highly skilled professionals, trained in the old school to give 'service' and that they surely did. I consider myself very fortunate to have served with them.

I was fortunate too, in the period in which I served in the Sudan. Up to World War I the administration, with no financial help from outside, was hampered by lack of resources; and after World War II came the period of political unrest and wide external urge to hasten our withdrawal. I served in that middle period between the Wars, and had the advantages of increasing revenue and being able to progress more easily. I salute the many friends, British and Sudanese, that I made during my sojourn in the Sudan and say — Thank you!

Appendix

JONGELEI

THIS was a real journey into the swamps! The word Jongelei has little significance until expanded into 'The Jongelei Cut', which was a scheme to cut a channel on the eastern side of the Sudd to pass a considerable fraction of the water in the Bahr-el-Jebel directly from a point north-east of Bor–Jongelei to a point on the White Nile between the mouth of the Bahr-el-Zeraf and Sobat Mouth, and thereby reduce the loss of water by evaporation in the Sudd. The scheme had been under consideration for many years. It would cost a lot of money, it was difficult and it would greatly upset the way of life of the cattle-owning tribes of the area. It might also cause serious trouble to navigation of the Bahr-el-Jebel by *sudd* blocks (caused by reduced flow), even to the extent of making the river unnavigable. The object was to make more water available for Egypt.

The area was a mass of *maiyas* (lakes) and *khors* (the interconnecting channels). When I visited it in 1945 the flood was hardly at its peak and there was 'no *sudd* running' (discharge). Landmarks or, even at this time of year, patches of soil, were scarce, and few people had any knowledge of its geography. None of our *reis* had any experience of its channels and so I arranged to borrow the second *reis* of the Egyptian Irrigation Department tug *Walad,* who had spent his working life in this area, to take me in and bring me out.

Whilst on the main river, the Bahr-el-Jebel, one had the advantage of travelling between river banks, albeit often submerged, with a Reference Pole driven into the river bank every 5 kilometres to give an idea of position. Once into the swamp, however, there were neither Reference Poles nor 'banks'. At low river bank or waters-edge would be visible but movement by water was difficult to the point of being impossible.

WHEELS AND PADDLES IN THE SUDAN

Our 'rendezvous' with *Walad* was a point near RP 118 and we arrived on *Melika* in the early evening to find *Walad* tied up. It was agreed that we would start at 05.30 hours. *Walad* would not be accompanying us as it would be required for some discharge gauge readings on the next day. We would borrow the second *reis* and return him by first available means.

Promptly at 05.30 hours we entered the swamp by 'Atem Head 1B' which was near RP 118. In the swamp itself all distances were by time. We travelled at an estimated 18 kilometres per hour. I sat on the bridge and had the benefit of a running commentary from the pilot. Readers may find the story a boring one, but it is the on-the-spot account of a journey which very few people have wanted, or been able, to make, and I have included it in the form in which I noted it down. My route report runs as follows:

'I entered Atem Head 1B, near RP 118 at 05.30 hours. All distances on a time basis. Estimated rate of travel 18 kilometres per hour. 05.34 joined by another *khor* from south (Possibly Atem Head 1A) to give a stream 50 yards wide. No trouble on entering system from sand-banks. Papyrus at present only 3 feet to 4 feet high and water only slightly more than bank high. 05.55 hours considerable *maiya* to east, parts of bank only grass and creeper covered to height of 1 foot. 'Kadi's' puddings very plentiful — an aquatic plant rather like a tough-leaved lettuce. *Maiya* to west 06.00 hours at three *tukls* — a great rarity here — bear away right to *maiya* on east. 06.18 hours considerable and lengthy *maiya* to east, width of channel about 40 yards. 06.25 hours cultivation and *tukls* at exit of large *maiya* lying to east also in distance mosquito nets and possibly small trees. Channel 50 yards wide, soon increasing to 60 yards. 06.33 hours two *khors* take off right to a *maiya* (not visible) to east. Small *maiya* to west. 06.44 hours *maiya* and *khors* join stream from west, stream now about 60 yards wide. Several large, prominent trees to west. 06.48 hours small *khor* takes off to west (said to be a *maiya*). Horizon of trees east. 06.54 hours small *khor* returns from west. 07.00 hours line of trees developing to west. Width of channel back to 50 yards. 07.11 hours *maiya* to west running parallel with channel, channel width 60 yards. 07.14 hours *khor* takes off east to *maiya* (not visible). 07.17 hours pass *tukls*; *maiya* to west joins stream with some *um-souf* about. Dinkas in canoe fishing. 07.20 hours *maiya* to west; stream width down to 40 yards. 07.27 hours *maiya* joins from west; width of stream now 50 yards. 07.29 hours at fork we take right (the left stream is said to rejoin us lower down) width of stream 40 yards. Clump of trees about ½ mile away to west. 07.37 hours a grassed *khor* joins from east, our width 50 yards, teal and plover in evidence. 07.37 hours stream splits, we take left (right said to lead to *maiya* not visible) both channels 50 yards wide and covered with a marvellous show of mauve convolvulus. No trees on horizon east. 07.45 hours *khor* width 30 yards from west increasing our width to 45 yards; patches of *um-souf* to our left. 07.50 hours small *maiya* west. Few trees visible ahead, and tops of trees visible on east horizon. 07.55 hours enter small *maiya* extensively fed from east; stream now more than 100 yards wide with *um-souf* edging and gradually narrowing. 07.59 hours leave our stream — 60 yards wide — turning right into stream 25 yards wide. 08.04 hours pass *tukls*, rejoined by stream from west 60 yards wide to increase our width to 50 yards. 08.15 hours large *maiya* west, and wooded horizon to east; our channel 60 yards, reducing to 40 yards. 08.40 hours *khor* takes off east; wooded horizon closing to 40 yards east. 08.45 hours small *khor* takes off west to *maiya*. 08.48 hours second *khor* in similar direction. 08.50 hours tail from west. 08.51 hours to 08.53 hours some obstruction by *sudd* islands and splitting but all rejoined after 2 minutes. 08.58 hours join large *maiya* from west. 09.05 hours extensive *maiya* to west continuous line of trees to east distant perhaps 2 miles. 09.07 *khor* takes off to *maiya* east. 09.08 hours *khor* takes off to *maiya* west. Our stream reduced to 30 yards. 09.10 hours enter complicated system of *maiyas* from east and west joining *maiya* ahead with shallow spots down to 4 feet but mainly 5 feet to 6 feet, a very extensive piece of water over a mile wide. Turned towards east approaching trees on horizon — reduced speed to troll a 'dolley' through *maiya* — with no success — considerable number of hippos.

10.00 hours called at Jongelei for a few minutes. 10.10 hours departed at normal speed. Trees and grass to east, stream 200 yards wide. 10.19 hours arrived trial cut to prove soil, stopped 20 minutes, took photos of hippos. 10.42 hours Dinka settlement to east. 10.44 hours large *khor* leaves to west said to rejoin shortly. 10.46 hours *khor* rejoins. Trees to east quickly fall away, our stream reduced to 45 yards. 10.51 hours small *khor* leaves east said to loop and we touch a parallel system to west, stream 60 yards wide. One tree ahead and one conspicuous palm ½ right. 10.58 hours at fork we go right. The left arm said to rejoin, stream 45 yards wide, *maiya* to east. 11.00 hours left channel rejoins from west (10.58) our width 55 yards. 11.02 hours fork. Left *maiya*, we take right, width 45 yards. 11.08 hours *khor* rejoins from west (prob 11.02 hours) 11.09 *khor* takes off to west, 70 yards wide; *um-souf* here and there along both banks. 11.15 hours stream widens to over 100 yards. 11.17 hours stream narrows to 45 yards with papyrus on both sides. 11.22 hours stream widens to 60 yards. 11.23 hours *khor* joins from east choked with *um-souf*; dead tree ahead. 11.28 hours number of palm trees of various types on horizon ahead, width of stream 60 yards. 11.38 hours *maiya* to west, trees on horizon west. 11.40 hours very large *maiya* to west (comparable with Shambe Lagoon), we skirt side of it. 11.50 hours another large *maiya* to west, stream 100 yards wide. 11.55 hours small *maiya* west. 12.05 hours *khor* joins from *maiya* east. 12.06 hours touch another *maiya* east. Dead *Doleib* palm trunk ahead (believed to be on bank of Bahr-el-Jebel). 12.08 hours. Big *maiya* from west joins our stream, our width 100 yards. 12.10 hours pass grassed up *khor* east. 12.11 hours *maiya* to west, number of clumps of trees and palms on horizon ahead. 12.13 hours width 45 yards, through papyrus. 12.15 hours widen to 50 yards, ten clumps of trees on horizon in east quadrant ahead. 12.21 hours very large *maiya* to east separated by narrow papyrus-grown strip with a similar but smaller item to west, which we touch at 12.24 hours. 12.28 hours heading for twin palms on horizon ahead. Complicated *khor* system joins from east, quite wide with island. 12.36 hours stream 60 yards, *um-souf* both sides. 12.41 hours small *maiya* joins west, stream 100 yards wide; some young *ambatch* thickets on west. 12.47 hours west horizon of trees and palms, pole in grass (sign of habitation) width of stream 50 yards. 13.00 hours large *maiya* west and trees on horizon west. 13.03 hours touch end of this (13.00) *maiya* west. Breakwater of young *ambatch* and large *maiya* east end of which we touch at 13.07 hours. 13.09 hours large *maiya* to west (perhaps same as 13.00 hours) 13.27 hours small *maiya* west. 13.31 hours small *khor* from west. Now said to be opposite (i.e. on a level with) RP 92 on the Bahr-el-Jebel. 13.34 hours big *maiya* to west and small *khor*, probably connecting, stream 30 yards wide. 13.35 hours *maiya* to east exposed soil west. 13.37 hours *khor* takes off to east possibly to *maiya* (13.35 hours) 13.42 hours big *khor* takes off to east, stream reduced to 45 yards and said to be a loop. 13.55 hours *maiya* to west. 14.01 hours *khor* rejoins from east (possibly 13.41 hours) but if so much reduced in size 14.10 hours grassed up *khor* west, width of stream 60 yards. 14.15 hours large *maiya* to east, stream 50 yards wide. 14.25 hours large *khor* joins from east, stream 70 yards wide and *maiya* ahead west. 14.36 hours into main river at Awei Tail 1B, RP 86. 15.45 hours enter Shambe Lagoon RP 84 and tied up at 16.00 hours.'

I was fortunate to have the opportunity of making this trip. The whole journey took 10½ hours gross. The corresponding distance on the Bahr-el-Jebel, a very tortuous section of hair-pin bends, was 158 kilometres. The river was still rising but approaching flood level and therefore no *sudd* was yet running. Speaking broadly, east meant looking towards the 'dry' land eastern boundary of the *sudd* area, from which the 'Cut' had to start. West meant looking towards the main river, the Bahr-el-Jebel.

It was my impression — but I only saw the conditions once and had no opportunity to check — that at low river, when much of the vegetation was burnt-off, 2 feet of dry land would be exposed; the *maiyas* would be greatly reduced in size and in many cases would have disappeared and similarly the *khors*. At the time of my visit several feet of water covered the whole land except for about ten spots where I noted a *tukl* on an exposed spot of land. Remarks on vegetation gave an occasional clue to what was underneath. For example, if there was papyrus it meant that there was earth on or close to the water surface because papyrus requires to have its roots in soil, whereas *um-souf* had its roots floating in water and gave no indication of soil. *Ambatch* grew on moist river bank conditions and could stand and even enjoy quite a lot of flooding.

It was interesting that some trees were observed between our route and the main river, indicating that there was some land in that area which was either above flood level or little troubled by flood. The ability of trees to survive flood conditions was very varied; more than four days would kill some whilst up to six months could be tolerated by others and it was not possible to determine the kind from our position.

I was much impressed by the bearing of my pilot-*reis*; I sat on the bridge with him throughout. At all times he appeared to know where he was going. He showed no hesitation and near landmarks were scarce. I had a high regard for these men who spent their lives in the backwaters efficiently carrying out tasks of real skill which pass un-noticed and un-sung and, along with my pilot, I think of Abdel-Rasoul, the king-pin of the Jur River Service.

The route I took had the specific purpose of visiting Jongelei. There were other known routes through the swamps which I have already mentioned, which might be useful in the case of a *sudd* block on the main river. For example, at this time it was possible to enter the swamp near RP 93, Awei Head 1, and come out at RP 86, either at Awei Tail 1A or 1B, very close together, only separated by 100 metres, but without regular use these channels tended to get blocked. Perhaps, with the commencement of work on the Jongelei Cut, it has become necessary to use them.

GLOSSARY

The following list of arabic words, though not exhaustive, should prove of use to the reader.

afsh — baggage
afrit — devil
aigl — Nile perch
amara — settlement
ambatch — very light wood
angareeb — native bed
anis — best type of grass for hareig
asara — oil seed grinder
Aur — Ingessana chief
awaid — Nuba traditions, folk lore
Bairam — two main Islamic holidays
bamsakir — ugly, flat-headed river fish
bayard — a quality sea fish
bintalig — a late maturing dura
Bul — a Nuer clan
bursh — palm frond matting
colbeita — Ingessana throwing knife
damoor — coarse native cotton cloth
debba — knoll, arising from past occupation of site
doleib — type of palm tree
dura — millet
'el sittat el Englezi' — 'The English ladies'
farash — attendant
fazda — recurring sand bank
feddan — acre
felucca — rowing boat
fiki — holy man
fula — shallow depression filled with water
ful sudani — monkey nuts
furwa — sheepskin worn as a seat protector
galabiya — male outer garment
gassis — clergyman
gattr — train
ghafir — watchman
goo-goo — grain store
gyassa — river sailing boat
'Hadret' — 'Your honour'
hafir — water reservoir
hareig — burning off grass for grain production
hashab — grey-barked acacia producing best gum
hegleig — tree-source of lalob oil
hosh — courtyard
jebel — hill

Kaid — Commander-in-Chief
kantar — weight: 100 lbs. approx.
kamadob — ground one year after burning
kanisa — church
khor — water course
kujur — Nuba medicine-man
la'ib — sports meeting
lalob — oil from kernel of stone of hegleig
la'ut — thorny bush, indicating worked out land
luak — large circular hut for cattle protection
mabsut *pl.* mabsuteen — happy
magnun — mad
maiya — lake
mamur — superintendent
marissa — beer
meshra — a landing spot
murasla — messenger boy
murhaka — corn grinding stone
müstaba — sitting-out extension
nahass — copper — a drum
nafir — policeman, private soldier, communal party
nagil — creeping grass
Niam-Naim — Yum-Yum, Zandee — a tribe
nugga — sailing boat
omda — local headman, a chief
osta — skilled artisan
radeef — army pensioners settlement
ras — cone of 3 lbs. of sugar. Abyssinian baron
reis — steersman — captain of sailing ship
saffia — 4 gallon petrol tin
sambuk — sea sailing ship
sib'r — cleansing ceremonies
sudd — massed floating vegetation
suffragi — table waiter
suk — market
tahteeb — plan — way of doing things
tauf — ambatch canoe or larger vessel
tebeldi — an obese, hollow tree
tisht — wide, shallow washing pan
toich — low-lying water meadow
wakil — agent, deputy
zaff — dried palm frond tips